738.09

D0409553

A History of Pottery

A History of Pottery

Emmanuel Cooper

Longman

LONGMAN GROUP LIMITED LONDON
Associated companies, branches and representatives throughout
the world

First published 1972

ISBN 0 582 15025 6

Acknowledgements

The illustrations used in this book have been obtained, gratefully,
from many museums in this country and abroad, as well as from
manufacturers and private individuals. Full credits appear with each
caption and I would like to thank all who have allowed their
photographs to be used.

My thanks, too, are given to all the people who have helped in
the preparation of this manuscript. In particular I would like to
mention Patrick Hardy and Treld Pelkey Bicknell of Longman
Lastly I would like to record my gratitude to David Ketteridge for
his help and patience in compiling the index of the book.

Maps drawn by John Flower

Designed by Treld Pelkey Bicknell

Printed in Great Britain by Butler & Tanner Ltd,
Frome and London

Contents

Introduction

Pots not only reflect technological developments at particular times but they are often works of art in their own right, over and above the demands of function. Such pots have been made ever since clay was first moulded and this is the sort of pottery with which this book is concerned. Much of the interest of pottery lies in the way it was made and decorated, the form chosen and the use to which it was put. Changes in style and type of pottery occurred in response to social, economic and technical demands, and for this reason pottery is closely integrated with the development of different civilizations from the earliest times up to the present day.

In this book I have attempted to fit pottery into its historical and technical background. Major countries have been dealt with as a unit and the pottery developments followed chronologically. Different techniques are explained as they occurred and are related to those which existed in other places at the same time.

It has not been possible here to deal with the many other uses to which clay has been put, such as the manufacture of bricks, tiles and drainpipes, or the great industrial development of the pottery industry during the nineteenth century when the use of the machine enabled the mass production of pottery for expanding home and overseas markets; soft-paste porcelain, too, is only referred to when its development influenced that of pottery.

The history of pottery is not a continuous story. It appears to jump in time and place for no known reason. However, there is a common thread of development and this is what I have tried to pick out.

Sufficient detail has been included to interest the more knowledgeable reader, yet all readers will, I hope, find the broad outline presented here an introduction to one of man's oldest and most exciting artefacts and a springboard for further investigation.

EMMANUEL COOPER

Pottery timeline chart (dates BC, scale from 6000 to 1000)

Area	Region	6000	5000	4000	3000	2000	1000
NEAR AND MIDDLE EAST	Anatolia / Syria / Asia Minor	Earliest pottery known	Painted pottery with white pigment on red body		Wares generally showed influences from Crete and Mesopotamia		
	Mesopotamia		Incised ware / Painted ware / Painted Samarra ware	Wheel developed and kiln improved / Olive coloured pottery / Richly painted style	Glass made	Lead glaze used	Glaze in general use / Unglazed wares generally made
	Egypt		Badarian pottery Finely made, well considered form, carefully prepared clay	Red burnished ware with black (smoke reduced) top	FAIENCE / Wheel introduced Meydum ware	Extensive trade brought foreign pottery and stylistic changes / Rich painted style developed	Wheel more efficient Faience developed / Roman Occupation
	Persia			Richly painted wares from Tepe Giyan, Susa, Tepe Sialk		Development of form and decoration for use in rituals	
	Crete				Minoan civilization. Richly painted style based on naturalistically painted decoration		
FAR EAST	India				Indus Valley Very well made. Painted decoration		
	China				Neolithic Period Urns, made out of red clay, richly painted swirling patterns in red, black and brown / Kansu Province Yellow River	Bronze Age metalwork had strong influence on form of pots Cooking vessels in grey clay with tripod feet	Experiments with more carefully prepared clay and high firing temperatures
	Korea				Little is known about early pottery but it is assumed to follow that of China		
	Japan				Hand-built methods followed	Joman style. Coil-built urns with impressed decoration of cords	
EUROPE	Greece					Mycenaean culture Minyan ware. Highly refined	Classical Greek Period / Geometric style / Black-figure style / Red figure style
	Italy					Villanovan civilization Hard, grey pottery	Etruscan grey ware / Rome established
	Byzantium						
	Spain				Beaker folk (?) emigrated to other parts of Europe	Iberians. Painted style influenced by Greek export ware	Coarse pottery Roman style
	Netherlands				Bowls and urns with incised decoration		Wheel introduced Pottery made in imitation of iron forms Impressed decoration
	Germany				Hand-built wares		
AMERICA	North						
	Central					Archaic Period Jars and bowls found — FORMATIVE PERIOD Wide range of forms, mainly for domestic use – cooking pots, storage vessels, water pots. Decoration – slip, painted and resist. Burnished surfaces. Incised patterns	
	South				Earliest pottery found in Ecuador	Archaic Period	Chavin and Cuprisnique style Mould-made ware. Stirrup handle. Incised decoration. Northern Andes region
GREAT BRITAIN					Pottery introduced from the Continent / Hand-built bowls for holding seeds / Cooking pots	Beaker folk Hand-built forms with incised forms / Cinerary urns with incised and applied decoration	Iron Age Simple wheel introduced Forms imitated more closely those of iron. Incised decoration

Isnik wares

ISLAMIC RELIGION (vertical)

Unglazed ware
Lead-glazed ware
Tin-glazed ware
Lustreware

Underglaze painting

Lustrewares

...man
...cupation   Christian
influence
Coptic

Rich lustre-   Painted
ware made   wares

Large storage vessels often moulded
Rich turquoise alkaline glaze

East Persia painted
style
Sgraffito wares

Kashan ⎫
Rayy ⎬ Centres
Seljuq wares
Artificial body
Decorated and lustrewares

Blue and white wares
Gombroon wares
Kubachi wares

...ade with Roman
...mpire brought
...d glaze

...heel used extensively.
...oulds used

...onze still most
...eemed material
...d forms imitated
...Kilns improved

Unsettled
period. Trade
disrupted.
Further
improvement
in high
temperature
firing

Settled period. Trade with
Islamic Empire brought lead
glaze. Rich lead-glazed ware
with splash decoration
developed
Yueh, green, white, and many
other high-temperature wares
developed

Classic period for
pottery. Stoneware
and porcelain made
Ting and Ch'ing pai wares
Chun wares
Northern Celadons
Ju ware
Tz'u-chou wares
Lung-chien wares
Chien wares, etc.

Ching-te Chen. Imperial
porcelain factory established
Blue and white wares
Copper-red decoration
Enamel decoration

Large export trade
Influence on form and decoration
"Famille verte" enamel
decoration
Swatow wares
Yi-hsing wares
Blanc-de-chine
Porcelain wares very refined
but forms sterile

High fired glazes developed
Strong Chinese influence

Celadon ware
Fine white wares

Style shows marked
differences to that of China

Closed country. Development of free, peasant
type of decoration of free and vigorous brushwork

Strong Chinese influence via Korea.
Olive-green stoneware glazes and
lead-glazed ware

Stoneware made in
Japanese style at six
main centres

Pottery made for tea
ceremony
Porcelain made at Arita
(Imari)
Exported to West. Raku made

Studio
potters
Hamada
etc.

...man
...upation

...an Empire
...gloss wares
...rse wares
...glazed wares

Domestic pottery
Lead-glazed and unglazed

Imported
Islamic
decorated
wares

Tin-glaze wares
Archaic style – Formal – Renaissance ⎪Lustre
Sgraffito wares – North Italy

Influence
of Chinese
porcelain

Constantinople established as capital. Influences from West and East
Lead-glazed and painted wares on buff body
Applied and sgraffito decoration on red body

Visigoths
Painted wares
Impressed decoration

Fine pottery imported from
Islamic countries

"Cuerda-seca"
technique used
Blue and white
painted bowls

Lustre
developed
at
Malaga

Blue, white
and gold
wares of
Manises

Alcora

Underglaze decorated ware at
Talavera de la Reina

Red
earthenware
made

Tin glazed
earthenware in
Italian style

Delft-ware similar to imported blue and
white style
Fine red unglazed stoneware

...man
...cupation
...gloss wares
...rse wares
...glazed wares

Higher fired
wares developed
Pingsdorf and
Badorf kiln sites

Buff ware with
red vitreous
slips

Ware
exported
in Europe

SALTGLAZE DEVELOPED
Raeren and Cologne brown wares
Siegburg white wares
Grenzhausen coloured wares.   Kreussen enamel wares

Bauhaus
influenced
much of European design

...blo Indians settle in south-east
...n undecorated pottery

...orated pottery made in Eastern
...odlands

Plain grey ware
in form of
gourds and
baskets. Built
in coils

Cooking pots.
White slip
decoration

Finest pots made
Black and white
slip decoration
Many individual
styles of decoration

Polychrome decorative style
developed. Patterns of
geometrical forms as well as
natural objects. Glaze used
only for decorative purposes

Spanish Conquest,
but many styles
continued to be
made in many areas

NORTH AMERICA
1800
Industrial firms producing a
wide range of functional and
decorative wares in earthenware
and low-temperature porcelain
1900
"Art" pottery produced, e.g.
Newark, New Jersey
1950
Studio pottery produced. Strong
Japanese influence
Free use of clay for objects and
sculpture, e.g. Voulkos
"Pop" influence

CLASSIC PERIOD
Further development of basic forms and growth.
of individual style. Teotihuacan, Maya.
Polychrome style developed

POST CLASSIC PERIOD
Break-up of peaceful city
states. Pottery forms
continued much as before.
Designs less vigorous

Aztec domination
Montezuma
Mazipan style
Cholula pottery

Spanish
Conquest

...chica: fine mould-made wares,
...h additional incised and modelled
...oration. South Andes: Nazca; mould
...de, wide range of rich painted decoration.
...ny other styles

Chimu pottery – con-
tinued earlier. Mochica
style. Chancay pottery –
simple forms, added
human figures

Incas
Limited pottery
range but
technically excellent

...man Occupation

...rse pottery made at
...y centres – Castor.
...w Forest, Aldgate.
...chester, St Albans
...s and wheels introduced

Anglo-Saxon urns.
Well made with
impressed and
incised decoration.
Dark firing body
Cooking pots

Technical improvements
introduced mainly
from the Rhineland
St Neots
Ipswich
Thetford
Stamford glazed ware

Fast wheels
Improved kilns
Lead glazes

Saxo-Norman wares

Medieval style
Jugs and pitchers.
Wheel-thrown, thin
bodied, finely thrown
wares. Lead glazes
dusted on unfired
pots. Simple incised
and slip-trailed
decoration. Made
mainly in south-east

Domestic pots

Tudor wares
with bright
green glaze
imitating
metalwork

Cistercian wares.
Dark brown glaze
over hard red
body. Made
principally in
monasteries

Tin-glazed
earthenware
London, Liverpool
and Bristol

Red earthenware.
Mainly for local areas.
Slipware decoration.
Especially in
Staffordshire

Saltglaze
stoneware

Art pottery
Doulton, etc.
Martin
Brothers

Studio pottery
Leach.
Cardew,
Staite Murray

Creamwares
Wedgwood
Industrial pottery
Porcelain

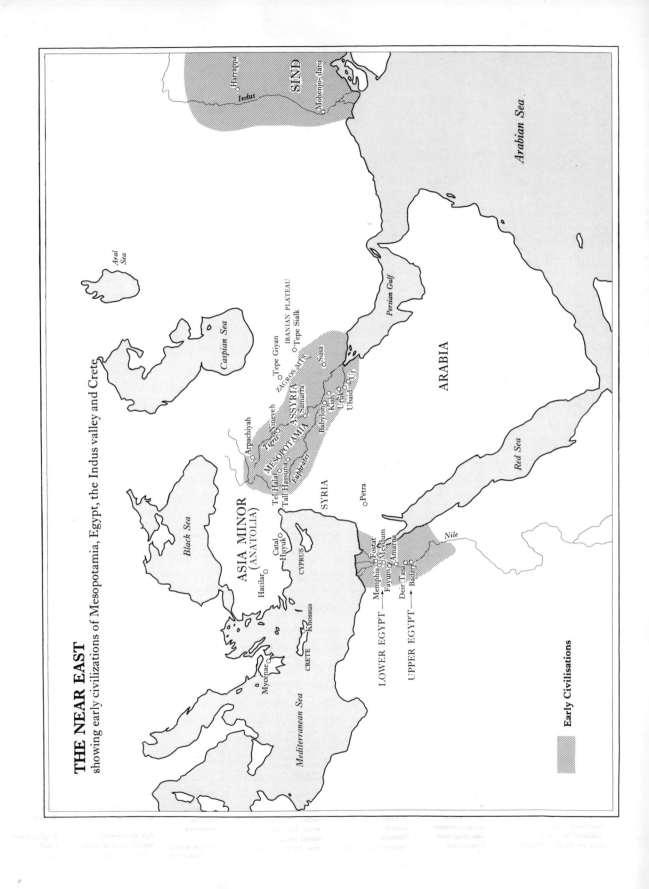

THE NEAR EAST
showing early civilizations of Mesopotamia, Egypt, the Indus valley and Crete

Early Civilisations

Aral Sea

Caspian Sea

Black Sea

Mediterranean Sea

SIND

Harappa
Indus
Mohenjo-daro

Arabian Sea

IRANIAN PLATEAU
Tepe Giyan
Tepe Sialk
ZAGROS MTS.
Samarra
Susa
Arpachiyah
Nineveh
Tigris
Tell Halaf
Tall Hassuna
Euphrates
MESOPOTAMIA
ASSYRIA
Babylon
Kish
Uruk
Ubaid
Ur

Persian Gulf

ARABIA

Red Sea

ASIA MINOR
(ANATOLIA)
Catal Huyuk
Hacilar
CYPRUS

SYRIA
Petra

CRETE
Knossus
Mycenae

LOWER EGYPT ⟶ Memphis Fostat
Fayum Meidum
Amarna
Nile
UPPER EGYPT ⟶ Deir Tasa
Badari

Chapter 1

The Beginning

The qualities which make clay immediately attractive to children are probably qualities which attracted Stone Age man. What could be easier than to pick up a lump of clay by the river or lake and press it into shapes with the fingers? From very early times magic played an important part in the life of man and it is more than probable that symbolic figures were modelled in clay at this stage.

Clay itself has no characteristic form. It occurs naturally as a dry, powdery solid, as a sticky but plastic lump and as a lumpy liquid. All these states are useful to the potter in different ways, but the plastic state is the one which responds most quickly to the potter's hands. Scientists tell us that the particles of clay are flat and plate-like, and the addition of water enables them to slide over each other without breaking apart. Too much water results in a formless mass, while too little

Clay

11

Egyptian oval bowl taking the shape of a section of melon or gourd. Pots have been made in many shapes and were not always round. c 3500 B.C. 6 inches across. Petrie Collection, University College London.

prevents any movement. Though almost any shape can be made from clay, some shapes are much better and easier to make than others. It would, for example, be possible to make a pair of scissors in clay though they would have little mechanical strength. Consequently clay imposes certain limitations on form which can only be extended at the risk of structural weakness. Form,

Round bowl with incised decoration recalling basket work, black burnished clay. Central European. c 2000 B.C. Height 3½ inches. British Museum.

12

The Beginning

too, is determined to a large extent by the method of manufacture. Wheel-made pots, for example, must be round and their shape can only be modified by further processes.

Objects made from clay have often taken on the form of things made in other materials. Throughout the whole history of pottery the imitation in clay of other objects and materials has been evident. There are many examples of this: some pots have imitated natural forms, such as gourds, and many have copied objects made from materials which impose a strong form, such as basketry. Such things as wooden trays, leather bags and bottles, ostrich eggs, sections of bamboo have all been copied at some time. Later, as metal-working developed, metal objects were the predominant forms which were imitated.

Most pots are circular, and even before the wheel was invented the majority were rounded as a result of the method of making rather than the demands of the clay. It is much easier, for example, to squeeze out a round pinch pot than a square one. In spite of this there are, however, many surviving early pots which are not circular: rectangular dishes, oval bowls and, from Crete, rectangular troughs divided into partitions.

The use of clay seems to have been developed independently by different people in different parts of the world. Nomadic races would have little time or use for fragile pottery and so it was with the beginnings of the more settled life of the New

Early Discoveries

Terracotta female figure. Mohenjo-daro. Indus Valley. c *3000–2000* B.C. With due courtesy of the Department of Archaeology of Pakistan.

Stone Age that the making of pottery developed. Before then images of men and animals were modelled in clay and were used for magical or religious purposes. Mother goddesses with enlarged sexual organs have been excavated in various parts of the world, including the Indus Valley and Mesopotamia, and date back to prehistoric times. These were part of the religious cult encouraging fertility in women. As the tribes settled, it is possible that such figures, along with shells and coloured stones could have been used for trade.

How the discovery was made that dried clay, subjected to red heat (about 600°C), would become hard and not disintegrate in water, is not known. It is probable that the idea developed over a considerable period of time and there are two theories to account for it. The first, and possibly the more valid, is the hearth theory. Fire was a valuable and vital part of man's early existence. It would be carefully tended, for it was much easier to control and maintain than to create. Holes were made in the ground and these could well have been lined with clay. The fire kept in them would turn the clay into pot and when the fire was eventually put out a crude vessel would be left.

The second theory is that baskets would have been lined with clay to render them waterproof and in due course, as the clay dried out and contracted, a simple pot would be formed which could have either held fire or been put into the

The Beginning

fire. Alternatively, such clay-lined baskets could have been burned in the fire which would have left a simple fired pot behind. Such a theory presupposes the existence of basketry. In some early cultures basketry existed without pottery but in others pottery without basketry. All that can be assumed is that a successful combination of social, technical and economic factors resulted in the discovery that clay changes to pot when heated sufficiently.

Clay occurs over most of the earth's surface and, while some of it may be more plastic or of a different colour, the basic qualities are much the same, though in early civilizations good usable clay was highly valued. Some tribes travelled many miles to collect workable clay and later the success of the Athenian and Corinthian potters was due to some extent to the fine smooth clays readily available to them. The Pueblo potters of Zuni in south-west North America brought clay from the top of a mountain because of its workable qualities. During the seventeenth century clay was taken from East Anglia to Holland to be used for Delft-ware because it was better suited to the needs of fine white majolica. For the establishment of a serious pottery industry a good working clay was essential; the clay had to be easily accessible, relatively clean and free from impurities or foreign matter such as stones or vegetation. It had to be plastic and able to withstand the heat of the fire without collapsing.

Clay Preparation

15

Before clay could be used it would have been prepared in two ways. First, any stones or other foreign bodies would have been removed, and secondly, it would have been made even throughout by a process called wedging. This was a combination of banging and kneading which was done either with the feet or hands. If large pots were to be made, some sort of filler, such as shells, sand or grit, would be added to the clay to open it, making it easier to control when modelling and, in the case of cooking pots, more able to withstand the rapid expansion known as thermal shock which had to take place when the pot was placed on the fire.

Making Methods Before the invention of the wheel, pottery was made entirely by hand by one of several methods or combination of methods:

1 Pinch pots were made in the hand by squeezing and manipulating clay between the fingers.
2 Coil or ring pots were made by placing rings of clay on top of each other, joining them together and smoothing them over. This enabled the construction of much larger pots.
3 Moulded pots, which required some sort of model, were formed either over natural forms such as gourds, or man-made forms such as baskets; or over moulds made specially from clay. Clay was smeared on the inside of a mould such as a basket or on the outside in the case of solid moulds such as stones.

The Beginning

4 Pots could also be made by patting out clay from a lump using an outside paddle and an inner support. These tools are known respectively as the paddle and anvil and were also used in the Indus Valley to complete the form of a pot thrown on the wheel.

Most of the early potters were women who sat on the floor and used either the inside of their thighs to support the pot or rested it on a disc or mat on the floor in front of them. This enabled the pot to be turned round much more easily. Such concave discs have survived from the Indus Valley. It was probably the women who were the potters of the early settled societies: along with caring for the household they prepared the family plots, ground and cooked the grain, spun, wove, made clothes, prepared ornaments and magical articles as well as fashioned and baked pots. It was probably the men who cleared the land, built huts, tended the livestock, hunted, and manufactured the tools and weapons. Only with the evolution of urban society and the establishment of fairly large groups of skilled workers, when pots were made on a wheel, did pottery become highly specialized work which was probably done by the men as an industry.

The introduction of the slow wheel enabled pots to be made much more quickly. The wheel was either pushed or kicked round and the impetus of the stone wheel was sufficient to enable

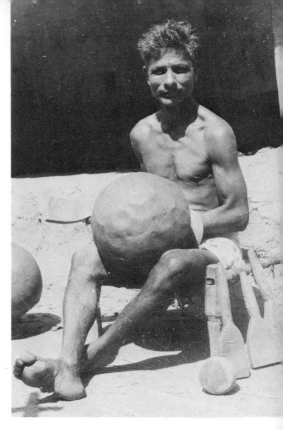

A potter of Ambikanagor using the traditional paddle and anvil to build the pots. Decoration is applied with an incised quartz pebble lying on the ground. Bengal.

17

pots to be made. This completely new technique had a strong influence on the shapes, as all pots made by this method had to be round. As they also had to be made quickly to prevent the clay from collapsing, they developed a new freedom and spontaneity, though the forms generally became more standard. Horizontal bands could be drawn quickly and easily on the revolving pots and this method of decoration began to predominate.

Finishing the Pots Pottery fired to the fairly low temperatures obtainable by the early potters was porous and fragile. Until glaze in the modern meaning of the word was in widespread use simpler methods had to be used to render the pottery impervious and give it strength. Such as:

1 Burnishing the clay when it was not quite dry. The surface was rubbed with a smooth stone or pebble which pressed the surface flat, giving it a dull, attractive shine and making it less porous.
2 Covering the surface of the pot with a slip of fine clay, prepared by removing the larger particles, such as was used by the Greeks on their red and black painted ware to give a decorated as well as a smooth surface.
3 Towards the end of the firing the pots could be covered with wet leaves. These produced smoke which penetrated the pores and made the whole pot a shiny black colour in the process known as "carbon smoking".

The Beginning

4 A vegetable "glaze" could be applied to the pot still hot from the fire, though the results were not as permanent as a true glaze.

To change clay into pot it must be heated as evenly as possible to red heat and above (600°C). The earliest firings were probably carried out in the domestic hearth. Open bonfires would also have been used and this method can still be seen in, among other places, Nigeria. In this method the fire is slowly started round the pots, gradually built up and then the whole is covered with grass, reeds or cattle dung to protect the contents from cold air. Only comparatively low temperatures can be obtained by this method and no glaze is used. The colour of the pots is affected by the flames and smoke, giving uneven results. Much heat is wasted and the method is uneconomic for the amount of fuel consumed.

Kilns were fairly specialized pieces of capital equipment and it was only with the establishment of pottery centres that they were developed. They were, at first, simple boxes made from clay; the fire was made underneath, the pots were stacked in the kiln from the top and this was then covered over with mud or earth, leaving a small hole for the smoke. Even so simple a kiln gave much more control than an open bonfire; it retained the heat and kept fire and pots separate; it allowed for a controllable draught and kept the pots together in one place.

19

Three pots from Haçilar, Turkey. The remarkable high technical quality of the pots and the painted geometrical designs are typical of the early wares of Anatolia. c 5500 B.C. Height of tallest pot 6 inches. Ashmolean Museum, Oxford.

Anthropomorphic vase from Haçilar, Turkey. c 5000 B.C. Height 6 inches. Ashmolean Museum.

THE EARLIEST POTTERY

On our present knowledge the earliest pottery appears to come from Anatolia and is associated with cave-dwelling communities of the late Mesolithic period and dates to not later than 6500 B.C. The earliest ware made here was undecorated and made from reddish-brown clay. This was followed in the same area by a group of well-known painted wares which date from around 5000 B.C. The decorated wares had designs of red pigment painted on to a cream slip in geometrical patterns. The whole pot was burnished to give a rich and pleasing effect. It is thought that the painting on pottery reflected the contemporary interest in art forms. Similar pigments could have been used for the pots and for painting as white clay and red and yellow ochres withstand the effects of heat.

From these early beginnings the basic style of Middle Eastern pottery developed which remained basically unchanged until the use of the wheel and of glaze became widespread some time after 2000 B.C. Hand-building methods were used and the surface of the pots was often burnished to give a smooth, slightly shiny appearance. Some pots were left plain while others were decorated, sometimes with impressed designs but more often painted with clays and pigments in simple geometrical patterns. Undoubtedly, potters of the Mesopotamian civilization owed a great deal of their skill to the Anatolian potters.

20

The Beginning

MESOPOTAMIA

In the fertile land between the rivers Tigris and Euphrates known as Mesopotamia, the earliest known civilization developed.

Early settlements in which the peasants lived in farmhouses, cultivated crops, kept cattle and sheep, wove materials and made pots date back to between 5000 and 4500 B.C. and are known as the Hassuna Period. Pottery made in this period was, for the most part, quite well developed and falls into two groups. The first group from north Mesopotamia comes from the area which was later to become Assyria. Bowls and globular jars have been found at, among other centres, Nineveh and Tall Hassuna. What makes the pottery characteristic is the simple incised linear designs. Samarra ware, named after the site where it was found, forms the second group. It is characterized by painted rather than incised decoration. Simple geometrical designs were painted in red and purplish-brown pigment on to a matt cream slip. Occasionally semi-stylized natural motifs of human and animal figures were incorporated into the designs. It is probable that Samarra ware originated in the Iranian plateau to the east and was either imported or brought by people moving into the more fertile country of Mesopotamia.

Hassuna Period
(5000–4500 B.C.)

In the Halaf Period, *c* 4500–4000 B.C., named after Tel Halaf, two technological developments were made which were to influence the manufac-

Halaf Period
(c 4500–4000 B.C.)

21

ture of pottery and culminate in one of the richest wares in the Near East. The first was the development of simple kilns which enabled pots with painted decorations to retain their clear colours after firing. Previously when pots came into contact with the flame and smoke of bonfires they were coloured red, black and brown; any painted decoration would, to a large extent, be lost beneath these firing colours. The use of a simple kiln in which the chamber for the pots was kept separate from the fire-box was a great step forward, though no kilns from this period have yet been excavated.

The other development was the attempt to reproduce the stone lapis lazuli which, probably because of its bright ultramarine colour, was highly prized. Its natural occurrence was rare, and efforts were made to reproduce it synthetically by carving small objects such as beads in soapstone, which is a form of talc stone, covering the surface with powdered ores of copper such as azurite or mala-

The Beginning

chite, and heating them until the surface melted and formed a simple glass. Though only indirectly related to pottery, it was probably in this beginning that the origins of glass and glaze lie.

Pottery now became more varied and complex. New shapes suggest metal prototypes. Rims, for example, were made which curled over in a way more suited to metal, and the profile of the pots often seemed to echo metal shapes. This was the beginning of the Bronze Age period when metal-working was to become highly developed and the metal products highly valued. Clay was more carefully prepared and the kiln-fired pots, having reached a high temperature, were quite hard. Thin-walled bowls, jars with rounded rims and sharply curved sides and a variety of round-bottomed vessels indicate the range of shapes. Red and black pigments were painted on to the pots before they were fired. Designs included geometrical shapes and floral and natural motifs which often developed into complete schematic patterns such as the so-called Bull's Head and Double Axe. Samarra ware continued to be made throughout this period and many modelled female figures of this date have also been found. These were made in limestone and pumice as well as in fired clay.

The Ubaid Period, *c* 4000–3500 B.C., saw the rise of Sumer at the head of the Persian Gulf with Ur, Uruk and Kish as the main cities. Stone was rare and they made clay bricks with which to

Ubaid Period
(*c* 4000–3500 B.C.)

23

Stone pottery wheel-head from Ur, Mesopotamia. c 2200 B.C. British Museum.

Mesopotamian bowl with brush decoration. Ubaid Period, c 4000–3500 B.C. 8 inches diameter. British Museum.

Mesopotamian pot with pouring lip from Ur. The greenish coloured clay is typical of this ware. Ubaid Period, c 4000–3500 B.C. 6 inches diameter. British Museum.

build their cities. It was here that the axle was developed which was later adapted for use on the potter's wheel.

The potter's wheel was not the fast, smooth machine we know today. It developed slowly: first the pot was set on a movable base such as a mat or potsherd; this base was then pivoted to enable it to turn more easily, and finally the slow wheel was developed. A heavy wheel-head of stone or wood was pushed round to enable the pots to be built up. It was not until much later that the free and fast-running wheels were developed. The effect of even a simple wheel was considerable as pots could be made much more quickly and with greater uniformity.

Improvements in kiln design continued and the first excavated kiln dates from this period. These two developments – the slow wheel and kiln – changed the whole nature of pottery. Clay which had been suitable for hand-building methods of manufacture now had to be more carefully prepared. Coarser particles of stone had to be removed as they hindered the working of the clay on the slow wheel. This was done by reducing the clay to a liquid state which enabled the finer particles to be tapped off while the coarser pieces sank to the bottom, in the process known as levigating. This process is also important as it was the basis of the decorative technique used on Greek and Roman pottery which will be explained more fully in Chapter Two.

24

The Beginning

Pottery from this period has a characteristic olive-green colour; the shapes were more uniform than before and were manufactured over a wide area. Extensive intercommunication over much of the Near East encouraged the distribution of techniques as well as of the pottery itself. Brushwork decoration became much more fluid and alive and the designs became more intricate and ambitious. The pots themselves were more finely made. During the period c 3500–2800 B.C., Uruk ware was made in the south of Mesopotamia at Warka (Uruk) in the area which was later to become Babylonia. A rich, painted pottery style developed in which complex designs were carried out in black, red and brown in ornate patterns including geometrical and stylized naturalistic motifs. In the north, pots were decorated with either painted decoration of animals in a single colour or incised with ornate geometrical patterns.

c 3500–2800 B.C.

Discoveries at this time in Mesopotamia were to lead to the use of glaze proper. Around 2000 B.C. true glass was made and though it was not moulded while it was a hot liquid, but carved and polished like precious stone, it was a step forward. During the period 2000–1000 B.C. glass was made which was worked while still hot and fluid and it was coloured by the metal oxides of copper to give turquoise, cobalt to give blue and tinstone to make it opaque white. All these metal oxides were later used to colour glazes. It was found that the addition of lead to glass not only gave greater

c 2000–1000 B.C.

25

brilliance but also reduced the shrinkage when the glass was cooling. This meant that glazing was now possible, as the main difficulty in using glazes containing only soda as a flux had been the amount they contracted on cooling which usually prevented them from sticking to the clay. The Mesopotamians thus seem to have developed a lead glaze suitable for use on pottery. An ancient glaze recipe on a clay tablet found in northern Iraq and dating back to 1700 B.C. is, in modern notation:

Glass	243.0	Saltpetre	3.1
Lead	40.1	Lime	5.0
Copper	58.1		

The amount of lead is significant in that this particular proportion enabled the glaze to be applied successfully to clay. Pots with a blue-green glaze have been found in northern Syria and date to the period 1700–1400 B.C.

Bricks and tiles were decorated with the lead glaze which was rendered opaque by the addition of the tinstone. Metal oxides were painted on to the surface to add colour. The decorated tiles were used with great effect on the doorways and gates in Babylon. Little effort seems to have been made to apply this glaze to pottery in general.

Alkaline glaze made from soda potash and sand seems to have been used in pots throughout the Near East at this time with moderate success.

26

The Beginning

PERSIA

Persia, lying to the east of Mesopotamia on the Iranian plateau, separated from Mesopotamia by the Zagros Mountains, has a long history of painted decorated ware.

Sites such as those at Tepe Sialk and Tepe Giyan have been excavated which reveal that around 2500 B.C. pottery similar to that of the Ubaid culture of Mesopotamia existed in this area. The style may have originated here much earlier and been taken to Mesopotamia by the movement of the people from the more barren highlands to the fertile lowlands.

Two finely made and painted beakers from Susa, Persia. c 3500–2800 B.C. Height 6 inches. British Museum

It is from Susa on the plateau that some of the finest pottery comes. Shapes were well thought out and achieved a high degree of technical ability. They included jars, bowls, chalices and goblets. The designs, native to Iran, were finely painted and well related to the shape of the pot. Combinations of geometric and semi-stylized natural forms such as the leopard were used to decorate the pots.

Later at Tepe Sialk a new series of shapes developed around 1000 B.C. Long-spouted vessels, perhaps imitating birds, were made and decorated with painted geometrical forms as well as animals. It is thought that these were made for contemporary ritual purposes, though the designs owe a great deal to the earlier traditions of painted wares.

Glazed tiles were used at the Palace of Darius, Susa, for wall decoration incorporating turquoise, brown, yellow, green and white colours.

Finely made pottery with painted geometrical decoration from Susa, Persia. c 35000–2800 B.C. British Museum.

SYRIA AND ANATOLIA

Syria, lying to the north-west of Mesopotamia on the upper reaches of the Euphrates, and Anatolia in Asia Minor have developments similar to that of Mesopotamia, but the nature of the area as a land-bridge linking east and west brought influences from both directions and it is difficult to isolate and identify the pottery styles. Fine pottery decorated with bold simple swirling patterns dates from

28

before 4000 B.C. in Anatolia and probably influenced later Mesopotamian pottery. Syrian contacts with Mesopotamia can be identified from as early as 3500 B.C. by similarities in architectural detail and fresco painting and it can be assumed that these contacts extended to the exchanging of information about pottery. For example, chalices, bottles, bowls and beakers found in Syria show a marked Mesopotamian influence. Western influence from the Mediterranean can also be seen in some of the pottery. Bottles, found in Syria, dating back to 2500 B.C. show influences from pre-Minoan Crete and the Aegean area. On some pottery the merging of the eastern and western styles can be seen.

All local styles were destroyed when the Assyrian armies destroyed the Syrian cities in the ninth to the seventh centuries B.C.

In 538 B.C. the Babylonians, who had conquered the Assyrians of north Mesopotamia, were defeated by the Persians in alliance with the Medes. Thus the whole area, including the Iranian plateau, fell under the control of a single ruler. This area, with its long history of finely decorated wares, saw the rise to power of the Islamic Empire and the decorated pottery which characterized it. This is dealt with in Chapter Four.

29

Badarian bowl. Egypt. Fine, thin, hard walls with "chattered" decoration and blackened rim. One of the finest of the Nile Valley wares. c 4000 B.C. Diameter 11 inches. Petrie Collection, University College London.

Pre-dynastic black topped pot. Egypt. These tall pots with pointed bases were typical of the early ware. c 4500–3200 B.C. Height 12 inches. Hastings Museum.

Early Period
(c 5000–3500 B.C.)

Pre-Dynastic Egypt
(c 3500–3200 B.C.)

EGYPT

The earliest Egyptian pottery is found in the central Nile Valley and forms one of the most aesthetically pleasing groups of Egyptian pottery. Between 5000 and 4000 B.C. the Badarian culture produced fine pottery of which the earliest wares from Deir Tasa consisted of deep bowls with flat bases and angular sides narrowing towards the mouth. Beakers with flared rims were often decorated with incised lines filled with white paste. From this beginning the finest Badarian wares were produced. Using carefully prepared red Nile clay the pots were finely made with thin walls, lightly burnished and well baked. Forms were simple and combined well with the black, brown and red colours of the body and occasional combed decoration. The entire production seems restrained and uncomplicated. Cooking pots with rounded bases and no rims or necks form the main part of the production.

Fayum, in the west of the Nile Valley, was also an early production area: the pots were fairly coarse and the body was filled with chopped chaff to increase the working qualities of the clay. No decoration seems to have been used and the shapes were irregular.

In pre-dynastic Egypt dating from around 3500 B.C. to 3200 B.C. pottery continued to be made much as in the early period. Essentially the style was monochrome and undecorated and made

30

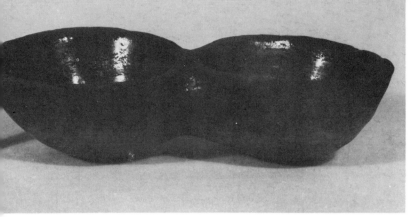

Red polished ware, double bowl with blackened rim, Egypt. c 4500–3200 B.C. *Height 2 inches* Petrie Collection, University College London.

from the red Nile clay, though new shapes and techniques were developed. Undoubtedly the main product was the black-topped red wares. Tall storage jars with pointed bases, and beakers, all highly burnished, were made and were probably fired upside down with their mouths buried in ash to achieve the black coloured top: the technique did not lend itself easily to shallow bowls and dishes. Occasionally animals in low relief were modelled on the pots and, rarely, incised animals.

The red polished Badarian pottery continued to be made with more regular colour, a higher gloss and in a wider variety of shapes. Dishes and bowls, narrow-necked vases, bulbous flasks and long-necked vessels were common. Double lobed and spouted vessels were more rare. All the pots were hand built and no evidence of the use of the wheel has so far been found.

Egypt was united as a single country in 3250 B.C. by Menes. The country was tightly governed by the priests who, having all scientific knowledge, were very powerful. Art formed part of the religious beliefs and as such played a part in religious practice. So rigid were the rules about the way paintings and sculpture should be carried out that in the following 3000 years little change was made. A statue was a representation in stone and it was thought that this enabled the person to be reconstructed after death and so live on in another world. Paintings, again executed according to strict rules on the walls of tombs, depicted scenes which

Red polished ware, oval bowl with white inlaid design showing women weaving. Egypt. c 3500 B.C. Petrie Collection, University College London.

Early Dynasties
(c 3250–2700 B.C.)

31

Flat-based bowl, burnished with inlaid incised decoration imitating basket work. Egypt. c 3500 B.C. Petrie Collection, University College London.

A typical Gerzean pot with lugged handles. Egypt. Full, globular form with rounded rim and painted spiral pattern. Other designs copied rope patterns as well as natural stone patterns of alabaster. c 3300 B.C. Height 5 inches. Petrie Collection, University College London.

would be useful to the deceased in the next world and were perhaps characteristic scenes from the dead man's life. Such a rigid and inflexible system did not allow, let alone encourage, movement in art. Pottery made in this period lost much of the vitality it had had earlier. With interest centred on the major arts little attention was given to pottery. Buff-coloured clay free from organic matter was used; it was found in desert valleys in Middle and Upper Egypt and, when fired, became grey or buff in colour. Decoration was painted on to the buff-coloured pots with iron oxide, which became purplish-red when fired, and white slip. The natural stone patterns of alabaster were often copied and more elaborate designs of boats, men and women, birds, trees and other objects were carried out. Little regard seems to have been paid to the symmetry of the designs. Handles fixed on to the side of the pots were made for the first time in Egypt. Forms became more cylindrical, imitating the results obtained from contemporary stone working.

Old Kingdom (c 2700–2100 B.C.)

During the Old Kingdom, about 2700–2100 B.C., the simple slow wheel was introduced into Egypt, probably from Mesopotamia. Shapes became finer but seem to owe much more to metal prototypes. Spouted ewers, lipped jugs, bowls with incurving rims, tall libation vessels, tall stands for ritual vessels and low stands for domestic pots are characteristic.

Around 2500 B.C. very fine bowls were produced

32

A fine Meydum bowl found on the site at which it was made. Egypt. The low sides with the rounded base make it an ideal shape for a cooking pot. c 2600–2200 B.C. Diameter 11 inches. Petrie Collection, University College London.

Gerzean jar. Egypt. Dark painted designs on buff clay show ship with emblem, aloe and flamingos. c 3200 B.C. Petrie Collection, University College London.

at Meydum which reflected the contemporary interest in metal-working. These carinate bowls had rounded bottoms and sharply angled sides; the clay was carefully prepared and the walls were thin and highly burnished. The simple forms and decoration gave the bowls a refined, precise, quality which other contemporary pottery lacked.

Gold, copper, precious stones, ivory, alabaster and wood were all worked with great skill and an artificial paste was developed to replace the soap-stone which had been used in the manufacture of small glazed objects in what is known as Egyptian faience. This artificial paste was made by mixing powdered quartz sand with an alkaline material known as a flux, which caused the quartz sand to fuse at a workable temperature. Potash, which occurs in wood-ash, or natron, which is a mineral containing sodium found in the western desert of Egypt, were the fluxes used. Small objects moulded in such a mixture would, when heated to a sufficiently high temperature, form a shiny surface; if small quantities of copper were present in the paste, rich turquoise colours were formed on the surface, while small quantities of manganese gave a purple surface.

The earliest faience objects in Egypt were made in Badari, Upper Egypt, in the form of beads. Small pieces of jewellery, figurines, amulets, vessels for precious liquids such as perfumes or oil, in-lays for coffins, furniture and temple walls came later. Small pots made in moulds were fashioned

33

Pot with stirrup handle and painted and banded geometrical designs shows evidence of foreign influences. Egypt. c 1000 B.C. Height 4 inches. Petrie Collection, University College London.

Cylinder jars. Alabaster form imitated in buff clay. Egypt. Wheel made. c 2100–1600 B.C. Petrie Collection, University College London.

Middle Kingdom
(c 2100–1320 B.C.)

in quite complex shapes, the range of which included baskets with lids and modelled pomegranates, though the objects rarely exceeded three inches in height until about 1000 B.C.

Foreign influence became more apparent in the manufacture of pottery in the period 2100–1600 B.C. Imperial expansion overseas and imported ware from Mycenae, Cyprus and Crete began to affect the forms of Egyptian pottery. Large numbers of small bottles with narrow necks and handles were imported from the Mediterranean and probably contained precious perfumes or oils, and these in turn were imitated by the Egyptian potters. The wheel became more efficient, and potters shown at work on the wall of the Egyptian tomb of Beni Hasan c 1900 B.C. appear to make the wheel go round by pushing it with the hand. The geometric patterns easily obtained with the wheel began to be used by the Egyptians, and carefully thrown pots were joined together to produce quite complicated forms. Pots with pedestal feet were made for the first time, imitating those made in the Mediterranean.

In the ruins of Akhetaten (Amarna) large quantities of painted pottery made for the use of the court for special religious purposes, dated to the years 1380–1350 B.C., have been found. Many of the pots were large and complex, some over three feet high, and demonstrate the skill of the potters. Painted designs were ornate and well related to

34

Flask in the form of a duck, used in burial rituals. Egypt. The black burnished body was inlaid with white pigment. c 1700 B.C. Height 5 inches. Petrie Collection, University College London.

Vase in green glazed ware. Egyptian. c 1567–1320 B.C. Height 4 inches. By courtesy of the Anthropological Museum, University of Aberdeen.

the shape of the vessel. Motifs of garlands of flowers, geometrical patterns and tomb scenes were painted in red, blue, white and black pigment after the pots had been fired. The decoration seems to reflect the strongly naturalistic tendencies which inspired the art of the period.

Painted pottery continued to be made after 1350 B.C., though changed in character. Designs on the pots were more crowded and less well painted. Decorated pottery that had been made specially for the use of the court was now made for anyone who could afford to buy it. Foreign influence continued and the loop handle came into general use. Amphora-type storage pots were made in large quantities.

Changes in the burial customs during the new Kingdom (c 1320–750 B.C.) led to a reduction in the amount and nature of pottery placed in the tomb. It may be that pottery was not now specially manufactured for burial purposes as in the past and the pottery which has been found is on the whole utilitarian and dull. In the late period c 750–325 B.C. a renaissance of Egyptian culture affected most arts and crafts but was less apparent in pottery. Shapes became more complex and the use of lead glaze became more general. The wheel, too, continued to gain in efficiency, lessons perhaps having been learnt from the Greeks. A tomb painting of about 300 B.C. shows the god Khum sitting at a wheel in which the

Late Period

heavy stone fly-wheel is shown being pushed round with the foot near the ground; the wheel-head is raised to a height of two feet. Such wheels were in use until the invention of the crank shaft in the late middle ages.

In 30 B.C. Egypt became a Roman province and the Romans introduced their own methods of making pottery. Around A.D 350 the Coptic branch of the Christian Church became a dominant factor and ancient Egyptian designs were fused with classical elements. At the battle of Heliopolis in A.D. 640 the Islamic Arabs took control of Egypt; pottery made in Egypt under Islamic rule is dealt with in Chapter Four.

CRETE

The Minoan civilization on the island of Crete was the first civilization in Europe. It rose around 3000 B.C. and lasted for about 1800 years, though pottery had been made in Crete before the Minoans and continued to be made after the civilization had finished. Unlike the other early civilizations, it developed not in a river valley but on an island. The sea, as well as protecting the islanders from attack, enabled the Minoans to develop an economy based on trade; they exported oil and wine in pottery vessels, in exchange for corn. This open and free trade brought with it a very cosmopolitan atmosphere. Unlike the Egyptians, the Minoans had neither an oppres-

The Beginning

sive priesthood nor a heavy and determined artistic style, and the culture which developed was rich, free and individual.

Chronologically the Minoan civilization is comparable with Egypt, and while Cretan sculpture and architecture were not as accomplished as that of Egypt, the pottery was superior, being more varied technically and aesthetically. In contrast to Egyptian pottery, the carefully observed and drawn natural objects used in the decoration of the Minoan pots give much of the work a freshness which is almost contemporary.

At various times immigrants from Egypt and Mesopotamia brought with them their skills, and such craftsmen as potters and metal-workers were received as honoured members of society. The King was not too rich to use earthenware on his table and the pots were often fine and beautiful. At their best Minoan pots were thought good enough to bury in the tombs of Egyptian noblemen along with their other treasures.

A wide variety of forms were made: tall-stemmed wine cups, imitating wooden chalices, handled vases, pitchers and large storage jars. Painted decoration was, however, the chief characteristic of Minoan pottery. Between 2000 and 1550 B.C. decoration derived from nature was used. At first the designs were stylized, but later during the middle Minoan period (1900–1700 B.C.) they became much more naturalistic. Several colours, including white, red, blue and black, were

Pottery jar, Knossos, Crete, with painted octopus design. Late Minoan. c *1450–1400* B.C. *Height 18 inches.* Ashmolean Museum.

37

used and designs were often painted on to a dark ground. Vivid pictorial representations of plants, lilies, octopus, seaweed and marine life in general were painted with great vigour, often over the whole surface of the pot. The results were fresh and naturalistically rendered and it is in this realism that some sources of Greek art are discernible. The pots were unglazed and the free-flowing, natural decoration echoed their smooth round forms.

The Minoan capital of Knossos was destroyed around 1400 B.C. either by the invading Mycenaeans from the Greek mainland or by an earthquake, or both, and it is only recent excavations which have revealed the enormous achievements of the Minoans.

Minoan pots seem, with their detailed observation and naturalistic decoration, to reflect a happy,

Mug with painted geometrical decoration. Crete. Late Minoan period. c 1450–1400 B.C. Height 2½ inches. Fitzwilliam Museum.

Three-footed tankard. Crete. Painted decoration probably derived from plants. Late Minoan period. c 1450–1400 B.C. Height 3 inches. Fitzwilliam Museum.

almost naïve society. No human figures are shown on the pottery and, unlike the Greeks, the Minoans seem to have had neither an obsession with the past nor did they make any attempt to record contemporary events. The designs are immediate, fresh and gay and, unlike the later Greek pots, demand little intellectual effort. Although in Crete we see the beginnings of Greek shapes and Greek vase painting there is none of the heaviness which Greek pots sometimes have; here are fresh, light, airy, completely unsophisticated designs on sound practical shapes. The work is unique and the qualities it possesses are rarely found in combination. Only with the destruction of Minoan society around 1400 B.C. and the diminished trade, did the standard of pottery decline.

INDUS VALLEY

The Indus civilization, developed in the alluvial valley of the Indus in north-west India, is thought to have started around 3000 B.C. and lasted until 1500 B.C. It seems to owe much of its technology to Mesopotamia and the immense cities of Harrappa and Mohenjo-daro, now gigantic mounds, leave evidence of the relative development of the two cities. They were complicated and well planned with running water and sanitation. Buildings were made of mud and fired bricks, irrigation was practised, copper and bronze were smelted, Egyptian faience was made

Painted pot. Mohenjo-daro, Indus Valley. Decorated with stylized animal figures. c 2000 B.C. With due courtesy of the Department of Archaeology, Pakistan.

and stamped seals were used for identification. Developments in other fields were made independent of Mesopotamia. New crops such as cotton were cultivated, and animals such as the ox were domesticated.

The pottery was technically excellent and much of it has been compared to the wares produced by the Roman Empire and the Victorians: technically accomplished, but extremely standardized and with a general lack of aesthetic sensibility.

Modern Sind potters continue to use a foot-wheel which is almost certainly a legacy of this period. Such wheels, which probably came from Mesopotamia, are still used in remote parts of Iran and north Africa. The arrangement of the wheel consists of a pit in which is set a central axis connecting a heavy fly-wheel at the base with a lighter wheel-head at the top, on which the pots are made. The potter sits on the edge of the pit pushing and controlling the fly-wheel with his feet.

Painted decoration took the form of natural motifs such as birds, fish, animals, plants and trees. Though the chemistry of glazing seems to have

The Beginning

been understood, little use was made of it. At
Mohenjo-daro many broken pots have been
found by a water stall; the pots are roughly made
and from the evidence it seems they were used
once for drinking and then thrown away. Such
pots must have been produced both quickly and
cheaply by the potters.

Painted pot sherds. Mohenjo-daro, Indus Valley. Hatched and plant decoration. c *2000* B.C.
With duc courtesy of the Department of Archaeology, Pakistan.

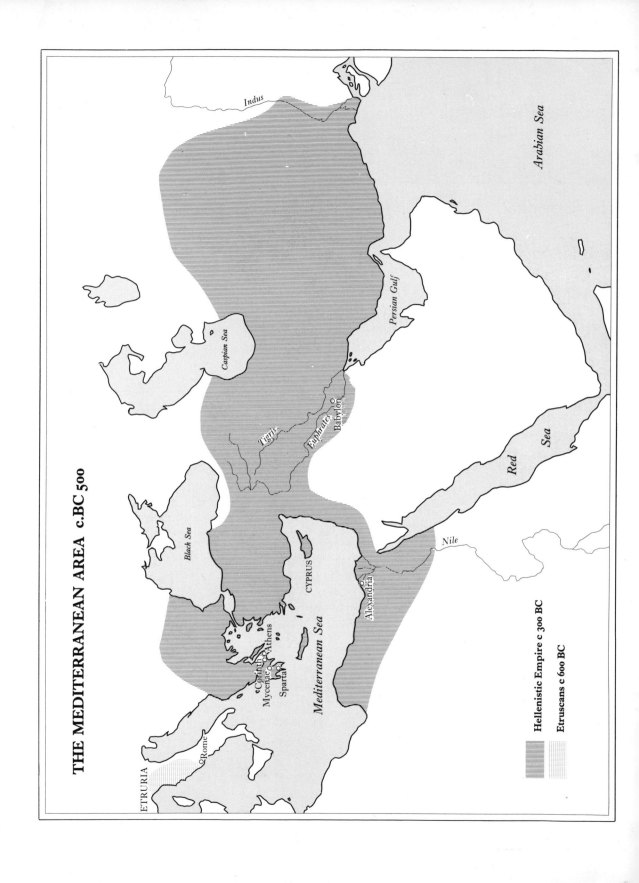

THE MEDITERRANEAN AREA c.BC 500

Indus

Arabian Sea

Caspian Sea

Persian Gulf

Tigris

Euphrates

Babylon

Red Sea

Black Sea

Nile

CYPRUS

Mediterranean Sea

Alexandria

Corinth
Mycenae Athens
Sparta

ETRURIA

Rome

Hellenistic Empire c 300 BC

Etruscans c 600 BC

Chapter 2

The Mediterranean
c 1500 B.C.—A.D. 500

MYCENAE

The mainland of Greece, unlike the Island of Crete, was much slower to develop a settled civilization. Mycenae, a city in southern Greece, flourished around 1500 B.C. and was strongly influenced by the Minoan and Anatolian cultures. The Mycenaeans were a fierce warlike people who built cities with strong fortifications in contrast to the Minoans who led a peaceful island existence. Gold seems to have been abundant and metal-working and ivory-carving were highly developed skills.

Pottery, in this society, was not regarded in the same way as in Crete. Metal was the chief source of wealth and pottery an inferior alternative. The early pottery was the grey Minyan ware, made around 1600 B.C.; the pots were soapy to touch and the shapes closely reflected those made

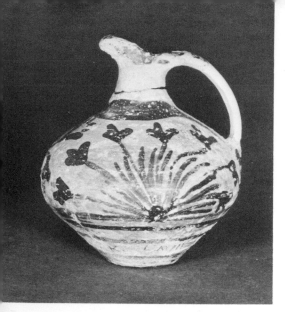

A History of Pottery

in metal. The influence of the warlike invading Achaeans from the north coast of the Peloponnese around 1500 B.C. combined with the Minoan influence from the south Aegean to produce distinctive if unexciting pots. Natural forms of cuttlefish, seaweed and shellfish, such as were used by the Minoans, were some of the decorative motifs, all reflecting a sea culture, but no longer were the designs painted over the entire surface. The introduction of the wheel, probably from Egypt, led to the banding of lines on the pot and these bands were soon used to confine the designs to borders, chiefly on the neck and shoulders. Minoan potters had filled all the available space on the surface with painted designs and the results were fresh and immediate. Mycenaean pottery seems to lack this freshness, and with the Dorian invasion from the north around 1200 B.C. pottery decoration became more limited and the beginnings of designs using geometrical shapes appeared; the lozenge, chequers and the meander were used in border patterns.

The shapes themselves began to evolve as basically Greek, though the forms lacked the strength of those which were to develop later. With the Iron Age well under way the Dorians, with their severe and militaristic temperament and superior weapons and armour, had a deadening influence on art as a whole. Artistic achievement seemed to decline in the entire Greek peninsula until the emergence of the Greek city states around 1000 B.C.

44

The Mediterranean

GREECE

From around 1000 B.C. the classical Greek culture as we know it today began to emerge. Art in Greece was of the people: the community, religion and the arts were closely linked. The State was the main patron of the arts, acting as such through the assemblies, councils and magistrates. Art was completely enmeshed in daily living and was not exclusive to the wealthy. Pottery was regarded in much the same way. The careful and highly sophisticated painted pottery was used at various times for grave monuments and as prizes for athletic success, but little pottery was produced merely for display: most of it had a function. Undecorated pottery probably formed the largest part of the total production; as this pottery was not so highly regarded it has not survived to the same extent. Much of the undecorated ware was made locally, leaving the painted pottery to be made in special centres such as Corinth and Athens. Most of the Greek painted pottery now in museums has been found in graves. Painted pottery was highly valued both for the amount of work such painting entailed and the nature of the scenes depicted — though the pots were decorated to make them attractive rather than to turn them into works of art. Paintings on Greek pots are a vital source from which to learn about the history of the Greeks and for this reason they have been studied intently.

Three-handled jar with formal bands and line decoration. Mycenaean. This shape was later developed by the Greeks. c 1200 B.C. Fitzwilliam Museum.

45

A History of Pottery

Greek pots have two unique characteristics. The first is the form, which was closely related to the use to which the vessel would be put, and the second is the decorative painting on the surface of the pot. The technique of painting on pottery had been used earlier by the Mycenaeans but was developed to perfection around the mid to late sixth century B.C. Greek pots are usually classified into four roughly chronological periods based on the style of decorations used.

Technique The use of the wheel was widespread throughout Greece around 1000 B.C. Pots made from carefully prepared clay were thrown on a wheel propelled by an assistant who was usually a boy apprentice. The clay used was highly plastic and fired a yellow-red colour in a kiln with an oxidizing atmosphere. Attic clay used by the Athenian potters and dug from the borders of the city fired a red much richer than the yellower clays used by the Corinth potters. Pots were thrown in sections which were joined together when the clay had become stiff enough to be handled yet soft enough to be moulded, known as the leather-hard stage. At this stage, too, the pots were placed back on the wheel and, in the process known as turning, surplus clay was cut off, using either a metal or wooden tool. In this way finger marks made while throwing could be removed and the profile, so important to the Greek pots, could be sharpened. It should be remembered that by this time (1000 B.C.) the wheel had become much more efficient

46

and smooth. Turning would have been very difficult without this improved wheel.

The painting on the surface was achieved by
using fairly simple materials in a sophisticated
way. Glaze had been discovered earlier, probably
in Mesopotamia, and may easily have been known
to the Greeks who, for some reason, chose not
to use it. The Greeks used a clay slip which lost
its mattness and became slightly shiny and glass-
like in the kiln. It was not completely waterproof
and it could not be called a true glaze. Simply, the
effect was achieved by using clay with a high
percentage of iron oxide – ferric oxide, Fe_2O_3 –
which fired red in a kiln where there was plenty of
oxygen; if the oxygen content was reduced (by
burning damp wood or closing the air inlets into
the kiln) the flame, hungry for oxygen, would
take it from the easiest available source – in this
case the oxygen in the iron contained in the clay
which, with a reduced amount of oxygen, became
ferrous oxide, FeO, which fired black. Using carefully prepared slip, red and black colours could
be produced on the same pot by the following
method:

1 The pot was made in finely prepared clay
   which fired red in an oxidizing kiln.
2 A slip was made from red clay and an alkali,
   such as wood-ash, was added to break down
   the ability of clay particles to cling together;
   large clay particles would sink and the finer

particles were poured off. Eventually a slip was made which contained only small-sized particles. Acid, in the form of urine or wine, was added to make the mixture flowing yet firm. It is thought that the slip was painted on to the surface of the pot.

3 The pot was fired in the kiln with plenty of oxygen present (oxidized atmosphere) up to 900°C; at this stage all the pot and decoration would be red.

4 Air inlets would now be closed and damp fuel used to lower the oxygen content of the kiln (reduced atmosphere); all the surface of the pot including the decoration at this stage would turn black.

5 An oxidizing fire, reintroducing oxygen into the kiln and lasting only a short time, finished the firing. This caused the body of the pot to turn red and the decoration painted in slip to remain black since it was much more dense because the clay particles were finer and there was a greater percentage of iron oxide; if this oxidizing fire lasted too long the slip, too, would turn red as the oxygen began to penetrate its surface. (Some pots have been found which show evidence of this.)

Shapes All the main shapes of the pots were evolved early on in the Greek culture and were a development of Minoan, Mycenaean and Dorian shapes. Most of the basic shapes were intended for holding

48

liquid of some sort. Wine and water containers predominated, but smaller containers for oil and perfume were also made. It was the Greek custom to drink wine mixed with water and the necessary vessels were the krater or large mixing bowl, the narrow-necked amphora for the wine and the three-handled water pitcher or hydria for the water. A tall-handled ladle or kyathos was used to pour the wine into jugs known as oinochoai or into flat, two-handled cups known as kylikes. Sometimes the wine needed cooling and then a psyketer, a vessel with a tall stemmed foot, was filled with wine and stood in cold water in a lekane which was a general purpose bowl. Personal toilet pots were also made. For the more precious liquids there were small bottles called aryballoi, lekythoi and alabastra.

The forms of the pots remained basically unchanged throughout the period of classical Greece, probably because they proved to be practical and convenient in use. The majority of pots were left plain or decorated with bands of black slip, or, later, covered entirely with black slip; and decorated pots represent only a small proportion of Greek wares. Cooking pots of all kinds were produced very cheaply; metal was still an expensive luxury while clay products were not. Storage pots, saucepans, ovens, frying pans, stoves, cooking pots and braziers were all produced. Water clocks were made for the law courts. These consisted of a pot with a small hole which let out the water

Krater. Greece. Design shows rowing boat and formal figures in the geometric style. Eighth century B.C. British Museum.

Jug. Athenian. The bands and formal meander design are typical of the geometrical style. c 900 B.C. British Museum.

Geometric Style
(c 1000–700 B.C.)

over a measured period of time; the force of the stream indicated the length of time left for the water to run out. Both plain and painted pots were exported in vast numbers as containers of olive oil or wine. Technically the ware was strong, but it chipped easily at the edges which were often thickened to strengthen them.

The earliest recognizable Greek painted style, known as proto-geometric, began to emerge roughly around 1000 B.C. Forms developed which, as previously explained, were to last throughout most of the Greek period. Decoration was clearly defined with light areas of clay and dark areas of slip forming simple balanced designs. Bands of slip were confined to shoulders and tops of pots; simple half-spiral designs and concentric circles were carefully drawn in slip and appear to have been done with mathematical precision. Completely abstract, the designs broke away altogether from the naturalistic style of the Cretans and the cramped convention of the Mycenaeans. Only black slip was used, though it occasionally fired dark brown.

Around 900 B.C. the geometric style emerged more fully, characterized by severely defined shapes with ornamental bands of patterns covering the entire pot. Decoration was still regular and abstract, but, later, human and animal figures appeared in very abstract forms, confined to the borders. Burial scenes were also depicted. Little art has survived from this period and these pots

Jug, late geometric style. Greece. Stylized birds and geometric designs, with plastic modelling of snake on handle. Eighth century B.C. British Museum.

The Mediterranean

may have been one of the main art forms; they were often used as monuments on graves.

The mature geometric style had a still more balanced decoration which usually incorporated the handle into the design. Decorative motifs included not only concentric circles, chequers, triangles, zig-zags and the meander, but also the quatrefoil and swastika. Towards the end of the style plastic modelling was introduced and rims, for example on the oinochoe or jug, were modelled.

Around 700 B.C. the Greek city states expanded, both geographically and artistically. The Greeks colonized much of the Mediterranean and came into much closer contact with the Near East and the oriental ideas of decoration. This influenced the decoration on the pottery and gave rise to the period known as oriental or black-figure because of the distinctive black figures painted on to the surface of the red pots. New ornaments, different animals and foreign plants were introduced into the designs; the curve of the pot became less restrained and there seems to be a great awareness of organic form. Experiments were made in drawing the human figure.

Later other colours besides black were introduced to heighten the designs. Small areas of purple, red, white and later yellow helped to break the designs away from the austerity of the geometric style.

Pots decorated with animals, which hitherto

Oriental or Black-Figure Style (c 700–550 B.C.)

Amphora. Athens. Black-figure design showing warrior fighting lion. c 520 B.C. Height 12½ inches. Victoria and Albert Museum.

A History of Pottery

had included only the goat and deer, were now incorporating the lion, bull, dog, hare, eagle, cock and goose as well as the mythological sphinx and griffin. All the animals were shown in peaceful, formal poses with little movement and no signs of aggression. It was the Corinthian potters, using the local yellow clays, who brought this animal style to perfection in the seventh century B.C. Detailed friezes beautifully carried out were shown in bands often no more than two inches wide. Incised lines were used in the designs to convey detail and the success of the designs was unequalled elsewhere in Greece. Bands of figures in complex arrangements were also shown.

It was in the study and drawing of the human figure that the potters of Athens found their greatest satisfaction; this was indigenous to the Greeks and owed little to oriental influence. Battles, races and processions were favourite themes and, later, scenes from mythology were introduced. No attempt was made to make the drawing absolutely anatomically correct; what seemed important was the recording of contemporary events. A profile was used for the head with a frontal eye view; limbs were shown in profile, while the torso was either in profile or front view. No attempt was made either to fit in a background or indicate depth.

Black figures were painted on to the red background and fine detail was scratched through to

Amphora. Corinthian. Lions and sphinxes with incised details. c 700 B.C. *Height $11\frac{1}{2}$ inches.* British Museum.

reveal the red body. The finest designs were often restrained and masterful, without any of the heaviness which developed towards the end of the period. Early designs included many border patterns, but gradually these were simplified and occasionally eliminated altogether. Purple was no longer used and by convention black was adopted for male flesh, white for female and purple-red was confined to drapery and accessories. Generally the colours were more sombre than those used earlier by the Athenian or Corinthian potters. The work of individual painters can be recognized and among the greatest are Lydos, Nearchos, Exekias and the Amasis Painter. While Corinthian potters developed a precise and elegant animal style, Athenian potters brought the black-figure style to its peak between 550 and 530 B.C.

The red-figure style was the last major Greek pottery painting style and developed in Athens around 530 B.C. The style may to some extent have been suggested by changes in contemporary art. Wall painting had become popular and painters were turning to this new and larger dimension in preference to the comparatively cramped and limited size and palette of the vase painter. Vase painting, therefore, required a technique which allowed greater emphasis to be placed on accuracy rather than stylization if it was to continue as a medium used by the best painters. The red-figure technique gave painters scope to practise their

Red-Figure Style
(c 530–330 B.C.)

53

Red-figure krater. Athens. Detail shows pots being decorated, by the Komaris Painter. c 430 B.C. Ashmolean Museum.

Amphora from Vulci by Dikaios, Painter, shows scene of warrior leaving home. c 510–500 B.C. British Museum.

newly acquired skills. Economic reasons may also have encouraged the new stylistic development as overseas competitors were producing work almost identical to black-figure pots and an attractive alternative had to be produced in Greece or export markets would have been lost.

The human figure, hitherto depicted stylistically and with a minimum amount of anatomical detail, now became the object of serious study. The incised method of showing detail was no longer thought satisfactory and a finer method of drawing had to be invented. Instead of painting the figure black on a red background the process was reversed and the background was painted black leaving the figure red in silhouette; detail was painted on to the figure with a thin raised black line, or else a thinner brown line. The early red-figure style was founded on line drawing rather than shading.

As the style developed, the figures were no longer used merely as decoration: attempts were made to suggest depth, using three-quarter views and foreshortening; draperies were detailed and ornate dots were used to suggest hair and texture; black-figure designs had had a solemnity lacking in the red-figure work which took a much more light-hearted view of life. Scenes from daily life became popular subjects. In later designs figures moved over the surface of the pot, no longer planted firmly on the baseline, and a variety of colours

The Mediterranean

were introduced. Perhaps the best work in this style was produced from about 530 to 500 B.C., expressing calm, refined, academic qualities and tending to reflect the best from the past rather than ape the contemporary vogue for free painting with its grandiose figures and compositions.

The red-figure style ceased to be used after 200 years or so. The overseas markets had been severely reduced both by emigrant Greek potters and the declining power of Greece; the industry failed to adapt itself to small production methods or to attract the better artists.

Only one other distinctive style of decoration existed. Around 580 B.C. potters started painting the background of the pot white and this was often supplemented by washes of colour, in red, purple or yellow ochre; this style was known as Attic white-ground ware. Since the white slip ground was fragile the technique was reserved for rather precious pots — for example oil-bottles or funeral pots. Scenes depicted on them tended to be of a peaceful nature and the pots as a whole were charming and delicate.

Gradually, as the Greeks warred with Persia and the city states became less strong, the fine, high quality of Greek pottery declined. Eventually the Romans took over those parts of the Greek pottery technique they required and adapted them for their own use.

Lekythos, white-ground style. Athens. The manufacture of successful white-ground ware was difficult and the technique was restricted to small objects. Scenes were often of a peaceful or quiet nature. Lekythos have a "false" container inside to hold the precious oil contents. c 460 B.C. Height 9⅝ inches. Victoria and Albert Museum.

White-Ground Ware

55

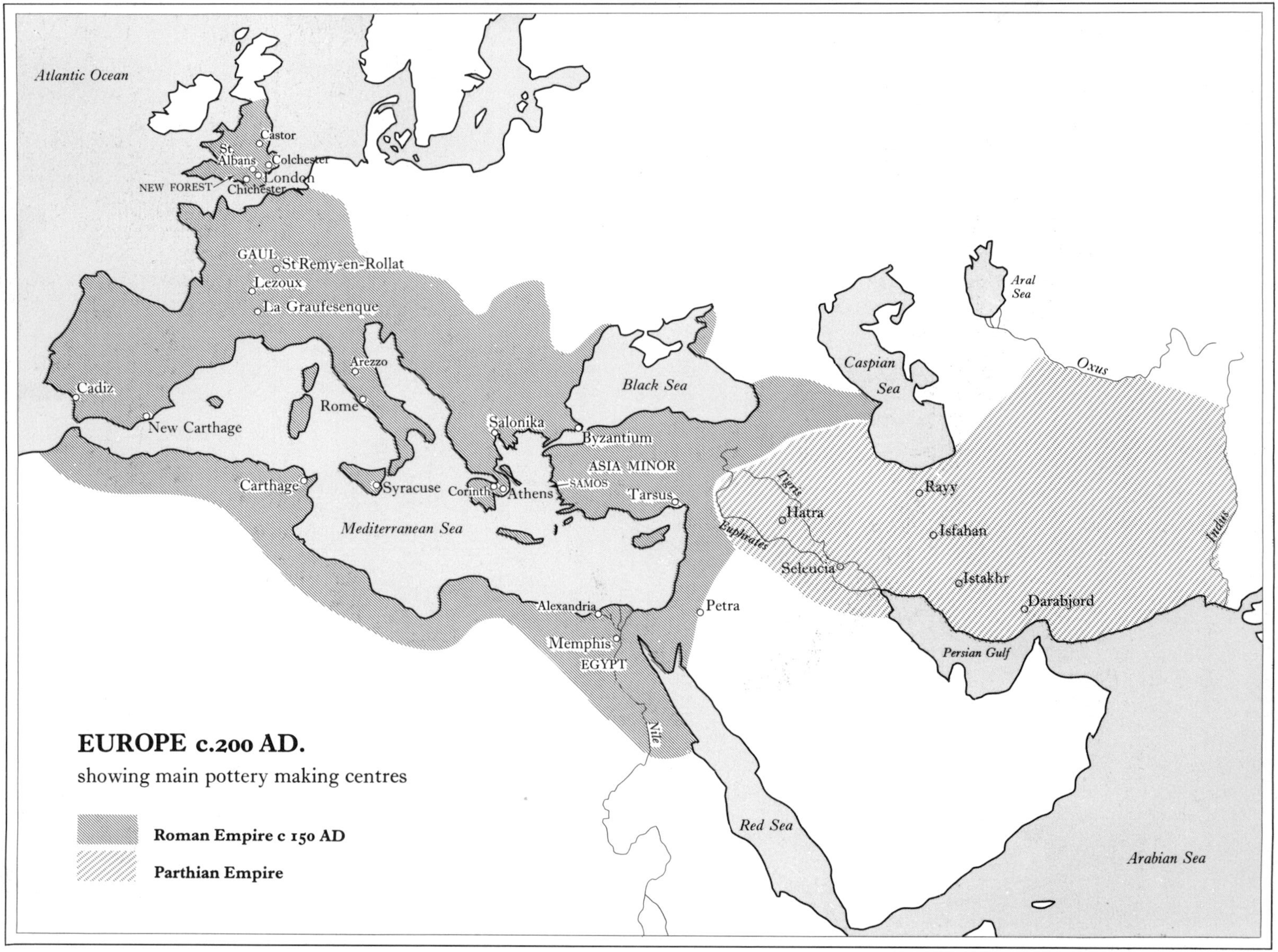

EUROPE c.200 AD.

showing main pottery making centres

Roman Empire c 150 AD

Parthian Empire

Atlantic Ocean

NEW FOREST

Chichester
London
Colchester
Castor
St Albans

GAUL
St-Remy-en-Rollat
Lezoux
La Graufesenque

Cadiz

New Carthage

Carthage

Arezzo

Rome

Syracuse

Salonika

Byzantium

ASIA MINOR

Corinth
Athens
SAMOS

Tarsus

Black Sea

Mediterranean Sea

Petra

Alexandria

Memphis

EGYPT

Nile

Red Sea

Arabian Sea

Persian Gulf

Caspian Sea

Aral Sea

Oxus

Indus

Rayy

Isfahan

Istakhr

Darabjord

Hatra

Seleucia

Tigris

Euphrates

THE ETRUSCANS

Etruria was a powerful, highly developed state situated in Italy, between Rome, Florence and the Appennine Mountains. The Villanovians, who lived in the region of Etruria before the Etruscans, were both skilled metal-workers and potters; their dead were cremated and the ashes buried in urns. They made pots by a combination of throwing and hand-building methods. Fairly coarse, iron-bearing clay was used and the surface was often burnished. Incised, often geometric designs decorated some of the pots, though towards the end of the eighth century B.C. an oriental influence was evident in the use of lotus flowers and mythological monsters.

Villanovians

Greek/Roman oinochoe, with moulded ribbed body and even black-gloss covering suggesting metal prototypes. c 200 B.C. Height 10 inches. By courtesy of the Anthropological Museum, University of Aberdeen.

Around 700 B.C. the Etruscan culture emerged. Many ideas from abroad, mainly from the Near East, were incorporated into their culture. They learned from Babylon how to construct the vaulted arch, from Egypt how to make faience, gold metal-work from Assyria and silver working from Phoenicia. Etruscan bronze-work was prized over the whole Mediterranean area. The native pottery was made from unpurified and roughly mixed clay which fired variable colours such as black, brown or red.

Around the middle of the seventh century B.C. grey-coloured pottery, often known as Bucchero Etruscan ware, was made. Technically the ware was sound and the shapes finely worked out and

Etruscans

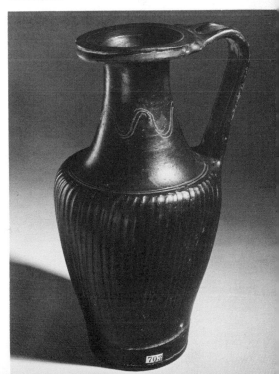

57

Amphora. Etruscan. Black polished ware with thin walls and engraved decoration of double spiral. Seventh century B.C. *Height* 5⅜ *inches.* British Museum.

A History of Pottery

executed. The decoration consisted of simple ornaments boldly incised on a shiny black or grey surface.

In the early seventh and sixth centuries B.C. Etruscan pottery was influenced both by immigrant Greek potters and imports of Greek pottery; firstly by the Greek geometric style and later by the red-figure style from Athens. The Etruscan style which developed was in fact slightly different from that used by the Greeks: Etruscan potters tended merely to copy the decoration they saw on the Greek pots rather than attempt to understand its significance, so that the results were often naïve.

THE ROMANS

According to legend Rome was founded in 753 B.C., but it was not until the fifth century B.C. that the Romans freed themselves from the Etruscans and the beginning of an Empire greater than any that had gone before appeared. By 275 B.C. Rome ruled the whole of the Italian peninsula. Greece had earlier colonized parts of Italy, mainly by the establishment of trade, while to the north of Rome the Etruscans had developed a Greek-inspired culture. Gradually Rome grew in size and strength and, in conquering neighbouring countries, absorbed a wider range of influence than had been absorbed by the Greeks.

It is difficult to look at Roman pottery without

Amphora. Etruscan. Bucchero ware with engraved and inlaid design. Seventh century B.C. British Museum.

comparing it unfavourably with that produced by the Greeks, but in doing so one must be aware of the needs of Roman society. The Romans were engineers and builders. They spread technical knowledge and ordered government and so encouraged the growth of industries which could produce the type and quality of goods they needed. The widespread introduction of mosaic and mural paintings led artists away from decorating pottery and so methods other than painting were developed. These methods had to be quick, efficient and effective to cope with the increased production. This led to the development by the Romans of the manufacture and use of special clay moulds for the production of a wide range of plain and decorated wares.

Pottery, being fragile, cannot easily be transported over large distances. Various centres were therefore established, at different times, in the Roman Empire, usually near the camps of the Legions or on a good trade route; for example at La Graufesenque in southern Gaul, and later at Lezoux in central Gaul. Whenever a new pottery centre was established little or no account was taken of local styles. Roman production techniques and knowledge were thus spread over the whole of Europe.

From the Greeks the Romans learnt how to prepare fine clay by adding an alkali, and so a slip of fine particles of clay was obtained. Suitable clay

Calix. Etruscan. The painted decoration shows Greek influence. Late sixth, early fifth century B.C. Fitzwilliam Museum.

Red-Gloss Ware

59

fired in an oxidizing kiln atmosphere gave a bright red sealing-wax colour and texture. The ware which resulted from the use of this clay is known by several names. Samian was one name given to it as the style was thought to have been developed on the island of Samos, but this is not now thought to be so. Terra sigillata is another of its names; again this is slightly misleading as it means pottery with stamped figures or patterns for decoration, though the term is also used to include much undecorated work made in this red clay. In general the pots can all be included under the heading red-gloss ware.

The pots, with raised decoration, were made in carefully prepared moulds, a technique which had been developed in late Hellenistic Greece and adapted by the Romans. Briefly, the method was to make a hollow mould in clay, known as a pitcher mould, and while the mould was soft a design, often based on contemporary metal-work, was impressed or incised on the inside of it. The fired mould was put on to the wheel-head and the inside smeared with clay which was smoothed as the wheel was rotated. A foot, and sometimes a rim, was often added to the moulded basic bowl shape. The decoration appeared in relief on the surface of the bowl. Early bowls were decorated with patterns of flowers and foliage used in a simple way. These designs were often copied directly from Greek metal-ware. The pots were

finished by being covered in a slip of fine clay which fired bright coral red in a clean oxidizing fire or black in a reduced kiln atmosphere (explained fully on page 47).

Arretium, modern Arezzo, gave its name to Arretine ware which was the most famous, most technically skilled and finest of the Roman red-gloss wares. The beauty and accuracy of the finish on the pots reveal excellent craftsmanship. Around 30 B.C. the industry developed very rapidly and lasted for about 100 years. Early Arretine pottery seems to indicate that Greek potters were employed, as the pots were fired black using the Greek reducing technique. Later the pots were fired red either because the process was easier or because the demand was for red rather than black ware. Early Arretine decoration was well balanced with sensitive groupings of figures of Hellenistic origin such as maenads, satyrs and fauns. Wreaths, masks, scrolls, swaths of fruit and flowers, birds, cupids and butterflies were all used. Often raised decoration on metal objects was copied directly by the potters, especially from the work of the silversmith. The fineness of the incised technique on the moulds allowed clear detail which perhaps encouraged the notable naturalistic decoration.

Plain, undecorated wheel-thrown pots were also made in red-gloss ware. Shapes were simple and undoubtedly influenced by contemporary metal shapes, having the clean, precise beauty associated

Arretine Ware

Undecorated Red-Gloss Ware

Decorated Red-Gloss Ware

with industrially produced rather than hand-thrown pottery. Best tableware at that time was made from metal, and the undecorated pottery set out to rival it. Flat dishes of various sizes were common as well as cups with slanting sides, bowls and other domestic pottery. The centre of manufacture was often stamped on the pot, sometimes falsely; "Genuine Arretine" has been found on pots made elsewhere. Potters also stamped their names on the pots; for example, Cerialis, a potter working at Lezoux in central Gaul during the reigns of Trajan and Hadrian, stamped his on the base of a red-gloss vessel.

As the Roman Legions moved farther west, the main production centre of the pottery industry moved first to southern Gaul and later to central Gaul. During the second century A.D. the central Gaulish factories were the chief suppliers of red-gloss ware to the British markets. Centres were also established in Britain at such places as Castor, Aldgate and the New Forest, but these were small industries in comparison with the potteries in Gaul.

The move of the industry away from Italy seemed to bring about a change in the style of the pottery. Decoration became livelier and more varied and, instead of using only metal originals, glass and leather forms were now also imitated. The cutting of leather-hard pottery imitating the cutting of glass became fairly widespread, and in some cases fine, detailed patterns were developed.

Thrown pottery decorated with applied ornament made by painting or trailing thick liquid clay slip on to the surface of the damp pot is often known as barbotine ware, named after the French word for slip. It was developed by the Romans to a high degree of control and early designs imitated those made in relief from moulds. Hunting scenes were a common favourite. White slip was often used over a dark-firing clay; because the technique required speed and dexterity rather than precision the results were often lively and pleasant.

The introduction of alternative methods of decoration, including rouletting made by a metal tool "chattering" on the side of the pot as it turned on the wheel, as well as patterns made with a tool with a revolving toothed wheel, saw a decline in the artistic and technical standard of moulded ware.

Roman coarse pottery used local clay fired without a coat of vitreous slip and was made with less carefully prepared clay. Wheel-made in a variety of forms it was the ordinary, everyday pottery for the majority of people, and was made at many different centres, mainly for local markets. The Romans, however, still managed, even in locally made pottery, to impose a Roman influence on form throughout the whole of the Empire.

Romano-British coarse pottery was made at numerous centres in Britain, each having its own characteristics. At Castor ware was produced with a dark, lustrous surface, often with barbotine decora-

Barbotine Ware

Coarse Pottery

63

Two-handled rich yellow/green glazed cup. Form, handles and moulded relief decoration recall contemporary silver forms, undoubtedly a contemporary luxury ware. From Soloi, Cyprus. Mid first century A.D. Height 2¾ inches. Fitzwilliam Museum.

Ewer with frieze of leaves and grapes. Roman, Asia Minor. Green lead glaze has deteriorated to silvery iridescence. First century B.C./A.D. Height 5 inches. Hastings Museum.

Lead-Glazed Ware

tion of animal figures or foliate scrolls, and was probably the most important centre in Britain. New Forest ware is characterized by a hard metallic surface with painted decoration. Bowls with rosette-stamped designs and pots decorated with faces were made probably as storage vessels. Cheese-presses, bowls, dishes, jars, beakers, bottles and mortars for pounding food were also produced. Local clays and local needs plus the throwing techniques brought by the Romans resulted in pots varying in colour, quality and decoration.

A minor but important Roman pottery technique involved the use of glaze. Lead-glazing had been discovered and used earlier by the Egyptians and Mesopotamians, though its use had never been widespread. Either it was technically too complicated to prepare and fire or the unglazed ware was preferred. A green lead glaze was used on pots made by methods similar to those used in the manufacture of red-gloss ware. Moulds with impressed designs or applied figures were used. By 100 B.C. the technique was practised in Asia Minor at Tarsus and at Alexandria in Egypt on pots which often had handles very like those made out of metal. The technique travelled through Italy, where it was very little used, to the Allier district of Gaul, at St. Remy-en-Rollat, Vichy. Subsequently it spread east into Germany and was established at Cologne by about A.D. 100. When the Roman Empire collapsed, much of the tech-

Jug. Roman, St Remy-en-Rollat, Gaul. Green glaze with design of floral wreaths with large flowers of four petals. c A.D. 100. Height 5 inches. British Museum.

The Mediterranean

nology the Romans had introduced lapsed, except for the lead-glazing of pottery in Byzantium where it formed the basis of later developments in Europe. Whether or not lead glaze continued to be used in Germany or was reintroduced at a later date is not known for certain.

Faience, developed much earlier by the Egyptians and Mesopotamians, continued to be made in Egypt during the Roman occupation. Brilliant blues were obtained from the addition of small percentages of copper; later the colours were extended to include black, red, green, purple, yellow and white. Because the paste had to be carefully prepared and the raw material was difficult to work they were very expensive to produce. A stronger and more workable body was later introduced by the Islamic potters, who developed the technique fully.

Under the Roman Empire the pottery industry was well organized and technical knowledge was taken to all parts of the Empire. To produce pottery in the quantity required by growing cities and large armies mass-production techniques were developed which foretold many of the production methods used by present-day industrial firms.

Amphora. Roman, found in Sardinia. Good green lead glaze, fired upside down. Seventh century A.D. Height $6\frac{7}{8}$ inches. British Museum.

65

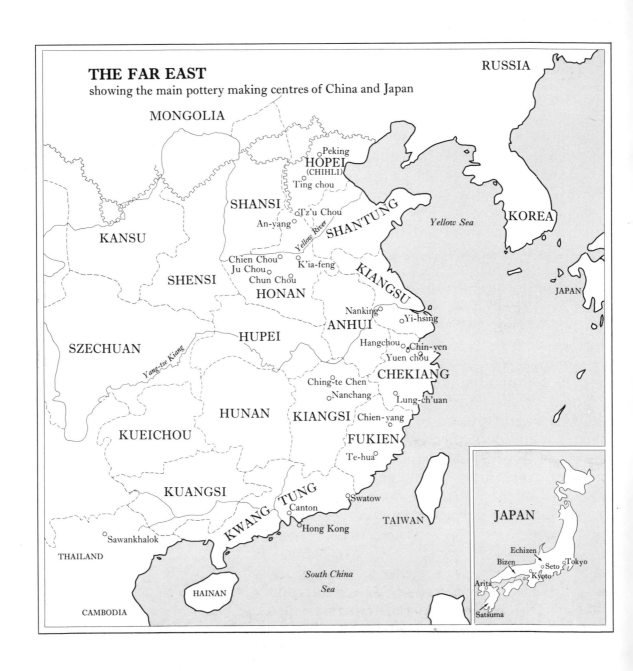

THE FAR EAST
showing the main pottery making centres of China and Japan

RUSSIA

MONGOLIA

KANSU

SHANSI

Peking
HOPEI
(CHIHLI)
Ting chou

T'z'u Chou
An-yang

SHANTUNG

Yellow Sea

KOREA

SHENSI

Chien Chou
Ju Chou
Chun Chou
HONAN

K'ia-feng

Yellow River

KIANGSU

JAPAN

SZECHUAN

HUPEI

Yang-tse Kiang

Nanking
ANHUI

Yi-hsing

Hangchou
Chin-yen
Yuen chou

CHEKIANG

HUNAN

Ching-te Chen
Nanchang

KIANGSI
Chien-yang

Lung-ch'uan

KUEICHOU

FUKIEN

Te-hua

KUANGSI

KWANG
TUNG

Swatow
Canton

Hong Kong

TAIWAN

JAPAN

Sawankhalok

THAILAND

Echizen

Bizen

Seto
Tokyo

CAMBODIA

HAINAN

South China
Sea

Arita
Kyoto

Satsuma

Chapter 3

The Far East

CHINA

The art of the Far East differs greatly from that produced in the West: a completely different philosophy encouraged the growth of a unique and, in many ways, fantastic art. The Greeks based their classic art on the idealization of the human form and as the decoration on pottery developed it reflected this. The Chinese were more contemplative and found enjoyment in the spiritual rather than the physical and this quality is evident in much of their pottery. At various times the expanding countries of the West and the settled and prosperous Chinese dynasties came into contact, each making an impact on the other. The fine ninth-century A.D. porcelain imported into the Arab world from China encouraged the development there of earthenware made in imitation of porcelain as well as instigating research into the manufacture of porcelain. From the West the

A History of Pottery

Chinese potters of the Han and T'ang dynasties got lead, with which to make low-temperature glazes, and later blue pigment, often called Mohammedan blue, which is a purified form of cobalt oxide unobtainable at that time in China. The lead was in the form of a frit, which is a manufactured material made by mixing lead with another material such as sand, heating it until it melts and then grinding up the glass so formed. The activities of the Dutch East India Company brought vast quantities of decorated Chinese porcelain to Europe which influenced the work of the Delft potters, and the Chinese themselves adapted many of their designs to the demands of the European market.

Decoration on Chinese pottery may appear confused and meaningless to western eyes. Yet to the Chinese each object and its arrangement had a meaning. In a country where the written language had developed from pictorial symbols this is hardly surprising. The lion, horse and elephant were used to symbolize Buddha, while the dragon represented the Emperor and the phoenix the Empress. The pomegranate stood for fertility, a pair of fish or mandarin ducks for wedded bliss; the pine tree, peach and gourd were emblems of long life; while the cassia bough and salmon leaping from the waves stood for literary success. Only when European decorative themes were introduced did the meanings become lost.

Pots were highly regarded from early times by both religious and secular leaders in China. The

The Far East

Imperial court commissioned work and later established an Imperial pottery factory at Ching-te Chen. Pots played an important part in the Buddhist ceremony, and alter vases, for example, received great care in their manufacture. Long and often lyrical descriptions of the different types of ware have left much literary evidence to assist in classifying pots, though sometimes such glamorous descriptions confuse an already large and complicated picture.

For the sake of simplicity the development of Chinese pottery will be dealt with in chronological order. China has one of the world's longest continuous civilizations, despite many invasions and foreign rulers. Each dynasty or period of hereditary rule had its own characteristics, though some dynasties were very short; only the main ones will be dealt with here.

Early Period

Neolithic Chinese pottery, produced on the plains near the Yellow River, was made in the period 3000–1500 B.C. Pots from Kansu province were made in reddish clay with boldly drawn geometric patterns in red, black or purplish-brown pigment and are related stylistically to those made in western Asia, southern Persia, Baluchistan and southern Russia, which suggests close communication at that time. Such examples of the ware as remain today are mainly burial urns or cooking utensils. The high quality of the painted decoration on the full swelling forms, and the vigour and life of these pots give them a quality which is both pleasing and refreshing. It is curious that later

69

Earthenware funerary urn. Tao Valley of Kansu, China. Red, black, purple and brown pigment painted on red clay. c *2000–1500* B.C. *Height about 12 inches.* British Museum.

A History of Pottery

Chinese pottery seems to bear no relationship to this early work.

Cooking vessels on three legs made out of grey clay have also survived. Incised textured patterns and the strength of the form, with hollow legs providing the liquid with a greater surface area from which to absorb heat, characterize this ware.

The Bronze Age in China saw the working of bronze and jade brought to a high degree of refinement, especially for religious vessels. These materials, far more precious than pottery, had a great influence on pottery forms. Many pots were made in almost exact imitations of bronze and jade vessels, and it was many hundreds of years before pottery began to be made once again with real regard for the qualities of clay.

The Chou Dynasty (1155–255 B.C.) The Chou Dynasty saw the establishment of basic government and the development of organized religion. Confucius (about 550–480 B.C.) introduced a religion based on filial piety, reverence for tradition, and moderation and harmony. At much the same time Taoism, following the teachings of Lao Tzu that impersonal nature permeates everything, propounded a high and compassionate morality; later cults developed the mystical element of Taoism.

Excavated graves are the richest source of pottery as well as other treasures of this period. It was the custom to inter with the eminent dead items which they might need in the after-life. Food in metal and bronze containers, as well as pots, were buried

70

with the bodies in specially constructed graves. Wives, servants and retainers were often immolated, though Confucius condemned this human sacrifice and clay or wooden models were later substituted. The majority of the pottery which has been recovered was fired to earthenware temperature and unglazed. Shapes often seem to be derived from those made by bronze casting, though occasionally decorated with painted patterns.

Two significant developments were made during this period which, though not widespread in their application until later dynasties, were of great importance to Chinese pottery.

The first was the use of a carefully prepared fine white clay decorated in relief in the style of contemporary bronzes. The second was the firing of clay to a higher temperature which gave a harder and more fused body. Some pots were also covered with a simple glaze made out of a mineral called feldspar which, when mixed with wood ash, melts to form a glaze at around 1200°C which is roughly the lower point of true stoneware firing. This technique seems to have continued intermittently until its use became more widespread in the Han dynasty.

A unified and powerful state provided a period of consolidation and expansion under an efficient centralized administration. Confucian philosophy had a profound effect while Taoism with its mythical and mystical beliefs also had many followers.

Han Dynasty
(206 B.C.–A.D. 220)

71

A History of Pottery

Buddhism, introduced from India in the first century A.D., did not have much influence until much later.

Trade was far-ranging and extensive. Silk was exported by the overland route via Turkestan to the East Roman Empire and by sea to India and Persia. Glass and the substance known as liu-li, thought to have been some sort of prepared glass mixture which included lead, were imported. Lead-glazing was practised at Alexandria around this time and it is probably from here that the Chinese learnt the art of glazing earthenware.

Pots were no longer made simply by hand but with the help of wheels and moulds. Bronze was still the greatest influence and pottery forms and glazes followed those of bronze as closely as possible. Green lead glaze enabled the colour of bronze to be copied. This glaze has become iridescent over the years and today appears more bronze-like than it did originally. Some vases had rings modelled on the outside in imitation of their bronze equivalents.

The so-called hill-censors and hill-jars form one of the largest groups of earthenware of this period. Made for religious or mortuary use, these jars had a lid on top of which was modelled a stylized mountain, hill or island representing the Taoist mythological Island or Mountain of the Blest. A reddish-grey clay was used and the lead silicate glaze was tinted green, probably with copper oxide. Other ornament usually took the form of a frieze round

Bronze wine vessel. Chou dynasty. Pottery forms were often made in imitation of such bronze vessels. c 200 B.C. *Height $12\frac{1}{4}$ inches.* Burrell Collection, Glasgow.

72

Left: *Food vessel for use on altar. Han dynasty. Form copied from contemporary bronze vessels. Feet show squatting animal with one paw on knee and the other to mouth. c 206 B.C.–A.D. 220. Height 4 inches. Hastings Museum. Below, top: Pottery censer imitating bronze. Han dynasty. The cup-shaped body is supported on a slender stem on saucer-shaped stand. Cover is of the "Hill vase" type moulded with mountains, leaves and animals. c 206 B.C.–A.D. 220. Height 9 inches. By courtesy of the Anthropological Museum, University of Aberdeen. Bottom: Finely thrown vase from Yang-chou. Stoneware with thin, greenish yellow glaze. c 206 B.C.–A.D. 220. B.M.*

the side and hunting scenes often included horses, dogs, tigers, deer and birds. These designs were often made in a mould and subsequently applied to the side of the pots. Miniature well-heads and miniature cooking ranges were also made.

Braziers, cooking vessels, ladles, various bowls and dishes, tripod kettles, candlesticks and cups have all been found, as well as such pottery objects as miniature tables.

The making of stoneware, which probably dated from the Chou dynasty, was extended during this time; it was made by firing the clay to the much higher temperature of around 1200°C and was to play a vital and fundamental part in the future development of Chinese pottery. This discovery was associated with the Yueh district of south-east China. The kilns used by the Chinese to some extent account for the discovery of stoneware. They were built into the side of a hill and the heat rose up the kiln, with the result that higher temperatures were achieved near the fire box at the bottom of the kiln and lower ones further up the kiln. With pots made out of clay able to withstand the high stoneware temperature without collapsing, kilns could be fired in which the hot areas were used for stoneware and the cooler areas for the lead-glazed earthenware. Simple glazes of the mineral feldspar and wood-ash produced thin olive-green glazes which enhanced the form, though were unnecessary from a practical point of view as stoneware is impervious to liquid.

73

Most of the stoneware forms are clearly based on bronze originals, having a stiffness and tightness of decoration associated with metal-working. However, when the forms did break away from the bronze originals and loosened up, they displayed the basic dignity and strength associated with the best Chinese art. Decoration was similar to that used on bronze. It was cut in relief and was usually limited to applied horizontal bands round the centre or shoulder of the pot; and incised combing was sometimes also used.

Invasions by central Asian tribesmen brought about the dark ages of China in which the art of lead-glazing was lost, but stoneware continued to develop. Buddhism flourished in these troubled times and strongly influenced the work which followed.

T'ang Dynasty (A.D. 618–906) The widespread adoption of Buddhism, with its doctrine of denial and renunciation, was consolidated during the T'ang dynasty. It was a peaceful, tolerant, prosperous and creative period which must be rated one of the richest and finest in Chinese history. Trade and religious toleration brought numerous foreign influences. The northern capital, Ch'ang-an, was the focus of Asia. To the west the Roman Empire had greatly diminished and the Mohammedans had not yet achieved their success. Trade spread by land to Iran and Mesopotamia and by sea to India, the Pacific islands and Japan.

Religious toleration encouraged the influx of Nestorian Christians, the Manichaeans from

74

The Far East

central Asia and the Zoroastrians and Mohammedans from Persia and India. From A.D. 638 a stream of western Asiatic refugees brought Persian Sassanian material culture to China and the metal-work in particular had a strong influence on T'ang pottery forms. In the ninth century, trade through the ports of south China with the Arabs was well established.

Lead-glazing was reintroduced when trade was resumed. During the troubled times between the Han and T'ang dynasties, trade had lapsed and so the lead frit necessary for the earthenware glaze was not imported. With the expansion of trade a much improved lead frit was brought, enabling brighter, clearer colours to be obtained which have not lost their brilliance over the years. Hellenistic influences can be seen in the shape of the flat pilgrim flasks as well as in ewers with handles and lips very similar to those made in Greece.

T'ang forms are characterized by a full, swelling, almost bursting body, contrasted with a light, fairly narrow neck. Each part of the pot relates to the other in a way suggesting movement and articulation, in contrast to the later Sung wares which have smoother, more continuous curves, suggesting stillness and peace. Decoration was bold and assertive, and was modelled, incised, stamped or painted. Necks on jugs often had five lobes which were probably derived from foliage. Bases were often casually finished with no turned foot.

Earthenware, made from a light buff-coloured

Lidded earthenware jar. T'ang dynasty. Buff clay with white slip, green glaze inset with white and blue plum blossoms between ribbons of yellow blue and white. Lead glaze. c A.D. *618–906. Height 10 inches.* British Museum.

75

Earthenware ewer with phoenix head on spout and floral moulding on body and foot. Clear Hellenistic influences are evident in the shape and decoration of this Chinese pot. Green and yellow splashed lead glaze. T'ang dynasty. c A.D. *618–906.* British Museum.

body and covered with a clear lead-silicate glaze, could be coloured yellow, amber and brown with iron oxide, green with copper oxide, and sometimes, but rarely, dark blue with cobalt oxide. Decoration was often simple but very effective. Geometric patterns were painted in contrasting colours on to the body employing such motifs as chevrons, dots and stripes. The fluidity of the glaze as it melted and ran down the pot softened the edges of the colours and dappled effects were common. Glaze was often applied to the top half of the pot, leaving a bare area at the bottom, enabling the pot to be glazed quickly as well as preventing the glaze running down the pot on to the kiln shelf.

In an attempt to prevent the colours running together, flat offering dishes were made with the design impressed into the surface so that the design lines acted as miniature ditches. On these flat dishes, again the designs were very simple, based on foliage, flowers and birds, and were painted in three colours: amber yellow, green and blue, usually on a white background. Much of this work imitates the Sassanian chased metal-work.

Stoneware was made during this period at various sites in China, and continual effort seems to have been made to perfect a white body. White, the Chinese colour for mourning, was important at the elaborate ceremonial burials.

Porcelain was the name given by the Chinese to any ware emitting a clear, ringing note when

76

Earthenware dish with design carved to keep coloured glazes separate. T'ang dynasty. c A.D. *618–906. Diameter 7 inches.* Victoria and Albert Museum.

struck; it did not have to be either white or translucent. For the sake of clarity it is simplest to refer to white translucent ware as porcelain and other high-fired ware as stoneware. The use of the term proto-porcelain for stoneware is both misleading and vague.

The exact origins of porcelain are unknown, but it is thought to have been developed in the south at Kiangsi. Suitable materials were available and it was in this area, at Ching-te Chen, that the famous Imperial porcelain factory was established under the Ming dynasty.

True porcelain is made by firing a mixture of white china clay (kaolin) and china stone (petuntze) to a temperature over 1300°C. Fusion of the particles takes place enabling thin walls to be made without loss of strength. Though this technique was probably mastered by the T'ang potters, it was not exploited by them; it was left to the Sung and Ming potters to develop it fully.

In the northern province of Chihli a fine whiteware with a transparent glaze was made. White slip was sometimes used over the grey body to achieve this. In Honan, fine grey-bodied stoneware with dark glazes and splashed with a creamy-grey glaze was produced. Such wares are now thought to precede the so-called Chun wares of the Sung period.

Yueh ware is a general term covering pots made at Chekiang province in east China. Various sites have been found dating back to A.D. 250, though

Stoneware glazed jug. Hunan. T'ang dynasty. c A.D. *618–906. Height 6½ inches.* By courtesy of the Anthropological Museum, University of Aberdeen.

77

Stoneware jar with four lugged handles and thin white glaze. Sui or early T'ang dynasty. Seventh century. British Museum.

Sung Dynasty
(A.D. 960–1279)

the best work was made in the T'ang period and later. It was here that the use of a pale green glaze, sometimes opaque, sometimes transparent, was developed. Generally they are referred to as green-wares, though the glaze was later called celadon and reached a peak of perfection during the Sung dynasty.

The Chiu-yen type of ware was made from a light grey clay with a thin creamy white glaze. Jars had looped handles, the vases had collar rims, and chicken-head spouts were often used on ewers. Decoration consisted of incised bands of diaper or star patterns.

A wide variety of pots were produced during the T'ang dynasty which included lidded jars, bowls, bottles, vases, ewers, offering dishes, cups, rhytons, spittoons and cosmetic boxes. It is also worth mentioning the fine and delicate tomb figures produced at this time. Originally made from wood, the figures retained a simplicity of form yet captured all the grace and movement the human figure could achieve. Horses and camels, too, were modelled with great sensitivity. Coloured lead glazes were used with great effect on some of the models, helping to heighten the sense of un-reality of the models. Other pieces were coloured with pigments which have now disappeared.

In opposition to the preceding T'ang period, the art of the Sung potters is peaceful and poised in contrast to the generally troubled times. The dynasty was not firmly established and the con-

78

tinual invasions by the Ch'in Tartars eventually caused the court to move, in 1127, from the northern capital of K'ai-feng in Honan province to the southern capital of Hangchou. The period was, however, enormously active artistically. Court patronage encouraged potters and ensured sales for their fine and often delicate work. Re-established in the south, the potters soon produced pots equal to those made by their predecessors in the north, and much of the work attained new heights. Vast markets were established both in China and overseas. It is difficult to believe that in those troubled times the arts of peace flourished so successfully. On the whole the court tended to patronize art which looked backwards, imitating the ever-popular bronze and jade, but this did not prevent the production of much more lively and inventive work.

Shapes tended to be less simple, and form was dominant over decoration. Contours were smoother than those made by the T'ang potters and a wonderful serenity and stillness pervades the best work. Stoneware pots were collected and savoured by the court. As Imperial patronage encouraged the study of the archaic the imitation of jade was considered to be the ideal in pottery glaze. Glaze descriptions such as "mutton fat", "congealed lard", "rich and unctuous" equally describe the best qualities of jade. Unfortunately, on wares made for the court the search for glaze quality as opposed to form often resulted in fantastically beautiful glazes over rather sterile forms.

Below, top: *Ting bowl with lid. The well integrated fluted decoration and the strong form are typical of the best pieces of Sung pottery. Dated* A.D. *1162*. British Museum. Bottom: *Porcelain stand and bowl. Ying ch'ing glaze. Thirteenth or fourteenth century. Height 3¾ inches.* Victoria and Albert Museum.

Northern Sung Wares

For the sake of simplicity, the pots can be divided into those produced in the north until 1127 and those subsequently produced in the south.

Ting ware was bought by the court and is undoubtedly one of the great Sung products. Made at Ting-chou in Hopei province in the north, this fine white porcelain has a coolness and simplicity which is technically excellent and visually enchanting. Bowls, plates, saucers, vases and lidded pots were all thinly coated with a dense ivory-coloured glaze. Three different colours were made: pai-ting was brilliant and white, fen-ting had the colour of ground rice, while t'u-ting had a coarser body and a yellower glaze. Foot rims were finely turned on the wheel and the pots were fired on their rims, which were unglazed and subsequently banded with metal. The best decoration was incised directly into the soft clay, and foliage designs were often used with great freedom. Moulded decoration was also used, though it lacked the clarity of incised work. Bowls foliated in six lobes and decorated with lotus sprays were particularly beautiful.

Chun wares, taking their name from Chun-chou in Honan province, date back to before the Sung period and continued to be made long after, but reached a peak of achievement during this time. Shapes were, for the most part, plain, with great emphasis placed on the thick opalescent lavender-coloured glaze which flowed from the rim, leaving it darker in colour. Often thick rolls of glaze formed near the base of the pot. Splashes of purple

80

Grey porcelain saucer dish. Transparent celadon glaze over carved foliage design. A good example of the so-called northern celadon wares. Sung dynasty. c A.D. 960–1279. Diameter 7 inches. British Museum.

on some ware gave a startling and not altogether subtle effect, though technically it is generally admired. The court tended to patronize forms imitating bronze, such as the rectangular bulb bowls with startling and rare purple glazes, rather than the less flamboyant globular jars, bottles, bowls, dishes and vases with rich and luminous pale blue glazes.

Celadon is the name given to green glazes obtained from iron-bearing glazes fired in a reduction kiln. The name derives from a character, Celadon, in a seventeenth-century French play who always wore green clothes. Different sites produced many shades of green, though the basic firing technique was the same. The main group of celadons, known as northern celadon, is characterized by a transparent dark shiny olive-green glaze, often over finely carved floral designs. The pots have a depth of colour and vigour of design distinguishing them from the more refined celadons made for the sole use of the northern court. Conical bowls, spouted ewers, circular boxes and high-shouldered vases were made.

Ju ware, from Ju-chou, was a group of celadon wares made from about 1107 to 1127 only for the use of the court. Known specimens are few, and when sold today command a price of many thousands of pounds. The forms are simple and well proportioned, but lack the vigour of other wares; their great beauty lies in the glaze, which is smooth, opaque and bluish-green.

81

Right: *Ju ware bowl with six lobes. Thickly applied celadon glaze. Sung dynasty.* c A.D. *960– 1279. Diameter 5¼ inches.* British Museum. Below, top: *Lidded pot, Tzu-chou ware. Cream slip with black painted decoration under transparent glaze.* c A.D. *960–1279. Height 4 inches.* Hastings Museum. Bottom: *Tzu-chou bowl with enamel decoration in red and greenish grey. Yuan dynasty.* c A.D. *1300. Diameter 5 inches.* Hastings Museum.

Southern Sung Wares

By far the largest group of wares from the north were those taking their name from Tz'u-chou in Hopei province. Made from light grey-coloured clay and covered with white slip, these wares possess all the life and vigour lacking in the contemporary Ju wares. Painted decoration characterizes these wares and separates them from any other contemporary group. With a dark brown or black clay pigment, flowers and foliage were freely painted in a direct and vigorous manner, having the clarity of calligraphy and the spontaneity of a rapid sketch. Sometimes the slip was scratched, revealing the grey body; peony designs combined with meanders, and diaper patterns were popular. Colourless or cream-coloured glazes were most common. Later, red and green enamels were used with great effect, as were green glazes. Vases, wine jars, brush pots, pillows, bowls and boxes were all produced for ordinary as opposed to court use.

The invasion of the north by the Ch'in Tartars caused the Sung Emperor to move the court to the south. Potters moved with the court, taking their techniques with them, and southern potters were not slow to react to this new stimulus. Celadon wares, formerly made at Yuen-chou, were now produced at Lung-ch'uan in the western part of Chekiang. A thick, dense, hazy, pale green glaze with a wide-meshed crackle covered pots made from a light grey clay which flashed red when exposed to flame, as, for example, on the foot ring.

82

The Far East

Some celadons had, as decoration, dots of iron pigments which turned a rich, dark, iridescent brown against the pale green glaze in the kiln. Lung-ch'uan celadons formed the largest and most productive group of wares at this time and were exported to Japan, central Asia, Persia, India, the East Indies, the Persian Gulf, Egypt and Africa. Much of the ware was mass produced and export ware was more crudely made than that for home use. Conical bowls, flat dishes, incense burners, vases and dishes or basins with pairs of fish or dragons in unglazed relief was made. Plastic modelling of dragons and other animals was often done on funeral vases.

Kuan, meaning Imperial, ware was produced in or near Hangchou for the use of the court. The thick bluish-green or grey-green glaze was applied in many layers, giving it a rare depth and luminosity. A crackled effect was deliberately sought to give the ware the look of jade.

Ch'ing pai wares originated at different sites in Kiangsi province. They are true porcelain and are the southern counterpart of the Ting wares. The pots were fired to a high temperature to achieve translucence and the pale blue or pale green glaze, sometimes called Ying ch'ing, was fired to a lower temperature. Shapes were fine and delicately potted and showed little or no influence of bronze shapes. The thin fluid glaze tended to run and settle in hollows, enhancing any finely carved decoration. One Chinese description of pots seems to fit this

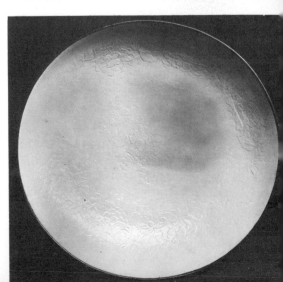

83

ware rather well: "Blue as the sky after rain, clear as a mirror, thin as paper, resonant as a musical stone of jade".

One large group of wares of this period still has to be mentioned. Chien ware made in Fukien province in southern China had a dense stoneware body which was used mainly for the production of tea bowls covered in dark brown glaze. Various different types of glaze were given appropriate names, especially by the Japanese, by whom they were greatly admired. Thick lustrous dark brown glazes which broke lighter brown on the rim or over relief decoration were given the general name "tenmoku". "Hare's fur" was a term used to describe a streaked glaze, while an "oil spot glaze" appeared to have spots of oil on the surface. Other wares with dark glazes were made at, among other sites, Honan and Kiangsi.

During the short-lived Yuan dynasty (1280 – 1367) a new ware was made called Shu-fu. It was a fine white porcelain produced near Ching-te Chen, covered in an opaque pale bluish-green colour, and was one of the forerunners of the fine Ming porcelains. Decoration was often in low relief and motifs included flowers and phoenix.

Ming Dynasty
(A.D. 1368–1644)

The breakdown of the Mongol domination of the East saw the return of a new Chinese dynasty and a subsequent renaissance of the arts. Movement was away from the quiet and austere ideals of the Sung period to colour and ornament. Great energy was put into building and most of China's

84

ancient architecture dates from this period. This energy and love of movement were reflected in the pots, which lost their formal contours and became much less constrained. Shapes became more diverse, with a continuously changing profile. Imperial wares were highly finished and no expense was spared in their production; Imperial kilns, for example, were, if necessary, fired half empty. This was to ensure that no inferior work was produced from unreliable parts of the kiln.

Three major developments in the production of pottery were made in the Ming dynasty. Pure white porcelain was manufactured at an Imperial factory established under government control; colour was introduced in the form of underglaze painting or enamelling and so superseded monochrome glazes; the majority of the production was at one large centre, Ching-te Chen in the province of Kiangsi. Ching-te Chen on the river Ch'ang was geographically well placed for the development of the industry. Both china clay (kaolin) and china stone (petuntze) were available locally, as was kiln fuel, while the river provided a quick and cheap method of transport. Many different sites were established in and around Ching-te Chen and all have not yet been identified.

White wares were produced throughout the period with incised, moulded or etched decoration. An hua or secret decoration was lightly carved into the body or painted in white slip, covered with white glaze and only became appar-

Stoneware bowl, provincial ware, early Ming, showing early and naïve underglaze blue designs. c A.D. 1369–1435. Height 3 inches. British Museum.

85

Below, top: *Porcelain stem cup, for standing on altars in Buddhist ceremonies. Example of the early use of cobalt-blue underglaze decoration. Yuan dynasty. c A.D. 1279–1368. Height 3 inches.* British Museum. Bottom: *Porcelain stem cup with underglaze blue painted decoration. Ming dynasty. c A.D. 1368–1644. Height 4¼ inches.* Victoria and Albert Museum.

ent under certain lighting conditions. During the reign of Yung Loo (1403–24) such decoration reached its peak. Small delicate cups and bowls resembling lotus pods were made for holding in the hand.

It is, however, the famous blue and white ware of this period which must claim first attention. Cobalt was brought in large quantities in the fourteenth century from Persia where it had been used much earlier to decorate pots. The fresh and pleasing combination of a fine white glazed body and blue painted decoration became very popular in China wherever the imported and expensive cobalt could be obtained. Painted either on to the unglazed pot or on to the unfired glaze the technique was simple, cheap and effective. Indigenous Chinese cobalt was an impure ore of cobalt and manganese which produced a grey pigment rather than a blue one. Mixed in the proportion of three parts imported ore with two parts of Chinese ore, a rich blue was obtained, called at various times Sumatran blue and Mohammedan blue.

Decoration on early blue and white ware was outlined in dark blue and thin washes filled in the enclosed spaces. Much use was made of flower and plant designs arranged in geometric divisions of borders and panels. Perhaps the best of this ware was made early in the fifteenth century during the reign of Hsuan-te (1426–35), when the designs became more orderly and the style as a whole became less cramped. During the sixteenth

86

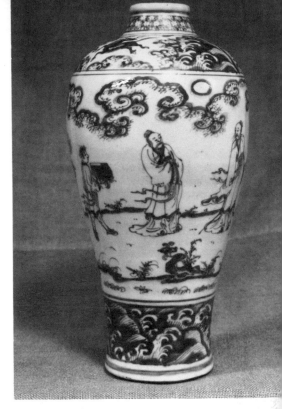

The Far East

century the human figure was more freely drawn and often set in landscapes. Later, Arabic or Persian inscriptions were incorporated into the designs. In Chia Ching's reign (1522–66) the blue became purplish and the designs broadened to include emblems and less formal subjects such as, for instance, children at play.

The skill of obtaining copper-red colours in the high-fired kiln, also associated with Ming pottery, was developed during the reign of Hsuan-te (1426–35). The rich tomato-red colour obtained by this method was used with great effect on delicate stem cups. Control over the colour was difficult and the red designs were limited to fish or fruit.

Painting in coloured enamels, which are low-temperature glazes applied to the fired glaze and refired in a low-temperature muffle kiln, was developed during the reign of Ch'eng Hua (1465–87). The so-called tou-ts'ai style of decoration, meaning contrasting colours, employed washes of apple green, red, aubergine and lemon over a lightly drawn design in underglaze blue. Small pieces such as wine and stem cups were decorated with chickens, fruit and so on. The chicken-cups, as they have come to be known, possess the feminine qualities associated with the reign and have never been surpassed in either skill or delicacy.

Another technique involved applying coloured glazes, separated by raised ribs of clay, directly on to the biscuited pot. The boldness of the tech-

87

A History of Pottery

nique resulted in simple floral patterns richly coloured in turquoise, yellow, aubergine and dark blue.

The five-colour or wu-ts'ai style is the general term covering all polychrome wares. Designs were outlined in dull red or black and the colours were thickly applied. A palette of tomato red, turquoise blue, yellow, green, aubergine and black was used.

Yellow, the Imperial colour, was developed especially successfully during the reigns of Hung Chih and Cheng-te (1488–1521).

Towards the end of the sixteenth century the china clay deposits which existed near Ching-te Chen were almost exhausted and the other fine materials necessary for the production of porcelain were difficult to obtain. At the same time, while no technical problem seemed too difficult, the general standard of design deteriorated. European trade demands were beginning to have an effect both on the form and on the decoration, and export wares were of a generally inferior quality.

From 1680 the Emperor took a personal interest in the arts and sponsored the development of twenty-seven different handcrafts in the palace at Peking. The Imperial pottery factory was rebuilt and working conditions improved. During the two successive reigns competent supervisors at the factory re-established and maintained a high standard of manufacture and the quality and finish

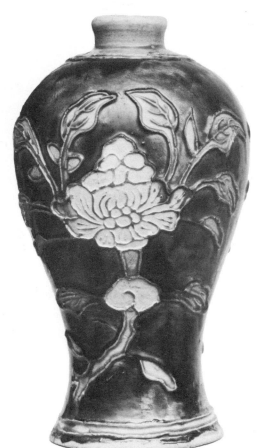

Ch'ing Dynasty
(A.D. 1644–1912)

Vase with three colour (san-ts'ai) decoration, the design outlined with ridges. Ming dynasty. Late sixteenth century. Height 8½ inches. British Museum.

The Far East

on pots were carefully sustained. A wide range of brightly coloured monochrome glazes was introduced, though on forms which tended to be sterile and dull.

The East India Company established a large and thriving export trade, and Spain, Portugal, Holland, England, France, Denmark and Sweden were represented at Canton. Special shapes and designs were demanded and supplied, though this had no noticeable effect on pottery made for internal use in China until about 1725, when salt-cellars, cruets, and tea and coffee cups with saucers were made. European motifs were incorporated into the Chinese designs, which became crowded and their meaning either obscured or lost.

Porcelain vases, exquisitely made though the shapes are lifeless and dull. (a) *Mottled crimson glaze. K'ang Hsi.* c A.D. *1700.* (b) *Crimson glaze. K'ang Hsi.* c A.D. *1700.* (c) *Crimson glaze. Ch'ien Lung.* c A.D. *1780.* Victoria and Albert Museum.

Porcelain teapot with design of buds, flowers and bird painted in "famille verte" enamel. K'ang Hsi. Ch'ing dynasty. c A.D. 1700. Height 5 inches. Hastings Museum.

A History of Pottery

Decorated porcelain ware, which was produced in fairly large quantities in the reign of K'ang Hsi (1662–1773), employed the traditional Chinese designs of prunus, peony, lotus and chrysanthemum as well as historical scenes. The main style of decoration was that employing families of enamel colours such as "famille verte", in which large areas were painted in different greens. Yellow, red, aubergine and black were also used in this way. Clear, fresh colours and adventurous subject matter gave these wares great charm and elegance. The colours, often painted directly on to the pot and known as on-biscuit, were covered with glaze and had a soft and subdued quality.

The reign of Ch'ien Lung (1736–95) saw the last great period of Chinese ceramic activity. Clay was used to imitate, very successfully, bronze, jade, shells, wood and lacquer. Western trade was at its height and much ware was decorated at Canton for export. Lace-work decoration, in which pressed or deeply incised holes were filled with glaze, was very popular.

Three major groups of wares not made at Ching-te Chen must be mentioned.

Swatow ware, a provincially produced porcelain during the seventeenth century decorated with great verve in green and red enamel, was exported to Japan where it was greatly admired. Boats, mariners' compasses, crabs and crayfish were often used as decoration, as well as the more conventional designs. Made for everyday use, the

Porcelain bowl decorated with enamel design showing ship. Chinese. Swatow type. Seventeenth century. Victoria and Albert Museum.

The Far East

designs have a freshness and spirit partly derived from their rapid method of production.

In the late seventeenth and eighteenth centuries, Yi-hsing ware and blanc-de-Chine wares were made and exported to Europe. They played a significant part in the development of European pottery.

Yi-hsing wares from Kiangsu province formed the largest group of unglazed wares. Made from finely prepared red-brown clays, they acquired a slight gloss at high temperature. Teapots seem to have been the principal product of this ware and were often smooth and round though occasionally square in shape. They were exported to Europe in large quantities where they stimulated Bottger, Elers and Dwight in their researches into the making of porcelain. These pots, often known as buccaro wares, had a pleasing simplicity of form and colour.

Fine red stoneware teapot based on bamboo design. Yi-hsing ware. Widely exported to Europe where they proved to be very popular, especially the teapots which were copied almost exactly by the Elers brothers in England among others. c A.D. 1700. Height 4 inches. Hastings Museum.

Unglazed dry red stoneware teapot. The ornately modelled body has been fitted with a metal spout and knob and a handle. Yi-hsing ware. Late seventeenth century. Height 4 inches. City Museums, Stoke-on-Trent.

Blanc-de-Chine, produced at Te-hua in Fukien province, was also exported in large quantities to Europe. It was low-temperature porcelain paste which was highly vitrified and translucent milky-white in colour. Plastic modelling of dragons and the like was sometimes carried out on the necks of bottles, but the chief product consisted of statuettes of the Buddhist goddess of mercy, Kuan-yin.

KOREA

Geographically situated north-east of China and forming a natural link with the southernmost island of Japan, it was inevitable that Korean pots should both reflect Chinese culture and be one of the means of conveying Chinese influence to Japan. Early Korean wares showed great similarity with the burial pottery of China. Jars, libation cups and food bowls were made and mounted, rather elegantly, on hollow stems which were often split and carved.

Silla Period
(c 50 B.C.–A.D. 935)

During the period known as Old Silla (A.D. 400–600) high-fired wares with ash glazes were developed. When the kingdom became united under one ruler in the period known as Unified Silla (A.D. 600–925), the Buddhist doctrine of cremation was followed. Many burial urns from this period have survived in the form of ovoid covered jars, cylindrical boxes and long-necked bottles. floral and geometric designs were used. Stoneware was often glazed an olive-brown and

92

Still life by Pieter Roestraten, 1627–1700, showing Yi-hsing teapot with silver chain and spout cover, indicating the high esteem and value in which this ware was held. V. and A.

Koryo Dynasty
(A.D. 918–1392)

Above: *Grey earthenware chafing dish, incised decoration. Korean. Silla dynasty. c 50 B.C.– A.D. 935. Height 7½ inches. V. and A. Below: Stoneware lidded boxes. Korean. Mishima decoration in which incised designs were inlaid in white, dark green and black pigment under celadon glaze. Koryo dynasty. c A.D. 918–1392. Height 1½ inches. V. and A.*

Yi Dynasty (A.D. 1392–1910)

some green lead-glazed earthenware was also made.

Influenced to a large extent by the pots of the Sung dynasty, Korean potters, after a transitional period lasting about 100 years, began to develop a distinctive style, subtly different to that of China. The best ware undoubtedly was the celadon, similar to the northern celadons of China but often taking on a bluish tint. Decoration was incised, carved or moulded with great vigour. Floral scrolls, boys holding branches, and the Buddhist motifs of ducks, water and lotus petals were all used. Porcelain similar to the Ting wares as well as the finer Ch'ing pai wares of China were also made.

A method of inlaying known as Mishima decoration, in which incised patterns were filled with white or black slip, was developed. Lacelike in effect, the technique was sometimes fine and delicate; at other times, fussy and over-ornate. The beginning of the Yi Dynasty saw the first native rulers of Korea. Koryo celadons continued

Right: (a) *Porcelain lidded wine ewer with sensitive and lively underglaze decoration. Korean. Yi dynasty. Seventeenth or eighteenth century.* British Museum.
(b) *Porcelain vase with rich underglaze decoration painted in iron oxide. Korean. Yi dynasty. Sixteenth century. Height about 10 inches.* British Museum.
(c) *Porcelain jar with blue painted decoration. Korean. Yi dynasty. Eighteenth century. Height 11 inches.* Victoria and Albert Museum.

The Far East

to be made, as did the white porcelain, and few new developments took place. The Japanese invasion during the sixteenth century weakened the country and afterwards the wares, generally, are of a rougher and less refined nature though often possessing great charm. Pots for daily use, such as bean pots, jars, wine flasks and bowls, were decorated with a remarkably direct iron brushwork, giving them strength and vigour rarely found in the more sophisticated Korean wares.

JAPAN

While the Korean potters developed their own subtle styles closely akin to those of China, the Japanese pots were, though still influenced by China, much softer and quite distinctive. Where Chinese pots had precision, severity of style, and were intellectually conceived, the Japanese forms were gentler and more intimate, reflecting perhaps the influence of the lower temperature and moister climate of the country.

Neolithic Japanese pottery was made entirely by hand-built methods. One type, Jomon ware, was made by coiling clay strips one above the other and was decorated by impressing cord into the surface. Open topped bowls tapering towards the base seem to have been a popular form. Later influences came via Korea from China, including the T'ang lead-glazed, splashed wares and the olive glazed stoneware.

95

A History of Pottery

Medieval Wares

Tea Ceremony

High shouldered stoneware vase with a narrow neck. Decorated with incised whorls under a transparent green ash glaze. Japan. Ko-zeto ware. Kamakura period. c A.D. 1300. *Height 10 inches.* British Museum.

There is a story that Toshiro, a Japanese potter, returned in A.D. 1227 from a visit to China, bringing back stoneware production methods, and, finding suitable clay, established a pottery at Seto in the province of Owari. True story or not, the thirteenth century saw the beginning of Japanese stoneware pottery. Tea was also beginning to be drunk ceremonially and demands were made for suitable vessels.

Other pottery centres were established, often by Koreans or under their influence. Little is known about this early period except that the fourteenth century saw the rise of recognized production centres, each developing its own characteristics. Six old centres are known: Seto, Tokoname, Shigaraki, Tamba, Bizen and Echizen.

It is at the end of the sixteenth century, when Hideyoshi's conquest of Korea caused the immigration of Korean potters with their potting techniques and knowledge, that the industry became most productive. Social changes at that time caused the priests and aristocracy to be supplanted as patrons by the more numerous groups of feudal lords and wealthy commoners. The tea ceremony also spread from the Zen Buddhist monasteries to the wealthier classes. Tea masters took a personal interest in the vessels required and often worked with the potter, who gained an elevated position in society. The ceremony employed the use of a small jar for the powdered tea, a drinking bowl, a washing bowl, a

96

Stoneware bowl with painted decoration of snow-covered pines painted by Ogata Shinsho at Arrat, east of Kyoto. Japan. c A.D. 1730. Height 4¾ inches. Victoria and Albert Museum.

cake dish and, occasionally, a water-holder, incense box, incense burner, fire-holder and a vase to hold a single spray of flowers. So highly regarded did the vessels for the tea ceremony become that Samurai would often choose a highly valued tea utensil as a reward for service.

Each centre produced its characteristic ware. Seto was perhaps the most important of these, and here pots were produced under the tea master Furuta Oribe (c A.D. 1580–1615). Thick opaque glazes containing feldspar were decorated with painted houses, flowers and geometric patterns in green and blue. Seto black glaze had a lustrous and lacquer-like quality.

Bizen ware was heavier and rougher and many vessels for daily use were produced here. The fine reddish clay was often left unglazed and dark grey or black "straw marks" caused by firing the pots in straw are characteristic.

Tokoname wares stand out with a strong masculine quality and large water jars are still produced there.

Raku was a method of producing pottery by firing it quickly at a comparatively low temperature. Much of the pottery was made with coarse-grained rough clay to enable it to withstand the firing process, but the forms were carefully considered and the glazes were often plain but attractive. Raku tea bowls were greatly liked by the tea masters for use in the tea ceremony.

The late seventeenth century saw a period of

Stoneware jar for containing rice, showing the patchy glaze caused by the high firing in a wood-burning kiln. Japan. Shigaraki ware. c A.D. 1338–1573. Height 13⅞ inches. British Museum.

Above: *Small box for holding incense in form of a sparrow. Raku with grey and red glaze. Japan. Eighteenth century.* British Museum. *Above, right: Porcelain covered bowl, Arita Enamel decoration of sprays of flowering prunus in red, blue, green, yellow and aubergine. Japan. Kutani ware. Seventeenth century. Diameter 6¼ inches.* British Museum. *Below: Porcelain square dish, Arita. Decoration in characteristic Kakiemon style with underglaze and enamel blue.* c A.D. *1700. Across 6 inches.* Hastings Museum.

Porcelain

sophistication in pots made for the tea ceremony. Studied roughness and asymmetrical effects on the raku pots eventually led to the debasement of the ceremony. Functional qualities of the pots became unimportant, and aesthetic and sensual qualities were the chief consideration; bases were often untrimmed and rough, and glazes thick and treacle-like.

Porcelain was not made in Japan until after 1600, when suitable clay was found at Arita. The style matured rapidly under early Korean guidance and bold enamel designs in red, yellow, green and blue were used in the mid-seventeenth century. Japanese designs tended to change the colours of nature, and water was liable to flow red, flowers to bear green blossoms and trees indigo fruit.

The so-called Imari wares, made at Arita, were elaborately decorated and mass produced, largely for export. Imari underglaze blue porcelain had a soft restrained quality. Exquisite porcelains were made during the eighteenth century and a transfer technique was developed to enable the duplication of designs for place settings.

The city of Kyoto expanded rapidly in the late seventeenth century and the so-called Kyoto wares became important, especially for the production of earthenware. Nonomura Ninsei was a potter associated with Kyoto who developed painted enamel decoration and influenced, among others, the great decorator Ogata Kenzan (1664–1743). Trained originally as a calligrapher, Kenzan

98

The Far East

developed an economical, near-abstract style of spontaneous and powerful brushwork. Soft browns, blacks and blues were his favourite colours. Other individual potters, Mokubei and Dohachi, followed him and the contemporary Japanese potter Shoji Hamada continues this tradition today.

Kyushu, the Japanese island nearest Korea, was the most sensitive to Asian and Korean influence. The wares made there reflected Korean influence in jars, large water jars, lipped pouring vessels, bowls and plates. Fine, dark clay was covered with thick, buff glaze, coarsely crackled. During the seventeenth century iron-brown pigment designs as well as black and white slip inlays were used.

The long tradition of local potteries and great master-potters continues today, as does the feeling of the use of "natural" clay qualities in the pots. Studied "accidental" decoration on asymmetrical forms are often highly valued. Japanese pottery, though owing much to Chinese influence, developed a studied freedom which is completely indigenous to Japan and today exerts a strong influence on studio potters, especially in England and the U.S.A.

Below: (a) *Porcelain jar with a lid, decorated in enamels in Kakiemon style. Japan. Late seventeenth century. Height 13 inches.* British Museum. (b) *Stoneware teabowl with painted decoration in brown, black and white over grey glaze by Kenzan, Kyoto. Eighteenth century. Height 2½ inches.* Victoria and Albert Museum.

99

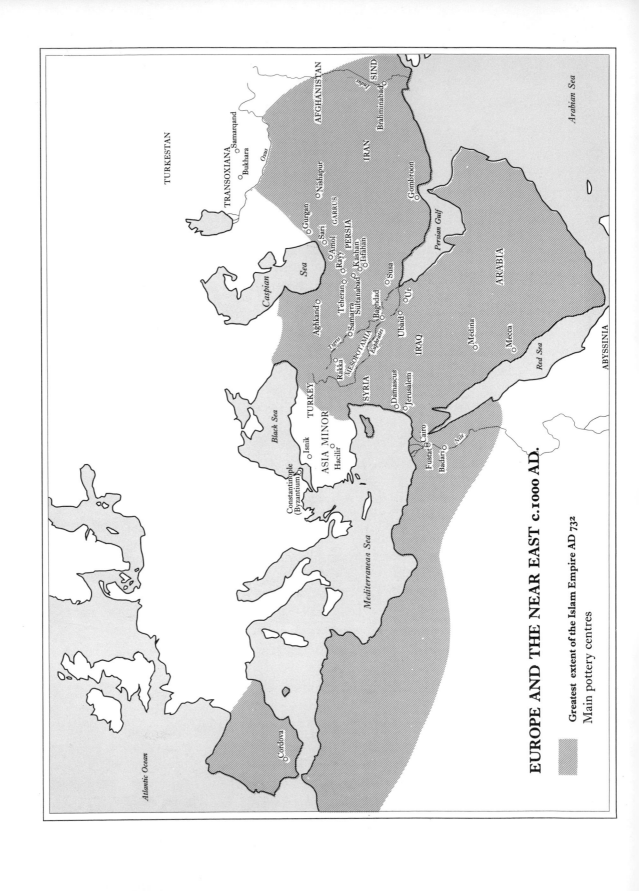

EUROPE AND THE NEAR EAST c.1000 AD.

Greatest extent of the Islam Empire AD 732

Main pottery centres

Labels on map:

Atlantic Ocean

Cordova

Mediterranean Sea

Constantinople (Byzantium)

Isnik

ASIA MINOR

Hacilir

TURKEY

Black Sea

Caspian Sea

TURKESTAN

TRANSOXIANA

Samarqand

Bukhara

Oxus

AFGHANISTAN

SIND

Brahminabad

IRAN

Gombroon

Nishapur

Gurgan

Sari

Amol

Rayy

Teheran

GARRUS

PERSIA

Kashan

Isfahan

Sultanabad

Samarra

Aghkand

Tigris

MESOPOTAMIA

Rakka

Euphrates

Baghdad

Ubaid

Ur

Susa

Persian Gulf

ARABIA

Medina

Mecca

Red Sea

IRAQ

SYRIA

Damascus

Jerusalem

Cairo

Fustat

Badari

Nile

ABYSSINIA

Arabian Sea

Chapter 4

The Islamic Countries

The countries of Islam at the end of the seventh century A.D. extended from the borders of India in the east, through Persia, Mesopotamia and north Africa into Spain. The Islamic faith had spread rapidly and in a matter of three generations unified many races, countries and people.

The ancient civilizations of Mesopotamia and Egypt had greatly declined politically and socially by the first century A.D. with a corresponding fall in the quantity and quality of arts and crafts. Persia, having fought Byzantium for so long, had exhausted itself. The fourth and fifth centuries saw a further decline throughout the Arab world in settled life and an increase in nomadism. The Arab tribes, which made up a considerable though largely nomadic and pastoral population, acknowledged no authority but that of their own tribal rulers. No major unifying force existed in the area until, in A.D. 622, the inhabitants of

Medina, a prosperous trading city, welcomed Mohammed and his religious teachings which formed the basis of the Islamic or Muslim faith. Mohammed quickly attracted a strong following and in due course the religious faith gave the Arabs their unity. The eventual result was a completely new and cohesive spirit, in which religious, political and social organizations were established.

Mohammed declared that the Koran was the word of God and forbade its use in translation; thus a single language was introduced which could be read throughout Islam and this had the effect also of unifying diverse peoples.

Muslims believe that the revelation of god is twofold, coming firstly from the writings of the Prophet, known as the Koran, and secondly from the relation of the manner of life of the Prophet. Traditionally the account of what the Prophet said or did was passed on by word of mouth, but in the ninth century a complete record of these accounts was made. This record was known as the Hadith or Traditions of the Prophet and it stated, for example, that idolatry in the form of human or animal representation was forbidden, as was the use of precious metal for tableware. Wine, too, was forbidden. These commands had some influence on the design and decoration of pottery. For example, geometric and abstract patterns were often used in preference to those depicting figures, though there are plenty of exceptions. The technique

The Islamic Countries

of lustre-painting, originally developed on glass, was adapted for use on pottery, probably because it imitated gold and silver. Much attention was given to the manufacture of fine decorated pottery, which was highly valued in the absence of vessels of precious metals. There is at least one record of verses dedicated to the beautiful bowls adorning the table of some wealthy man. The prohibition of wine meant the absence of wine jars, which in Greece, for example, had provided such useful containers for the export trade and, as a result, had been sent throughout the Mediterranean area.

Pottery was not used in Islam for religious purposes until the thirteenth or fourteenth century when the production of tiles to decorate mosques became widespread. The tiles were often decorated with Arabic script; the angular kufic or the cursive neskhi was used, though these often developed into mere patterns rather than inscriptions.

The establishment of an ordered government over a large area and the growth of towns and industries favoured the development of extensive internal and international trade. The route to China through central Asia brought the Arabs into contact with the Chinese and this had a major influence on Islamic pottery during three successive periods. The white-wares and richly painted earthenwares of the T'ang dynasty (A.D. 618–906) inspired the Muslim potters in the ninth century, the fine Sung porcelains of the eleventh and twelfth centuries were a second influence and, finally, the blue and white wares of Ming China produced further changes and developments.

A comparison of the backgrounds and approach to pottery making in China and Islam, however, reveals important differences. No royal patronage or court pottery existed in Arabia nor was the craft ever developed from a purely aesthetic point of view as it often was in China. All pots made by the Islamic potters had a use, mostly in the daily life of a Muslim, and qualities in the pots were never developed merely for their beauty. But when finely made Chinese pots, especially the porcelains, were imported into Islam, they were admired by the Arab potters, who imitated and copied them, often slavishly, using completely different pottery techniques, before adding ideas of their own.

All the pottery made by the Muslim potters was fired to earthenware temperatures which are lower than those required for stoneware and porcelain. The necessary knowledge and raw materials did not exist for firing pots to a higher temperature and many experiments were made in an attempt to imitate the whiteness of Chinese porcelain at earthenware temperatures.

The results of these developments were not limited in application to Islam but were, in time, to affect the whole of western pottery. The use

The Islamic Countries

of white opaque tin glaze with coloured painted decoration, as well as lead glaze over coloured slips, were techniques which spread across Europe; the former technique into Spain, Italy and then to the rest of western Europe, and the latter into Europe through Byzantium and Italy.

Much of the beauty of Islamic pottery lies in its decoration rather than in its form. The long tradition of painted and decorated wares of Mesopotamia and the Near East was continued and developed by the Islamic potters. Whether the designs were painted, carved, moulded, or built up in relief, they were always well thought out and carefully arranged on the pot.

The potters of Islam made almost all the utensils for day-to-day living. Form related to the function of the pot was always a primary consideration, though Islamic pottery is thought of as one of the most richly decorative styles. The range of vessels made was extensive and included water containers, water pots with long tapering spouts for ablution rituals, cups, beakers, braziers and spittoons, though it is the numerous bowls, often richly decorated, which receive most attention today.

Because the geographic area of Islam was so large and many techniques were used in different centres at varying times, it is impossible to cover all of them. Only the main types of ware are described here in detail.

Two-handled bowl with blue alkaline glaze. Syria. Fourth century A.D. *Height 4¾ inches.* Fitzwilliam Museum.

PRE-ISLAMIC PERIOD UNTIL A.D. 632

Before the growth of Islam there had been a long tradition of painted pottery throughout the Near East which is fully described in Chapter One. Goblets, painted with zig-zag patterns and tigers, have been excavated at Susa and date back some 3700 years. By 1700 B.C. the dead were buried in graves in cemeteries, and pottery, weapons and jewellery were buried with them. A variety of well preserved pots have been found in these graves, many with a long spout imitating both in form and decoration the beak of a bird, for use probably in religious ceremonies. Geometric decoration was also used on the pots.

The use of glaze had been developed in Mesopotamia around 1500 B.C. and had come into fairly widespread use around 500 B.C. Beads made from soapstone and glazed a turquoise colour had been made at, among other places, Badari in Egypt. Later a lead glaze was discovered in Babylon during the time of the Kassites (1750–1170 B.C.) and the technique was eventually brought to Persia. Tin oxide was added to opacify the lead glaze as early as the eighth century B.C. and was used to glaze building bricks used in Nimrud in Assyria. The most famous example of the use of this technique is the Ishtar Gate, built by Nebuchadnezzar (604–562 B.C.). Iron, copper and antimonate of lead were used to colour the tin glaze. Lead glazes allowed a wide colour range

106

The Islamic Countries

that was functional at a fairly low temperature (1000°C) and made possible the production of some brilliant colour effects. The use of tin oxide in a glaze died out until the ninth century A.D. when it was used by the Mesopotamian potters to imitate the whiteness of Chinese porcelain.

The Empire of the Sassanian Kings (A.D. 224–650) in Persia saw little development in the art of the potter, apart from the manufacture of large liquid storage vessels. These were wheel thrown with moulded designs and decorated in a blue glaze. Similar pots are still made in remote parts of Persia today.

EARLY ISLAMIC WARES (A.D. 632–c 1150)

Pottery was slow to develop in the Islamic expansion, mainly because the movement was primarily concerned with establishing political control rather than patronizing the arts. The Umayyad dynasty A.D. (661–750), with its capital at Damascus in Syria, was, for example, largely engaged in conquest and in the spreading of the faith throughout the Near East, where the Arab army was often welcomed as a great liberator. Through conquest the Greco-Roman art of Syria and Egypt and the Sassanian art of Persia and Mesopotamia were all absorbed into the Arab culture. Syria had been a Roman province and had been under strong western influence which included Greco-Roman type ornament with strong

Earthenware jar, applied clay decoration, turquoise blue glaze. Mesopotamia. Eleventh century A.D. Height 19 inches. Victoria and Albert Museum.

107

naturalistic foliage, animals and figures. From the West, however, came also the influence of Assyria and Babylon, with emphasis on formal designs of repeating symmetrical patterns with a strong abstract tendency. These two styles merged into what has come to be known as the arabesque style. The new Muslim decorators indulged in all-over patterns infinitely repeated. While many of their patterns retained an abstract quality, naturalistic renderings of flowers and foliage were used in largely symmetrical compositions.

In A.D. 750 the Persian house of Abbasid took over power and the capital was moved east from Damascus and established at Baghdad on the Tigris, moving the centre of artistic influence back from Syria with its strong western background to Mesopotamia. A beautiful and exotic city was built which rivalled Constantinople, the capital of the Byzantine Empire, in both splendour and commercial success. Arts and scholarship were pursued in a rich and colourful oriental atmosphere.

Most of the pottery of this period was made in and around the new capital of Baghdad. At Samarra, north of Baghdad, the Abbasid Caliphs built, occupied and left a large and rich palace during the ninth century. From the ruins of the palace it has been possible to identify the four main groups of pottery of the period: unglazed ware, lead-glazed ware imitating the Chinese T'ang splashed ware, tin-glazed painted ware and lustreware.

Vessel for holding water, unglazed, relief decoration. Mesopotamia. Eighth century or earlier. British Museum.

108

The Islamic Countries

Until the influence of Chinese pottery was felt, the Muslim potter continued to work much as his predecessors had done. Unglazed water pots, made in buff clay, had been made for centuries throughout the whole area of the Near East and even today the industry continues. Because the unglazed clay was slightly porous, water continually seeped through the walls of the pot to the outside where it evaporated. This caused loss of heat which helped to keep the water inside cool and fresh. Such pots were often made up in quite complex biscuit moulds filled by pressing in the clay. Intricate designs were carved or stamped into the clay mould, before it was fired, in a way similar to that used by the Romans for the production of their red-gloss wares.

Unglazed Ware

T'ang splashed wares from China arrived in the ninth century and were at first copied almost exactly by Islamic potters. Red clay was used and covered with white slip which was splashed with various colouring oxides to give yellows and browns. A subsequent transparent lead-glaze covering resulted in the colours running down the pot as lead glazes are very fluid. Later, purple, aubergine and black were added, widening the colour range on the pots. The Islamic potters added their own methods of decoration, using, for example, sgraffito decoration, which was the technique of scratching a pattern through a clay slip of contrasting colour, usually white, to show the dark body beneath. Traditional patterns of

Lead-Glazed Splashed-Wares

109

Tin-glazed earthenware bowl with blue painted decoration. Mesopotamia. Ninth century. Diameter 8 inches. Fitzwilliam Museum.

A History of Pottery

palmettes and rosettes were used. This was the main difference, in appearance, between the Chinese and Arabic splashed pots. Inspection of the clay body of these pots would also help to make the distinction clear as the Chinese pots were fired to a higher temperature. (Sgraffito technique was also used widely on other types of Islamic pottery, often with great success, as will be explained later.)

White Tin-Glazed Wares Tin oxide had been used between about 1000 and 600 B.C. by Babylonians for turning transparent glaze opaque-white; the glaze had been used with great success on bricks and tiles though, as far as is known, not on pots. The technique was now rediscovered in Mesopotamia. The sight of Chinese porcelain was the spur to this rediscovery. A good, reliable, even white surface, like porcelain, became the aim of the Islamic potters and tin opaque glaze was one method of achieving that aim. White tin glaze was simple to apply to the pot as it did not need to go over a white slip and it was more stable in the firing than transparent lead glaze. Little did the Islamic potters realize what a fantastic and far-reaching discovery tin-glaze would prove to be. Not only was the white surface relatively simple to achieve but its clean, even quality was ideal for painted decoration of all sorts. The technique was improved as the materials were more carefully prepared and in time the art of tin-glazing spread through north Africa and was taken by the Arabs into Spain where it formed the basis of Hispano-

The Islamic Countries

Moresque ware. From there it spread into Italy
and formed the basis of Italian majolica. In due
course it spread throughout Europe to France,
Delft in Holland, and Bristol and Lambeth in
England.

The Arabs themselves were not content to leave
the dishes and bowls plain. They recognized the
possibilities presented by the white surface and
decorated the unfired glaze. Various colouring
pigments were used but the most popular was
cobalt oxide, deposits of which are found in
Arabia. This oxide gives blue when used on or in a
glaze. Early dishes decorated with cobalt blue
tended to have simple, rather naïve designs. Occasionally green obtained from copper was used and
later a purple-brown from manganese was developed. Early tin-glazed dishes can be recognized by the fuzzy quality of the decoration, as
the pigment, when applied to the raw tin-glaze,
tended to spread and lose definition. Later, cobalt
ore was exported to China where it encouraged
the blue and white porcelain of the Ming period.

The fourth major technique used by the Muslim **Lustrewares**
potters at this time was that of lustre. To achieve
the effect of lustre, the potter must have detailed
knowledge and great skill, for the difference
between success and failure is very slight. Too
much heat and the lustre will burn away, too little
and it will not shine. Lustre is said to have been
inspired by the famous gold dishes made by Sas-

sanian goldsmiths and was in widespread use towards the end of the ninth century. It is one of the few techniques used in Islamic pottery which can truly be said to be entirely indigenous to the Near East rather than to China. The technique is thought to have been invented in Egypt for use on glass around A.D. 700–800 and was brought by craftsmen to Mesopotamia. Briefly, the technique involves preparing a special mixture of the sulphates of gold, silver or copper, and red or yellow ochre to act as a painting medium. This mixture is painted on to the fired glaze and the pot is fired a third time in a smoky (reducing) atmosphere at a low temperature. The metal oxide, reduced to metal, is suspended on the glaze and appears as a dull metallic film at this stage. Burnishing removes the ochre and reveals the lustre in all its brilliance. Unfortunately, the lustre does not retain its brilliance and over the years often changes colour and becomes dull.

Early lustrework tended to be more colourful and used in combination with other types of colouring pigment. On some pots plain gold lustre was used on a white tin-glaze, on others ruby lustre was used on a white background either alone or in combination with other colours, and lustrework in gold and silver was also carried out. When the lustre coating was very thin it appeared as yellow-brown or olive. Because the technique was so difficult, some centres, for example Nishapur in Persia, failed to produce it successfully and here

Earthenware bowl with tin-glaze decorated with brown monochrome lustre. Floral decoration. Mesopotamia. Ninth century. Diameter 12 inches. British Museum.

112

The Islamic Countries

the technique of underglaze painting was to be developed, as will be explained later.

By the end of the ninth century the use of yellow-brown lustrework predominated. Early centres were mainly in Mesopotamia. The decoration on lustrework made at Samarra was characterized by an absence of the human figure; floral and geometric motifs were used instead, though other lustrework centres included representations of humans and animals in their designs.

The lustrewares of Baghdad were widely exported to such places as Samarqand, Brahminabad in Sind, Egypt and Medina Azahra near Cordova in southern Spain. By the end of the tenth century, however, the industry was greatly reduced in size, the majority of lustreware potters having moved to work for the newly established Fatimid Court in Cairo.

Only one more major group of wares was made in this period: these were covered with glazes over relief decoration. Rich green and yellow lead glazes had been used during the Roman occupation of Egypt, and the relief decoration had often been of the Greco-Roman naturalistic style. In the ninth century the Egyptian potters brought their skill to Mesopotamia where the style of decoration changed; the use of kufic script, for example, became more popular. Some larger pots were covered with alkaline glaze which enabled bright blue and turquoise to be achieved.

East Persian painted pottery, often known as

Lead-Glazed Wares

East Persian Painted Pottery (A.D. 820–999)

113

A History of Pottery

Samarqand ware, was made at centres such as Samarqand, Nishapur and Sari. It demonstrated a unique quality long before pottery of great interest was made in the rest of Persia. The eastern provinces of Persia and the lands beyond the river Oxus, often known as Transoxian, were united under the Samanids, a Persian dynasty from A.D. 874 to 999: Bukhara was their capital city, Samarqand the chief city. The trade routes to the East lay through Samarqand and this must have had an indirect effect on the pottery in the province.

The ninth and tenth centuries saw what, in many ways, was one of the highest and purest interpretations of Islamic ideas in pottery. The potters of east Persia, being unable to make lustreware, turned their attention to other ways of decorating the white ground of the pots. They discovered that pigments could be prevented from running under a transparent glaze if first mixed with fine white clay. This resulted in pigments less fluid in use and so the designs were often simple and formal. White slip, over a red body, was decorated with a black or purplish underglaze pigment. Dark brown, dark red and aubergine colours were also used. Using the basic colours of the calligrapher, simple bands of designs in kufic script were painted on to the white pot, often round the rim. Large areas of the bowls were left white which gave them their most striking characteristic, in contrast to the later decorative tech-

Earthenware plate, tin-glaze, with blue and green painted decoration which has run on the raw glaze to give the characteristic blotting-paper effect. Eighth or ninth century A.D. Diameter 15 inches. Victoria and Albert Museum.

The Islamic Countries

niques which developed in Persia, where most of the surface was covered with patterns. Such phrases as "Generosity is (one) of the qualities of the blessed", "Peace and blessing", "Good fortune", "Blessing" or "Good fortune and perpetuity" were used. Simple patterns were developed from the kufic script, decorative dots were used and occasionally very stylized animals and birds can be found. No examples of human figures have been discovered, reflecting perhaps a strong religious influence.

At Sari, in Persia, a pottery centre on the Caspian Sea pots were decorated by similar methods but a wider range of colour was used and a particularly beautiful green was added to the palette. Stylized birds moving across bowls, and radiating stalks and flowers, are typical. The pigments used have retained a brightness of colour and the almost modern conception of the designs gives the bowls great charm.

The sgraffito technique of first scratching or carving through a fine white slip over a red body and then covering the pot with a transparent glaze was further developed in Persia in the tenth century. Mesopotamian potters had used the technique on their lead-glazed bowls under splashed colour decoration, but the Persian potters developed the technique much more fully. Sassanian engraved metal-work must have influenced both the technique and the designs of the Persian work. The so-called "champlevé" or carved style of the Garrus

Persian Sgraffito Wares

Earthenware bowl with bird design painted in coloured slips over white slip. East Persian, Sari. Tenth or eleventh century. Diameter 7½ inches. Victoria and Albert Museum.

Earthenware bowl, design carved through white slip to show dark body. Monochrome glaze. Persian, Rayy, Garrus type. Thirteenth century. Diameter about 7 inches. Fitzwilliam Museum.

Bowl with sgraffito decoration through white slip showing dark body, recalling Sassanian engraved metal-work. Green coloured rim. Twelfth or thirteenth century. Diameter 9 inches. Fitzwilliam Museum.

Egyptian Fatimid Dynasty
(A.D. 969–1171)

district, lying south-east of the Caspian Sea, is characterized by large areas of white slip left on a dark ground and was an extremely successful use of the technique brought to perfection around the late twelfth and thirteenth centuries. Sometimes the transparent glaze was colourless, sometimes coloured green. Fine lines scratched through the slip in simple geometric designs produced an effect very much like that of chased metal-work. In the Amol and Aghkand district colouring oxides were painted on to the carved slip and animals and birds were incorporated into the designs. Green, brown and purple were the colours used.

The Fatimid dynasty in Egypt established their independence of Baghdad in A.D. 969 and became the new cultural centre of the Islamic world. The artistic traditions of Baghdad were continued in Egypt probably by the immigrant artisans. While failing to surpass the potters of Mesopotamia in the shape of the pots, they produced technically excellent and beautiful lustreware, with colours ranging from rich, deep copper-red to pale lemon-yellow. The designs combined the classical naturalistic style and the formality of oriental patterns with a strong Christian influence. Fantastic birds, animals and human figures were shown, as were priests and incense burners. Nasir-i-Khuaran, who visited Egypt from A.D. 1046 to 50, wrote: "At Misr [the Arabic name for Egypt] pottery of all kinds is made. . . . They make colours for them like those of the stuff called bugalimun. The col-

116

The Islamic Countries

ours change according to the ways in which the vessel is held." Bugalimun was a sort of shot silk which describes exactly the changing colour of lustreware.

With the fall of the Fatimids there came a decline in the production of pottery in Egypt; many potters moved east again into Mesopotamia and Persia, and some may have moved as far as southern Spain.

MIDDLE ISLAMIC PERIOD (c A.D. 1150–1350)

Major changes were brought about in the Islamic Empire by the invasion of a number of Turkish tribes from central Asia. The Seljuqs entered Persia and Syria, accepted the Muslim faith and gradually gained control of the Empire, entering and conquering Baghdad in 1055. In 1171 the Ottoman Turks overthrew the Fatimid house of Egypt and in the thirteenth century captured Asia Minor from the Byzantine Empire. Unlike the early Islamic period, no permanent court was established and the centre of culture moved from place to place. This period, lasting some 200 years, is considered to be the classical period of Islamic arts. New techniques were employed in architecture and many new ideas were forthcoming in both science and arts. Ceramics were not excluded from this flowering of the arts. Pottery centres had been established at Baghdad, Cairo and Samarqand in the early period, but

117

new schools were now started in northern Persia, notably at Kashan. Potters tended to work where their wares would be most easily available, and so many centres were found on trade routes.

The fine white porcelain wares imported from Sung China (A.D. 960–1279) encouraged the Islamic potters to experiment further to produce these wares for themselves. Unlike the potters of the early period who only copied the surface colour and shape of the Chinese wares they now tried mixing up a new white artificial clay body with which to make the porcelain.

Centres of Production Kashan in Persia, 125 miles south of Teheran, is perhaps the most famous centre in Persia and work of a high technical and artistic standard continued to be produced there well into the fourteenth century. Complete genealogies of potter families, some dating from the tenth century and continuing for 400 years, are known. Never a seat of government, Kashan developed as a peaceful industrial centre. Vases made in Kashan were given special mention in lists prepared after the capture of Baghdad by Hulagu Khan in 1258. Tiles were produced in large quantities to decorate the walls of mosques and tombs. As well as having finely painted designs these tiles were also made in complicated shapes in the form of crosses or stars which interlocked to form complex patterns.

Lying on the main route across north Persia, Rayy (Rages) was, along with Kashan, one of the

118

The Islamic Countries

major centres of production of a wide variety of pottery. It was the main centre for the production of the monochrome carved ware often known as the Seljuq ware.

Rakka was an ancient caravan city on the Euphrates in north Mesopotamia and was a major production centre, very much associated in style with pots made at Cairo.

Gurgan, to the south-east of the Caspian Sea, was a production centre for lustreware and other types of pottery. In 1942 a discovery of treasure in Gurgan, buried in the early thirteenth century, proved to be of extraordinary beauty. In 1221 the town was destroyed by invading Mongols and the inhabitants buried their possessions. Vessels were packed in earthenware jars which were carefully buried in sand. Much of the work is attributed to the Kashan and Rayy potteries, but archaeological evidence suggests that some pots were also made at Gurgan. All the pots can be dated between A.D. 1200 and 1220.

Three major developments in the pottery of this period enable convenient divisions of the type of ware produced. Firstly, a fine white, semi-vitrified body similar to porcelain was artificially made for the production of white and coloured wares which formed a large part of the so-called Seljuq wares; secondly, coloured and painted decoration was developed; and thirdly, alkaline glaze was introduced on a large scale for the production of the famous rich turquoise-blue wares.

Saucer dish with foliated rim. A fine example of the Islamic potters' attempt to imitate the imported Chinese T'ang porcelain wares by mixing a special earthenware body and covering it with a white glaze. Mesopotamia. Ninth or tenth century. British Museum.

Footed bowl with pierced and carved decoration filled with transparent glaze. Painted rim. Persia, Rayy. Thirteenth century. British Museum.

Fine Seljuq Monochrome Wares

Ting ware and Ch'ing pai wares of the Chinese Sung Dynasty (A.D. 906–1179) were imported into Persia towards the end of the tenth and beginning of the eleventh centuries. Both were fine white wares with either an ivory-white or bluish-white glaze. These wares stimulated the Islamic potters, who invented a new artificial body with which to try and make similar pots. An artificial clay body had been used much earlier by the Mesopotamians and Egyptians for the production of faience wares, but whether or not there is a direct connection is not known.

A long treatise on the technique of the Seljuq potters, written in A.D. 1301, explains how the body was made. Quartz pebbles, crushed and powdered, plus an alkaline frit of potash and borax were added to the clay. The result was a low-temperature, translucent soft-paste body, similar to that produced in eighteenth-century Europe, and quite a good imitation of genuine porcelain. As a clay body it could not have been very plastic, but it was quite strong when fired and allowed pots with thin walls to be made. The result was a whiter, finer and harder body than that of previous wares. Further translucent effects were achieved by piercing the walls; these holes were subsequently covered with glaze and heightened the whole transparent effect to one of great delicacy. Many of these bowls were decorated with carved designs. The powdered quartz

120

Earthenware bowl, moulded and decorated with piercings under a clear glaze. Persia, Rayy. Thirteenth century. Diameter $4\frac{3}{8}$ inches. Fitzwilliam Museum.

and alkaline frit, when mixed with water, served as an excellent glaze. Because the glaze and body matched so closely and fused so well, they fitted together with no danger of the glaze flaking. Sometimes these glazes were coloured by the addition of the metal oxides of copper or cobalt which, in the alkaline-based glaze, produced rich, deep colours of blue and turquoise. Other colours, including soft purple, yellow, green and brown, were also made.

Early white-wares dating from the middle of the twelfth century are rare and must have been difficult to produce from the artificial white body. The refined nature of the pots made in the thirteenth century can hardly be overpraised and their delicate, sensitive quality has rarely been matched.

Later, moulds were used for the production of faceted bowls which closely imitated metal-work. The definition of the moulded ornament lacks the clarity of carved decoration, but their appearance is pleasant and rich. Moulds were also in common use for the production of tiles.

The decoration on the so-called Seljuq wares was often carved in bands round the bowls or in panels on faceted bowls. Subject matter was dealt with in a rhythmic style and neskhi inscriptions were often interwoven with foliage.

One of the problems confronting the Persian potters was the production of colourful decorated

Earthenware bowl with carved and moulded decoration under a monochrome turquoise blue glaze. Persian, Rayy. Twelfth or thirteenth century. Diameter $7\frac{1}{2}$ inches. Fitzwilliam Museum.

Painted and Decorated Wares

121

Seljuq white earthenware bowl. Incised floral decoration under purple glaze. Persia, probably Rayy. c A.D. 1150. Diameter $7\frac{3}{4}$ inches. Victoria and Albert Museum.

Earthenware bowl with design incised on a white slip, green, yellow and brown splashed colour under a transparent glaze. Persia. Thirteenth century. British Museum.

ware. Various different methods were used to produce this ware, which forms the second major group of wares of this period. It had been found earlier that colouring oxides run under lead glazes because they were too fluid, and attempts by the east Persian potters to make the pigments stable by the addition of white clay had resulted in pigment which had lost its fluidity altogether.

A new technique, known as "laqabi", meaning painted, was developed in which the artificial clay body was carved with lines to prevent the pigment running. An almost jewel-like effect of a coloured carved design, set on a white background, was achieved. Flat dishes with formal designs of animals, birds and figures coloured with rich blue, yellow, purple and green worked well. Kashan seems to have been the main production centre.

In time this painting technique led, in Persia, to the production of a highly sophisticated and technically complex ware using coloured enamels in what is now known as Minai decoration. The haft-rang technique was developed and was often used in the production of Minai decoration. It was a method of underglaze decoration in which pigment was painted directly on to the biscuit-fired pot which was then dipped into a clear glaze. Unlike enamels, underglaze colours only developed their brilliance during the subsequent firing. Pale blue, purple and green underglaze colours were used and acted as a background to the enamel decoration which was added later.

122

Earthenware cup on tall stem with Minai, meaning enamel decoration over underglaze painted decoration. Persia. Thirteenth century. Height $4\frac{5}{8}$ inches. Victoria and Albert Museum.

The Islamic Countries

At least three firings are needed to produce the Minai decoration: first the biscuit, then the glaze which would usually be white but sometimes blue, followed by the much lower temperature enamel firing.

Enamels are low-temperature glazes prepared in frit form by melting the ingredients in a crucible and grinding them before applying them to the pot. Mixed with a suitable oil medium they can be made to stick to the shiny glaze surface. Rich and varied colours can be obtained at the low temperature and the enamel technique allows detailed designs to be painted as the colours do not run and lose definition. Since the enamels have already been carefully prepared as frits, which reveal their colours, the subsequent firing does not change these, so the enamel artist has a true palette from which to work. This is comparatively rare in pottery as most raw materials only reveal their colour after being fired. Black, chestnut brown, red, white and leaf gilding were used. Many of the designs were outlined in black. Early Minai decoration depicted large figures, formally arranged. Later, the figures got smaller, reflecting perhaps the contemporary interest in illuminated manuscripts and miniature painting generally.

Lajvardina ware used an enamelling technique in which a limited range of colours, usually black, red and white and sometimes gold, were painted on to a cobalt-blue or a rich turquoise glaze.

The greater control over colours and the fine-

Earthenware dish with lajvardina (painted) design. Coloured enamels were painted over fired glaze – usually dark blue or turquoise – in ornate designs. Opaque red, black, white and gold leaf were most common. Persia. c A.D. *1300. Diameter $5\frac{1}{8}$ inches.* V. and A.

123

Footed earthenware bowl with incised design through black slip under rich turquoise glaze. Persia, Rayy. Twelfth century. Height 4¼ inches. Burrell Collection, Glasgow.

Underglaze Painting with Alkaline Glaze

ness of the enamel technique encouraged artists who had worked on illuminated manuscripts to decorate bowls. Many designs show contemporary scenes in great detail and act as an accurate social record of the time. Narrative scenes are also fairly common, as are ornamental arrangements of horsemen, hunters and court scenes.

It had been found that coloured pigments were less likely to run under a glaze which was made of alkaline material such as potash or soda rather than one made of lead, and pots decorated with this technique form the third major group of wares. The so-called silhouette wares made in Persia in the twelfth century had solid designs painted under the glaze. Thick black pigment was applied direct to the pot with designs made either by painting or carving through the pigment. Foliage and figures, often used in combination, were favourite themes. The designs were covered with either an ivory-white glaze or a rich turquoise glaze.

Gradually the colour range was extended and painted decoration in which colouring oxides were painted on to the pot or on to the unfired glaze was developed. At Rakka in north Mesopotamia hunting scenes in black, blue and red-brown were painted under clear or turquoise-coloured glaze. Production at Rakka was brought to a halt in A.D. 1259 when the city was invaded by the Mongols, though the technique was further de-

Left: *White earthenware bowl with silhouette-type decoration painted in black under clear turquoise glaze. Persia, Kashan. Early thirteenth century. Diameter $10\frac{1}{4}$ inches.* Victoria and Albert Museum.

Below: *Two earthenware bowls. Persia, Sultanabad district. Fourteenth century.* Victoria and Albert Museum.
(a) *Painted design of animal and foliage in black, blue and green. Diameter $8\frac{3}{8}$ inches.*

veloped and practised in other parts of Syria until the fifteenth century.

In Persia the painting technique was used at Kashan from the beginning of the thirteenth century and from about fifty years later in the Sultanabad region in west Persia. Here decorative schemes usually involved scroll work, geometric patterns and leaves. Animal figures were rare and human figures and inscriptions were entirely absent. Painted ware is usually attributed to the Sultanabad region in the late thirteenth or fourteenth centuries. The range was further extended to include pierced ware, with painting under a turquoise glaze. Later, more naturalistically painted decoration was developed. It is probable that master potters travelled widely and settled wherever and whenever their products were most valued.

The overthrow of the Fatimid court in Egypt in A.D. 1171 and their subsequent loss of power caused many artisans to emigrate. Many lustre potters moved back to Mesopotamia and Persia.

At Rakka, in Mesopotamia, lustreware was produced similar to that made earlier in Egypt, though the style of decoration changed later and the more miniature style of the Persian decorators was copied. Following the style of the contemporary production of Minai wares, the designs became generally smaller and more complex. Figures were often set in formal foliage designs, sometimes on

(b) *Painted design of scroll work, geometrical pattern and leaves in black, blue and green. Diameter $7\frac{1}{2}$ inches.*

Lustreware

125

Earthenware bowl, white tin-glaze with yellow lustre decoration. Persian, Rayy. c A.D. *1200. Diameter 7½ inches.* Victoria and Albert Museum.

Mameluke Wares of Egypt and Syria

horseback; animals and birds were common and, later, panels were used to divide the designs.

The earliest known Persian lustreware was made at Rayy, near Teheran, with decoration very much like that produced in Egypt, though painted with a broader style, and is dated A.D. 1179. Generally, the wares lacked the refinement of those made earlier in Egypt or those which were made later in Persia. Designs were often used in combination with blue painted under a greenish glaze. Occasionally the pots were carved in high relief with arabesque ornament combined with neskhi inscriptions.

Kashan was the other main centre of production in Persia. Kashan lustreware is distinctive because of the density of detail which was scratched through the painted but unfired lustre.

The Mongol migration originated from China and brought with it much Chinese influence, evident in the dress and ornament subsequently depicted on pots. Kashan was one of the few cities to survive the invasion, though one report suggests that the gunpowder-equipped Mongols often spared the craftsmen, allowing them to continued working, and the production of lustreware continued well into the fourteenth century.

The Ayyubids, who succeeded the house of the Fatimids in Egypt in A.D. 1171, were themselves overthrown in 1250 by the Mamelukes, who ruled over Egypt and Syria until 1571, when they in turn were defeated by the Ottoman Turks. The

Bowl with sgraffito design of equestrian rider carved through white slip, painted in brown and green. Syria. Thirteenth or fourteenth century. Diameter 10¼ inches. British Museum.

Mamelukes checked and defeated the Mongols and gave refuge to artists fleeing from Mesopotamia and Persia. Centres of pottery production were re-established at Damascus and Cairo. The main products seem to have been pots made for containing strong oriental spices and medicine which were exported to Europe. Designs in relief were painted in blue and black.

LATE ISLAMIC PERIOD (*c.* A.D. 1350–1900)

Tamerlane or Timur the Lame (A.D. 1336–1405) was a ruthless and merciless Turkish leader who established Samarqand as his capital and himself as sovereign over conquered Islam in 1369. A brief revival of the arts took place as Tamerlane had a great love and respect for art and architecture and surrounded himself with the best craftsmen of the time. However, it was not until the third great period of Islamic history, which began with the conquest of Constantinople in 1453 by Mohammed II and the establishing of the Ottoman Empire, that the arts had their next major revival. The Ottoman Empire extended into Egypt and Syria as well as into Europe. Much of the Empire remained intact until the nineteenth century.

Ottoman pottery overshadowed many contemporary Islamic wares and, with its main manufacturing centre at Isnik near the west coast of Asia Minor, it became known as Isnik ware. This pottery has often been known as Rhodian or Damascus

Bowl, richly painted design of plants and foliage on white slip under clear glaze. Turkish, Isnik ware. Sixteenth century. Diameter about 11 inches. British Museum.

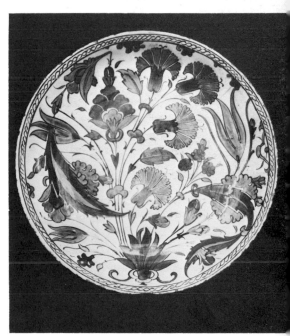

Isnik Ware

127

Earthenware bowl, design painted in blue on white body under transparent glaze. Turkish, Isnik ware. Early sixteenth century. Diameter 17 inches. Victoria and Albert Museum.

ware and is characterized by a bright and richly painted decorative style painted on to a fine white clay slip and finished with a clear shiny transparent glaze. Large dishes, standing-bowls, jars, ewers, lamps, pen-boxes and wall tiles were made in a sandy, whitish clay body.

Colours used include cobalt blue, turquoise, green and purple. Later a rich brown-red colour was added known as Armenian bole. This had to be applied thickly and is consequently raised above the other decoration. Patterns and designs were based on naturalistic renderings of such flowers as carnations, roses, tulips and hyacinths, while borders were often filled with arabesques and scrolls. The style, starting in the late fifteenth century, deteriorated and finally ceased towards the end of the seventeenth century.

Blue and White Wares

Ming blue and white wares were imported from China in the late fourteenth century and once again the Islamic potters were stimulated by a Chinese influence. Blue decoration was painted on to the unfired clear transparent glaze over a white ground. Foliage, often delicately interlaced with birds, is typical of early designs. The break-down of Chinese trade in the seventeenth century at the end of the Ming dynasty caused European traders to place orders for blue and white ware with Islamic potters. This further encouraged the copying of Chinese designs and these were often outlined in black. Some blue and white wares were

128

made in Syria but most were made in Persia at Meshhed and Kirman where production continued until the nineteenth century.

Shah Ismail became the first King of the Persian dynasty of the Safavids in A.D. 1499 after 850 years of foreign rule. Two hundred years of stable government followed, the peak of which was under Shah Abbas the Great (A.D. 1587–1620). His capital, at Isfahan, was filled with and surrounded by many skilled craftsmen. He himself was a collector of fine pottery and his collection still exists in the shrine of the Safavid family at Ardabil in Azarbaijan. Renewed interest in all types of pottery brought about a major revival of the craft.

Kashan again developed as a pottery centre and the technique of producing a soft paste type of porcelain was revived. Famous Chinese green-glazed ware, known as celadon ware, was also emulated using a smooth grey-green glaze. Gombroon ware, so called because it was shipped through the port of Gombroon (modern Bender Abbas) on the Persian Gulf, was also made in Persia. It was shipped to India and Europe where, in the seventeenth century, it became very fashionable, especially in England. The pots were characterized by a fine white translucent body sometimes with pierced decoration. Jars, bowls, plates and ewers were produced.

Lustrewares were reintroduced in the late

Safavid Period and Later
(A.D. 1499–1736)

Earthenware stem bowl, painted in blue and green in a design of foliage and roses under a clear glaze. An example of the ware known as "Golden Horn". Turkish, Isnik. About A.D. 1635. Height about 12 inches. Victoria and Albert Museum.

seventeenth century and were painted in a copper colour on a white or blue ground. Sometimes the body was fine and white and much of the decoration consisted of stylized flowers showing little or no evidence of foreign influence.

The so-called Kubachi wares were made in northern Persia and used the technique of underglaze painting. Large plates were painted in brown, green, yellow, dull red, black and white under a clear colourless crackled glaze. Early designs included animals, figures and even portraits but, later, plant and foliage designs predominated.

The general standard of most crafts declined in Persia during the nineteenth century, though traditional pottery of a high standard is still made there. Recently it was possible, for example, to replace old tile-work on mosques and tombs with contemporary work in quality equal to that produced 500 or 600 years ago.

130

The Islamic Countries

Islamic art is an amalgam of Byzantine, Persian and Chinese influences but, no matter how strong the influence, the Muslim potters soon adapted what they saw for their own use. To regard Islamic pottery as a sort of inferior Chinese ware is to do it a gross injustice; the two approaches to pottery were completely different. But though Islamic pottery was always utilitarian, few people can fail to admire the vigorous Samarqand wares of the ninth and tenth centuries or the fine white Seljuq bowls from Kashan.

Earthenware dish, polychrome enamel painting recalling the early Minai wares. Persia. Kubachi type. Early sixteenth century. Diameter 12½ inches. Victoria and Albert Museum.

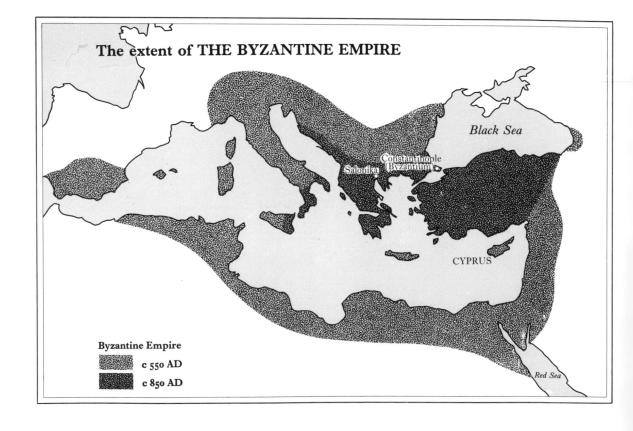

The extent of THE BYZANTINE EMPIRE

Black Sea

Constantinople
(Byzantium)

Salonika

CYPRUS

Red Sea

Byzantine Empire

c 550 AD

c 850 AD

Chapter 5

Europe *c* A.D. 500–1900

In A.D. 330 Constantine declared the ancient Greek city of Byzantium the new capital city of the old Roman Empire and the Byzantine Empire was founded. The city became thought of as the new Rome and its name was changed to Constantinople in honour of the Emperor. For a further 1000 years many aspects of the old Roman Empire continued with a government centred on Byzantium, though gradually a new civilization developed. Only in 1453, when the Turkish armies over-ran Constantinople, did the last vestige of the Roman Empire disappear. Geographically, Constantinople had a powerful and commanding position: situated at the meeting point of Europe and the Orient, on a waterway connecting the Mediterranean with the Black Sea, well fortified and with a good harbour. Little wonder Constantinople has been described as the crossroads of the world. It was attacked at different times by Christians, Muslims and pagans, and absorbed many aspects of the different cultures. When trade was at its height Constantinople must have been an incredible warehouse, with goods and people from many countries moving through it.

Early influences may have come mainly from the West, but the collapse of Rome as the centre of the Empire brought significant changes. The oriental influence in art soon manifested itself with an emphasis on formal style, vivid colouring and rich ornament. In most of the art that remains today this change can be seen quite clearly, though the development in pottery is difficult to trace because of the relatively small number of pots found.

Unlike Islam, Byzantium placed no ban on the use of gold and silver vessels for domestic purposes. Therefore pottery was not as highly valued and the craft, as a result, was not as highly developed. There is no evidence, for instance, that lustreware was made.

The red-gloss wares which had been widely produced throughout the Roman Empire continued to be made in parts of the Byzantine Empire for some time after A.D. 300, though the pots lacked the precision of those produced under the Romans. The art of glazing practised by the Romans was retained and during the eighth and ninth centuries was used on a wide range of thrown forms. Green and pale yellow lead glazes were used, as were other more colourless glazes. During the Isaurian Period (A.D. 717–876) simple green glazes were often used on some of the most pleasing Byzantine ware.

Theophilus, a monk writing about the arts and crafts in what is now thought to be the eleventh century, speaks of the crafts of glass-making and gilding which are closely related to pottery, and pottery is referred to in passing but is not dealt with at length. This seems to indicate that pottery was not highly regarded at that time. Only during the period of the Palaeologans (A.D. 1261–1391), when the country became impoverished by constant wars and religious and social upheaval, and the gold and silver vessels on the royal table were changed for ones made out of clay, did the craft gain in stature.

Insufficient excavation has been carried out to identify positively the sites where pottery was made, but the chief ones were probably at Constantinople, Salonika, the Caucasus in south Russia, Corinth and Cyprus.

Byzantine art did not begin to develop as a distinctive style until the eighth and ninth centuries. It was, primarily, a style based on religious belief but was derived artistically from two sources. One was the classical Greco-Roman style and the other was the oriental style from the East. Byzantine art, unlike the Greek style, was not naturalistic but ritualistic, shown, for example, in the treatment of Greco-Roman themes in a stylized formal way.

Earthenware dish with sgraffito design of bird scratched through white slip, touches of brown and green under a pale yellow glaze. Byzantine. Fourteenth century. Diameter 9¼ inches. Victoria and Albert Museum.

A History of Pottery

The wide origins of many of the designs used on Byzantine pottery can be seen by glancing at the animals depicted in them. The dove, a common Christian symbol, is shown, as are ducks which were commonly used in Egypt as decorative motifs of symbolic or pictorial importance. Fish, too, depicted with open mouths, recall those used by the Egyptians. Lions and leopards of a heraldic type with long waving tails reflect western influence. Hares and the human-headed lion are very Persian in character. The griffin and centaur were mythological rather than representational of nature. Deer, dogs and gazelles were among other animals shown, but the favourite animal, however, appears to have been the eagle, symbolizing goodness, alertness and power. The human figure, usually in grotesque or formal poses, was sometimes represented; it was very rarely shown naturalistically, reflecting perhaps the attitude of the Byzantine Church that forbade the representation of the human form as being idolatrous.

Byzantine pottery can roughly be divided into two main types: the first is that made in a whitish body, glazed and often decorated with underglaze painted designs, and the second is pottery made out of red clay covered with a white slip, often with sgraffito decoration.

White-bodied wares were the largest and the most impressive group of Byzantine wares and were developed around the ninth century A.D. Plates, dishes, bowls, cups, goblets and fruit bowls

Jar in red clay with impressed bands of geometrical pattern, dark green lead glaze. Byzantine. Tenth or eleventh century. Height 7½ inches. Victoria and Albert Museum.

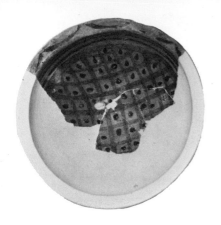
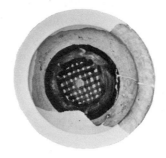

Two white earthenware bowls, largely reconstructed. Examples of Byzantine white-glazed wares with painted decoration. From Athlit, Palestine. Thirteenth or fourteenth century. Widest bowl diameter 5½ inches. Victoria and Albert Museum.

with long hollow stems were among the pots made. Colour in the form of an underglaze was painted directly on to the whitish biscuit pot and the whole covered with a transparent glaze. Various shades of brown were used as were yellow, green, blue and occasionally bright red in the form of small dots and outlines.

Undecorated ware covered in a yellowish glaze was both cheap and quick to produce and was in widespread domestic use. Liquid containers in the shape of jugs and beakers were the most common forms, while dishes, plates, strainers, cups and cooking vessels were also made.

One group of white-bodied ware was decorated with applied clay and is often known as petal ware. Flattened balls of clay were applied to the pot while it was still soft and one side of the pellet was smoothed into the side of the pot. The result looks like fish scales or petals. Impressions of stamps made from clay or wood were often used to decorate the insides of bowls. Real or imaginary animals were popular decorative subjects.

The use of fine white slip over red clay was developed around the tenth century and was used on the inside of bowls. This usually had sgraffito decoration covered with clear or coloured transparent glaze. Early sgraffito ware had a linear decoration in which the design was scratched with a fine point. Geometric patterns of scrolls, dots and zig-zags were used. Spatial decoration was achieved by using a flat chisel-like tool to take

Red-Bodied Slipware

137

Bowl, light red earthenware, incised design through white slip under pale green glaze with added painted decoration. Byzantine. Diameter 8½ inches. Victoria and Albert Museum.

Earthenware bowl, sgraffito design of two figures carved through white slip under yellow transparent glaze. Byzantine. Fourteenth century. Diameter 6½ inches. Victoria and Albert Museum.

away large areas of the slip, thus leaving the darker body to show up the white design in slight relief. Circles, wavy lines, formal trees, chequered patterns, crosses, rosettes, five-pointed stars, animals, fish and birds were common designs. The human figure appeared only occasionally. Slipwares were sometimes painted with green and brown underglaze colours. Marbled ware, produced by using different coloured slips, was made around the middle of the fourteenth century.

On the evidence of present excavations Byzantium would appear to be essentially a repository. It was here that the Greek language and learning were preserved, the Roman Imperial system was continued and Roman law codified. Much early technology was retained and developed during the expansion of Europe in the Middle Ages. In pottery the use of lead glaze was retained and improved technically and in the ninth century its use spread to Germany, the Low Countries and England. However, the later birth of a new Greco-Oriental

138

Urn made from red clay painted with stylized floral pattern. Iberian from cemetery of Oliva, Valencia, Spain. c 500 B.C. Height 22 inches. Museo Arqueologico, Barcelona.

Europe

art dedicated to the glorification of the Christian religion is evidence of a rich and thoughtful civilization. More excavation will undoubtedly bring to light further pottery and then perhaps the Byzantine pottery style will become more fully known.

SPAIN

The most distinguished pottery made in Spain before the Roman conquest (218 B.C.) was that made in the east of the peninsula by the Iberians. Celtic invaders had settled there by the sixth century B.C. and established an Iberian culture. Trade with Mediterranean countries brought, among other goods, Greek decorated ware. Iberian attempts to copy this were unsuccessful but led to the development around 500 B.C. of a painted style indigenous to the Iberians. Light-coloured clays, firing yellow or pink, were used to make thin-walled, wheel-made pots. Goblets, flat-based jugs, low-footed bowls and urns were produced. Their most distinguishing feature was the decoration painted on to smooth, slip-covered pots. Iron and manganese oxides were used which fired a wine-red colour. Designs were rich and varied, employing geometric shapes as well as stylized birds, fish, plants and the human figure.

The Romans introduced their own pottery style and methods of manufacture into Spain during their occupation of the country, but with the

Roman withdrawal in the fifth century A.D. many
of the technological improvements lapsed.

Visigoths (c A.D. 500–756) The Visigoths, invading from the north at the
beginning of the sixth century A.D., established a
kingdom which lasted until the Moorish invasion
in A.D. 756. They made Toledo in central Spain
their capital. Little is known about the pottery
made by the Visigoths, but it seems to fall into
two groups and to reflect two major influences.
The first group was the low-fired, red earthenware
decorated with impressed and moulded designs,
and generally left unglazed. This reflected, per-

On the map:

SPAIN c. 1550 AD.
showing tin-glazed earthenware centres

Oviedo
Leon
CATALONIA
Saragossa
Tarragona
Barcelona
ARAGON
Alcora
Talavera
de la Reina
Toledo
Tagus
MAJORCA
Valencia
Manises
VALENCIA
BALEARICS
Guadiana
Cordova
Guadalquivir
MURCIA
Almeria
Mediterranean Sea
Seville
Granada
ANDALUSIA
Malaga

Europe

haps, a continuation of the methods of decoration used by the Romans. The second group of wares was decorated with simple yellowish or greenish glazes. Trade and contact with the Byzantine Empire during the seventh and eight centuries may have been the means by which the glaze was introduced into Spain. Further excavation will no doubt reveal more about the Visigoth pottery.

It was the Moorish invasion of Spain and the establishment in A.D. 756 of the Caliphate of Cordova under the Umayyads that a new and completely different culture was introduced. This Muslim culture was, in time, to lead to the development of a new pottery style, the influence of which would be felt throughout Europe.

Cordova became the intellectual centre of the western world during the Umayyad period (A.D. 756–1031); Christian scholars from France and Italy studied Arabic and exchanged ideas there. Trade, especially with Islamic countries, was extensive. Excavations indicate that considerable quantities of pottery were imported from Mesopotamia. Lustreware fragments, for example, of Mesopotamian origin dating to the latter part of the tenth century have been excavated at Medina Azahra on the outskirts of Cordova. Such fragments have only been found on the sites of palaces, which also indicate that lustreware was a luxury item, much admired and expensive to acquire, and certainly not produced in Spain at that time.

It was not until the thirteenth century that the

141

potters of Spain, using techniques developed in Islam, began to produce a new and exciting style of their own. They used white tin-glaze and decorated it with designs in rich lustre as well as with colours painted on to the raw glaze. It is possible that potters capable of making lustreware emigrated from Egypt during the twelfth century to Spain and eventually established their own potteries.

Ibn Said (A.D. 1214–86), writing around the middle of the thirteenth century, refers to glazed and gilded earthenware made at Muravia, Almeria and Malaga in southern Spain. It was in this region, known as Andalusia, that the first Spanish lustreware was made in any quantity at this time. This came about for two reasons. The first was that Christian armies had conquered much of Muslim Spain and by 1248 only a small area in the south was left under Muslim control. The second reason was that Iranian potters, fleeing from the Mongol invasion of Arabia, settled in fairly large numbers in Malaga in the thirteenth century, bringing with them their detailed knowledge of the production of lustreware and underglaze techniques. They also introduced cobalt blue, the use of which was hitherto unknown in Spain. So the necessary knowledge and skill were available and formed here the basis of an industry which was to thrive so successfully for nearly 300 years.

The Hispano-Moresque wares can be divided

142

into three main groups each roughly following the other in time and divided on a stylistic basis. The first group, employing predominantly Moorish designs, was made at Malaga in Andalusia and later at Valencia. The second group, made around the end of the fifteenth century, continued until *c* A.D. 1700 at Manises, a suburb of Valencia, and combined Gothic and Muslim decoration in what is known as the mudejar style. The last and least interesting group of wares was made in the eighteenth century and showed a strong French influence.

Early Wares (*c* A.D. 1200–1450)

Comparatively little is known about the early wares, considering the length of time during which they were made. Bowls, dishes and pitchers as well as storage jars were produced and exported to Sicily and Egypt as well as to England. The forms and designs on the pots clearly owed much to Islamic influence and especially to the Islamic centres at Rayy, Kashan and Rakka. Designs were usually carried out in two shades of blue on a white ground and finished with copper-golden lustre. The kufic script was used as decoration as well as foliage designs of great complexity. Geometric designs were also popular.

Large decorative vessels, made in sections, probably in a mould, are perhaps the most famous products of Malaga. The Alhambra vase, named after the Alhambra palace in which one was found, is an example of these. Special niches were built in the Castle of Alhambra, Granada, to

143

Earthenware dish, decorated in the "ceurda-sea" technique in which unglazed lines pick out the design painted in blue, green, yellow and brown enamel on a white tin-glaze. Seville. Fifteenth century. Diameter 14¾ inches. Victoria and Albert Museum.

accommodate the magnificent pieces. The vases, standing nearly four feet high, are remarkable technical achievements. High, flat, wing handles immediately mark them as decorative objects. Painted decoration often consisted of bands of kufic script and some had panels depicting animals such as deer. That it was considered worth while to produce such ornaments in pottery decorated with lustre is a measure of the wealth of the country at that time and its high regard for lustreware.

Hispano-Moresque ware also sometimes exhibited the so-called "ceurda-seca" (meaning "dry cord") technique. Areas of dry pigment, usually black, separated different coloured glazes and prevented them running into each other. The technique was developed mainly for use on flat dishes during the eleventh and twelfth centuries in Valencia, probably because of the failure at the time to produce lustre. However, "ceurda-seca" technique became popular again in the fifteenth century when formal designs were carried out on vases as well as dishes.

The pottery industry seemed to lose its vitality with the Catholic reconquest of Andalusia in 1487 and virtually no lustreware was produced in this area after the beginning of the sixteenth century. Changing trade routes also moved the centre of production from Malaga to Valencia and it was here that lustreware of a different style thrived in the fifteenth century.

144

Small flat bottle, probably for holding precious liquids, Egyptian faience. From around 2000 B.C. *small votive objects and cosmetic containers had been made in the artificial body known as faience. During the Roman occupation of Egypt the technique was developed to enable larger forms to be made and the colour range widened to include yellow, white and purple.* c 800 B.C. *Height 3 inches.* Petrie Collection, University College, London.

Above, left: *Two painted pots from Arpachiyah, Mesopotamia (page 22). Halaf period, c 4500–4000 B.C. Height of bowls 2 inches.* Above, right: *Wine jar with a cover. A tall elegant pot made in buff-coloured clay from Amarna (page 34). Egyptian, New Kingdom. c 1370 B.C. Height 2 feet 7 inches.* Left: *Corinthian vase. Lively and crisply executed designs with rich colour contrasts and scratched detail show all the characteristics of Corinthian pottery at its best (page 52). c 600 B.C. Height 22 inches.* Right: *Athenian amphora. Black-figure style. The scene shows Dionysos on the left holding a cantharos. Oinopion, on the right, is holding a myrtle wreath in his left hand and an oinochoe in his right (page 51). c 600 B.C. Height 16½ inches.* Below, left: *Vase, Athens in the red-figure style. The scene shows Triptolemos sitting in a winged car holding corn. In front of him stands Persephone with a torch and a fluted oinochoe in her right hand. Purple was used for the inscriptions, snake's tongue and other details (page 53). c 550 B.C. Height about 10 inches.* Below, right: *Oinochoe with black design painted on a white ground. Neck, handle and foot have black slip. A white slip was used on body. Purple slip was used for fillet bracelets, sandals, spindle and other details, light brown for inner markings on body (page 55). Height 8¾ inches. c 500 B.C. B.M.*

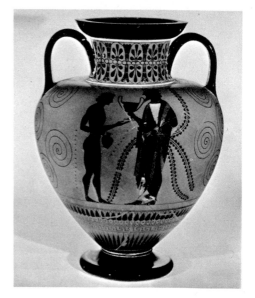

Above: *Roman chalice, red-gloss ware. The body of the pot was made
in a decorated hollow mould. Handles and a foot were added later.
The moulded design consists of a band of six pointed rosettes, a row
of beads above a wreath and vertical objects.* c A.D. 1. *Height about
2½ inches (page 61).* B.M. *Below: Bowl, stoneware with a thick
green (celadon) crackled glaze. An example of the Imperial Kuan
(meaning official) ware made specially for the court but subsequently
copied by other potters. The quality of the glaze, which was meant to
imitate jade, and the forms those of ancient bronze, were qualities
highly regarded by the court. South Sung dynasty, twelfth or thirteenth century. Diameter 7¾ inches (page 83).* Below, right: *Small
porcelain cup with "famille rose" enamel decoration. Ch'ing dynasty,
Ch'ien-lung.* c 1750. *Height 2½ inches (page 90).* Percival David
Foundation of Chinese Art.

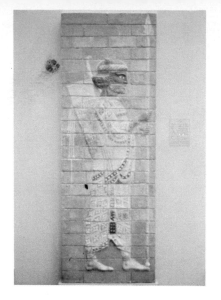

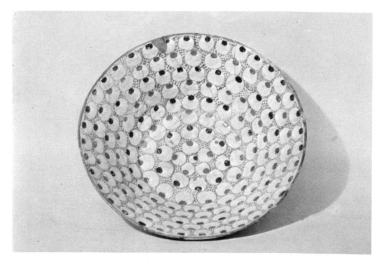

Above: *A panel of modelled and painted tin-glazed tiles from the Palace of Darius, Susa, Persia. An archer is shown and several coloured glazes were used to achieve the rich and permanent effect (page 28). c 500 B.C. Above, right: Earthenware bowl painted with rich ruby-coloured lustre in simple floral patterns set symmetrically on the bowl (page 112). Mesopotamia. c A.D. 850. Diameter about 5½ inches. Right: Bowl from Samarqand. A slip-covered ground was painted in thick coloured pigments (page 114). East Persia. Tenth century. Diameter 13½ inches. Below: Bowl decorated with underglaze colours and enamels, in the Minai style, Persia (perhaps Kashan). Miniature figures and the fine detail are in keeping with the illuminated manuscripts produced at the time (page 122). Late twelfth or thirteenth century. Diameter about 8 inches. Below, right: Bowl decorated with a design of paired horsemen set in a foliage pattern. Painted in black pigment under a rich turquoise glaze. Persia, Kashan (page 125). Thirteenth century. Diameter about 7½ inches. B.M.*

Above, left: *Bowl with a lid. On the white slip-covered ground a rich natural-istic pattern is painted in coloured pigments giving a bright and colourful effect (page 127). Turkey. c A.D. 1550–1660. Height about 6 inches. Above: Plate decorated in blue on a white ground. The fine detailed intricate designs show this pot to be of the so-called "Golden Horn" type (page 128). Turkey. c A.D. 1550. British Museum. Below, left: Earthenware bottle with a stirrup handle on side. Pot is moulded in form of a man playing a tambourine (page 234). Mochica, Peru. Seventh–eighth century. Below: Earthenware jar with a rounded base. A white slip ground is decorated with two colourful bands of sacrificial heads with protruding tongues. The subject shows the warlike nature of these people (page 236). Nazca, Peru. Seventh–eighth century.* City Museums, Stoke-on-Trent.

Left: *Jug with slip-trailed decoration in white clay on red body. The tall form with the close-fitting handle which is moulded well into the pot, and the rich but simple decoration, gave these medieval peasant jugs a strong quality which was only equalled by the Staffordshire slipware potters of the late seventeenth century. Fourteenth century (page 183). Height about 14 inches.* Below, left: *Large dish by Thomas Toft. Slipware decoration was brought to the peak of its achievement under the Toft family. In this scene, set in a trellis border, a cavalier is shown drinking a toast (page 187). Late seventeenth century. Diameter about 14 inches.* Below: *Large dish by Ralph Toft. Here Catherine of Braganza is shown (page 187). Late seventeenth century. Diameter about 14 inches.* City Museums, Stoke-on-Trent. Bottom, left: *White tin-glazed earthenware oval dish with relief modelling after the style of the French potter Bernard Palissy. His style was closely imitated. In this scene a strong Renaissance influence is evident. London (page 192). Length about 14 inches. c 1635.* V. & A. Bottom, right: *Bowl with brown and white decoration of the Ralph Shaw type. Saltglaze. Robert and Ralph Shaw were brothers working in Burslem who attempted in 1733 to patent a saltglaze ware with striped decoration on the outside and plain on the inside (page 197). c 1725. Height about 8 inches.* City Museums, Stoke-on-Trent.

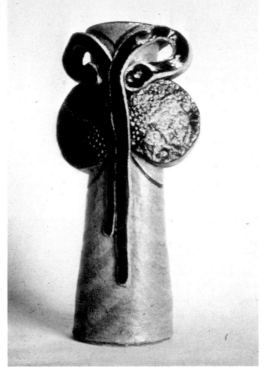

Above: *Bottle, stoneware. Lucie Rie. A tall, elegant bottle thrown in two or three sections and then joined together (page 250). Height 15 inches. 1967. V. & A. Above, right: Stoneware Baroque vase. Jerry Rothman, U.S.A. Height 30 inches. Below: Earthenware plate. Thomas Samuel Haile. Influenced by the work of Picasso and other painters who have decorated clay, Sam Haile explored freely the uses of slip and underglaze colours at earthenware temperatures (page 250). 1948. Diameter 18 inches. Marianne de Trey. Below, right: Two stoneware pots with lustre decoration. Tony Hepburn, one of England's leading ceramic sculptors, who uses a wide variety of techniques to obtain his effects (page 252). 1970 Height 18 inches.*

Below: *Group of tall pots by Toini Muona, Finland. The plain shapes with the contrasting glazes form an interesting group.* Right: *Group of three stoneware goblets with rich blue and turquoise glazes contrasted with unglazed areas.* Annikki Houisaani, Finland.

Europe

Manises, near Valencia, became the main centre of production in the second part of the fifteenth century and there are at least two references to Manises potters travelling to France at the request of local officials, which is an indication of the success of the Spanish pottery industry. Valencia had earlier been taken from the Moors and had come under the influence of the Catholic Church and a strong Gothic influence. Decoration on Valencian pottery is distinguished by the merging of the two major influences in Spanish culture of the time. From the north came the Gothic and from the south the Muslim. The resulting style became known as "mudejar". Originally the Valencian potters had made pots in imitation of their Andalusian predecessors, but gradually they developed a style of their own in which the blue and white and lustred wares show a distinctly European character.

European Gothic influence was characterized in general by more naturalistically rendered ornament, the use of heraldic devices and shields, and inscriptions of a Christian nature in Gothic script. Muslim influence was evident in the treatment of ornament, and intricate designs continued to be made. Kufic script, used as stylized decoration, was often combined in the same design as Gothic.

Plants and foliage shown in the designs included berries, flowers, briony leaves as well as golden and blue vine leaves. Animals such as songbirds, falcons, cocks and long-legged waterbirds,

Mudejar Style
(A.D. 1450–1700)

Earthenware dish with "mudejar" style of decoration. Imitation bands of Arabic script lead into the centre shield of the Arms of Castile and Leon. Probably arms of John II of Castile, 1407–1454. Blue underglaze and gold lustre. Valencia. Fifteenth century. Wallace Collection.

145

Drug-jar or albarello with bands of briony and vine leaves painted in lustre and enamel on a white tin-glaze. This was a standard pattern popular with the Manises potters. Valencia. Early fifteenth century. Height about 12 inches. British Museum.

bulls, goats, pigs and hunting dogs were popular design motifs – the human figure rare.

Heraldic devices include the eagle as well as the lion and dragon. Armorial motifs were popular and designs were carried out for many of the royal families of Spain as well as other parts of Europe.

Gothic inscriptions included such expressions as "Ave Maria gratia plena" and "Senora Santa Catarina guarda nos".

The designs were still stylized, though they were painted with more naturalism than hitherto. The combination of arabesque ornament and animal motifs encouraged a free decorative treatment which often produced beautiful results. In one example a naturalistically painted deer sits happily under a beautiful arabic "Tree of Life" design. Around the middle of the fifteenth century Manises ware became very popular in Italy and for this market the ware was decorated with the coats-of-arms of famous Italian families. Such pottery, exported in Majorcan ships, became known in Italy as majolica.

In the late fifteenth and early sixteenth centuries came the influence of the Renaissance style from Italy. Shapes imitated more closely those of precious-metal-work and the designs those of painting, though classical motifs of leafy garlands and swaths of fruit and flowers, grotesques, masks and acanthus scrolls never became really popular. Dishes became more elaborate with petals,

146

scollops and raised repoussé work incorporated into the designs; and woven brocade velvets seem to have influenced some of the more ornate work. While the magnificence of the painted dishes can be admired for their technical skill and richly patterned decoration, the underside of the dishes often carried a simpler and more attractive design.

Lustreware was highly regarded and valued, and most of the magnificent decorated dishes were made for special occasions. Tables were not laid with individual place settings; instead individuals took their portions of food from central dishes which encouraged potters to make these as ornate as possible since they were large and static.

Shapes, other than dishes, were generally few and simple. Following the oriental tradition, cylindrical jars with concave sides, known as albarellos, were widely made for the use of the apothecary. Gallipots, used for storing dry foodstuffs, bowls, drinking mugs and round platters were also produced.

With the unification of Catholic Spain, the growth of strong trade and the absence of Muslim law forbidding the use of precious metals, lustreware lost its exotic quality and was replaced by imported Venetian glass, Chinese porcelain and fine metal-work.

Hispano-Moresque ware was revived in the eighteenth century at Alcora in Valencia. Artists were brought from France to teach the contemporary popular styles of form and decoration found there.

Underneath of dish shown above, showing simple but vigorous design of eagle painted in gold lustre on a white glaze. British Museum.

Eighteenth-Century French Style

147

Little or no lustreware seems to have been made and instead painted decoration was carried out in blue or in a combination of blue, yellow, green and brown on a bright white background. Arabesque designs of great delicacy were popular, as were subjects copied from engravings and rococo floral motifs. The work produced was chiefly remarkable for its extravagant, ambitious and grandiose forms, consisting of busts, elaborate chandeliers, large wall-cisterns, basins and similar objects. Production ceased around A.D. 1800 in the face of competition from English cream-coloured ware and European soft-paste porcelain.

Talavera de la Reina   Pottery made at Talavera de la Reina in central Spain forms a separate group of wares. It was not decorated with lustre but with underglaze colours painted on to or under the glaze. It is first referred to in 1484 and the characteristic milky-white glaze painted with blue, emerald green, yellow and orange was produced in a great variety of shapes. Talavera pottery, it was said, stimulated the appe-

148

Europe

tite because it enhanced the savour of food with its shining purity. In 1575 the pottery received royal patronage and it was successfully traded throughout Spain. A group of potters was also sent to establish a pottery at Puebla de los Angeles in the then recently acquired colony of Mexico.

The individual character of Talavera pottery is noticeable in its coarsely made large white dishes which were vigorously painted with dark blue figures of songbirds, deer, rabbits and heron, enclosed in borders of rough foliage and tendrils. Other colours such as manganese purple and reddish-orange were added later. Many of the pots were very large, consisting of dishes, two-handled jars, basins for lemonade, jugs, barrels and cisterns. Candlesticks and inkstands were made in fanciful human or animal shapes. Attempts were made in the sixteenth century to fall in with the fashion from Antwerp which had a decorative style based on pierced ironwork and strapwork, interwoven with caryatids and stylized floral motifs.

During the seventeenth century the palette was extended to include intense copper greens, yellows and purples. A monochrome blue and white style was developed which was strongly influenced by

Bowl with design painted in underglaze green, brown and blue on white tin-glaze. Spain, Talavera de la Reina. c 1650. Diameter 12 inches. Hastings Museum.

contemporary engravings depicting, for example, landscapes, wild beasts or children at play. A writer in the seventeenth century favourably compares Talavera plates with those from China, and the pottery was generally highly regarded. The quality of the work deteriorated during the eighteenth century, but pottery with vivid green decoration still appears from this area to this day.

ITALY

Early Wares
c A.D. 500–1200

Little is known about the pottery made in Italy between A.D. 500 and 1000. The earlier Roman pottery tradition continued in some form, but the break-down of central government and the consequent decline in the arts meant that few developments were made during this time. Contact with the Byzantine Empire, through Venice and Ravenna in the north, was probably responsible for the wider use of lead glazes. Recent excavations have brought to light a range of domestic pottery produced around the seventh and eighth centuries glazed in a dark green or yellow lead glaze. Vessels have also been found at Ostia, the port of Rome, and also in Rome, dating to the ninth century on which decoration for the most part was limited to combed lines or applied pellets of clay in the shape of rosettes.

During the eleventh and twelfth centuries decorated bowls were imported from the Muslim countries. These were often set into outside walls

150

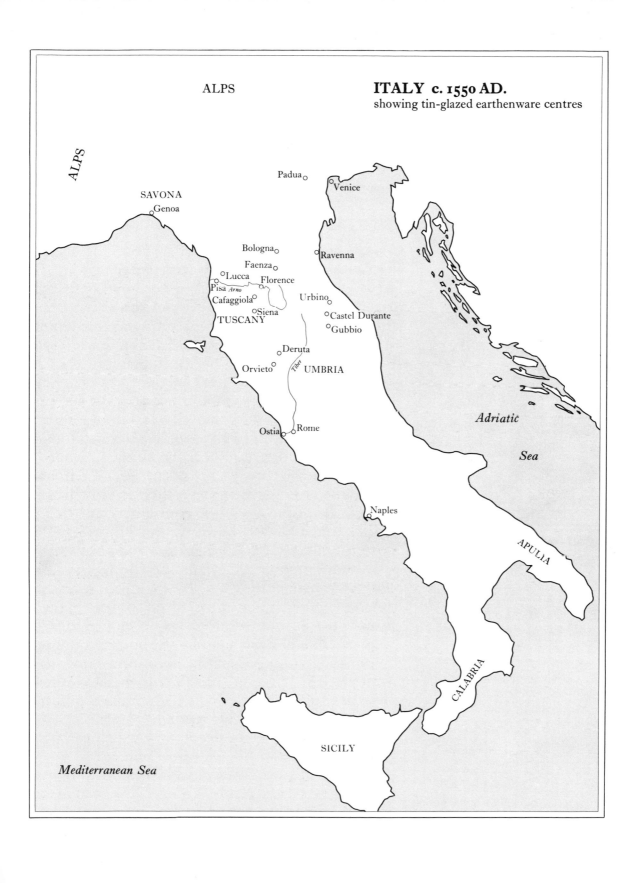

ALPS

ITALY c. 1550 AD.
showing tin-glazed earthenware centres

ALPS

Padua

Venice

SAVONA

Genoa

Bologna

Ravenna

Faenza

Lucca

Pisa   *Arno*   Florence

Cafaggiola

Urbino

Siena

Castel Durante

TUSCANY

Gubbio

Deruta

Orvieto   *Tiber*   UMBRIA

Adriatic

Sea

Ostia   Rome

Naples

APULIA

Mediterranean Sea

CALABRIA

SICILY

Earthenware bowl found in the masonry of a church tower at Pisa, Italy. The design is painted on a white slip over red clay. It is thought that the bowl was made in Palestine. Thirteenth or fourteenth century. Diameter about 9 inches. Victoria and Albert Museum.

of churches, such as those at Pisa, for use as decoration. Special niches were often left in the walls to hold the bowls. The bowls, though greatly admired, were never put inside churches, probably because they came from a pagan country. It was not long before this decorated ware was being imitated in Italy by the Italian potters.

It is interesting that Italy, a country with a long tradition of painting, should adapt the technique of painting on pottery and develop it as a branch of the arts of the Renaissance. Decoration on much of the pottery, especially in wares made in the sixteenth century, is often superior to the form, and it is the painting which is most highly valued. In some ways this contradicts one of the basic principles of pottery, that form should dominate over surface decoration, and goes against the usual criterion for evaluating the work of the potter. Italian pottery must be looked at from a different point of view if it is to be enjoyed, though the decorative processes developed in Italy were essentially those used by the potter. A limited colour range imposed by the colouring oxides and a method of painting directly on to the unfired, absorbent glaze surface, which eliminated rubbing out or over-painting, led to the development of a bold and fresh style of decoration which can only be thought of as a branch of ceramic art.

Tin-glazed earthenware only became known as majolica in the fifteenth century. The name was derived from tin-glazed ware imported from

Europe

Spain on boats from Majorca. Italian majolica ware can be divided into three distinct groups based for the most part on decorative treatment.

In Italy the use of white tin-glaze on light red bodied pots began around A.D. 1200. At first it was used only on small areas or confined to the inside of bowls, the remainder having a clear glaze. The use of the glaze seems to have spread slowly, appearing first in Sicily and later in northern Italy. Colouring oxides were painted directly on to the raw glaze and colours were limited to copper green painted in broad areas and often outlined in manganese brown or purple. Blue was not introduced until later. Early painted designs often reflected the Romanesque style of decoration in which natural forms were freely translated into linear patterns which were, at their best, calm and severe. For example, birds or beasts supporting a coat-of-arms were shown, but decorative themes echoing those of the Islamic potters were also used. Vegetables, foliage, animals, abstract patterns and geometric forms are found in the decoration though the human figure was rarely included. Little or no attempt was made to create an illusion of depth, volume or movement and the designs tended instead to be static and peaceful. Occasionally the design was enriched by modelling details in low relief. Trailing vines, bunches of grapes and coats-of-arms were, for example, modelled on pots in Orvieto.

153

Archaic or Early Period
(c A.D. 1200–1400)

Earthenware drug vase or albarello. White tin-glaze with majolica decoration painted in purple and green. Simple geometric or floral designs in a limited range of colours are characteristic of early majolica wares. Italian. Late fourteenth century. Height 7½ inches. Victoria and Albert Museum.

Forms were mainly those used in medicine or on the table. Albarellos, based on the bamboo shape, were widely made to hold medicine, as were ovoid jars and water pots with stirrup handles. Globular jugs, derived from the Greek vases, and very tall elegant jugs, which seem to have a more Gothic appearance, were produced for the table.

Fifteenth-century Italian tin-glazed ware developed more formal designs due to two major foreign influences. From northern Europe came the Gothic style and from Spain came the Oriental style.

Shapes generally tended to be those which had been made during the early archaic period, though in general they became more elaborate, and designs and form were purposefully related in a way which was later to be ignored. The undersides of bowls and the insides of pots were glazed white and were often decorated. Different regions produced distinctive ware, much of which was local in character. The palette became larger and richer and included a range of primary colours as well as green, purple and brown.

Extensive trade in the fifteenth century between Florence, Pisa and Lucca in Italy and Barcelona and Valencia in Spain brought the rich Hispano-Moresque wares of Valencia to Italy. Around 1420 the green and purple Valencian wares inspired a novel Italian style painted with foliage and from this developed a decorative style of great

Severe or Formal Style
(*c* A.D. 1400–1500)

Two-handled majolica jar with design on white tin-glaze painted in manganese purple and blue. Florence. Early fifteenth century. British Museum.

154

Majolica vase painted in the "severe" style. Italy. Design of a youth is set in ornamental field of oak leaves in raised cobalt blue. A typical example of this group of Florentine wares. c 1450. Height 14½ inches. British Museum.

Europe

distinction known as the "Florentine green family". The pattern consisted of formal repeating designs recalling peacock feathers, painted mainly in green on a white background.

In Tuscany, in particular at Faenza, a series of two-handled globular jugs was made, using a rich ultramarine blue or, more rarely, green, in slight relief. Oak leaves, derived from a Valencian design, formed the main decorative motif.

Fifteenth-century Italian potters were unable to make lustreware and imitated its effects in yellow and purple colours painted on to the raw glaze. From these imitations several superb types of decoration developed with thoroughly Italian figure painting added to the original Spanish ground motifs.

Gothic ideas on decoration were reflected in the more formal designs on pottery. The motifs used appear as types or symbols and not as pictorial images. Foliage, radiating beams of light, initials, sacred monograms, heraldic emblems, religious figures and animals all appeared in designs during this time.

A period of more settled government during the second half of the century saw the beginning of a new style of decoration related more to the Renaissance. The palette acquired warmth, and orange was often used instead of lime yellow. By 1500 the technique of majolica was well established throughout much of northern Italy. Individual centres were clearly established with their

Drug jar, majolica, with twisted rope handles. Design, painted in blue and orange, showing the Arms of Ranieriof, Perugia. Florence. 1475. Height 6 inches. Hastings Museum.

Renaissance Style
(*c* A.D. 1500–1600)

155

Plate, majolica. Castel Durante. Painted in blue and greys by Nicola Pellipario. Dated 1526. Wallace Collection.

own recognizable characteristics. The whole nature of pottery decoration had departed from that based primarily on Spanish and Gothic influence to one which reflected the attitude of the Renaissance and a completely indigenous style developed. Favourite local meeting spots at that time were the pharmacies, which were lavishly decorated with ornately painted majolica drugvases. This fashion, together with the contemporary style for displaying large decorative dishes on sideboards and tables, reached its height in this period. This encouraged potters to produce richly decorated ware. Individual ceramic artists, too, began to emerge, due probably to the patronage of wealthy noblemen. Their work was often as highly valued as that of the oil painters and had, besides, the advantage of an imperishable medium. Local schools of painting influenced pottery decoration and many designs were copied directly from drawings by famous artists.

While forms generally became more complex they were often overshadowed by the decoration. A plate or bowl would simply be used to provide the background for a detailed painted composition. Nevertheless, the painting was still related to that achieved by majolica painting rather than oil painting, though in the new pictorial style, often known as "istoriato", because it usually illustrated a story, elaborate scenes were depicted in great detail. Mythological subjects began to replace religious ones, and cupids, satyrs and

Plate, majolica. Deruta. Painted in gold lustre and cobalt blue. It was at Deruta that lustre was first achieved in Italy, probably by immigrants from Spain. c 1510. Wallace Collection.

156

dolphins were introduced. However, in Umbria, the home of St Francis, religious subjects remained most popular.

Pottery centres in different areas developed distinctive independent designs and it is only possible here to look at the main ones.

Castel Durante in the Duchy of Urbino saw the height of the "istoriato" style in the work of Nicola Pellipario. Engravings often stimulated his work, though these were never merely copied. His drawings of animals had a supple liveliness as if they were poised for easy movement, and they often appeared in idyllic landscapes. Colours on his designs were delicately graded.

Deruta, near Perugia, saw the first production of lustre in Italy, the technique having been brought, perhaps, by Moors fleeing from the Christian conquest of Spain. From about 1501 onwards a golden mother-of-pearl and a ruby lustre were made at Deruta. Lustre decoration allows no tonal changes, relying for its interest on surface reflections. At first, simple combinations of lustre and one other colour on a white background were used; later, surfaces were made in relief to enhance the effect of lustre. Scales, bosses and gadroons were introduced in imitation of precious metals. Early Deruta ware was fairly conventional with the rim used as a border around the central motif of a bust or heraldic arms.

Cafaggiola potteries enjoyed the patronage of the Medici family and produced their best work

157

Dish, majolica, painted in Baroque style. Faenza. Moulded externally with palmettes in relief, the inside carries a light and swift sketch of a female head in blue and yellow. c 1570. Diameter 10 inches. Museum of the Decorative Arts in Prague.

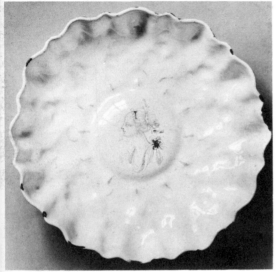

Baroque Style
(c A.D. 1570–1650)

Dish, majolica with lustre decoration. Gubbio, Umbria. Here lustre decoration was brought to perfection. Rich ruby and gold lustre are used in this scene, The Judgement of Paris, with Cupid shooting from the clouds. An inscription on the back reads "Lalto Gin dizio di'l Trojan Pastore". First half sixteenth century. Wallace Collection.

A History of Pottery

from 1500 to 1525. Jacopo Fattorini was a famous pottery painter whose work often had a characteristic dark blue background. It is probable that he studied in the workshop of Botticelli or Donatello. At Gubbio, in Umbria, lustre decoration was brought to perfection with a rich ruby and gold lustre. Tinted backgrounds were used about the middle of the century, grey and pale blue being the most common colours. White was often added for highlights. At Faenza, work on coloured backgrounds was highly developed.

The counter-reformation around the middle of the century led to a movement against the "istoriato" style of pictorial representation. The development of a fine, smooth white glaze at Faenza encouraged the reduction and restriction of decoration to small areas, often painted entirely in blues or yellows. Here the roots of the baroque style of decoration which developed at the beginning of the seventeenth century can be seen. In this style shapes were not limited to those traditionally produced but based on the forms of objects made in precious metal. Table services of many pieces, plates, dishes, ewers, wine coolers, candelabra, drug pots, flasks, inkstands, busts and obelisks were all produced, often in complex forms. Decoration, at its best, was delicate and limited to a palette of dark and light blue, yellow and orange. Drawing was often lively, having the freshness of a sketch, and avoided the elaborate and colourful detail of the "istoriato" style.

158

Plate, majolica. Urbino. Decoration, painted lightly and quickly, is based on the work of the followers of Raphael and is typical of the Baroque style. c 1590. Wallace Collection.

Later Majolica

Europe

Ware exported to France became known as faience after Faenza, one of the production centres, and potters travelled from Italy throughout Europe to teach the technique. Industries were established by Italian potters at Rouen and Nîmes in France and Antwerp in Belgium.

The seventeenth century saw the return of religious subjects in decoration and a general dislike of unpainted areas. New colours were introduced, such as pea green, but the palette was generally restricted. Baroque shapes were often complicated and largely based on gold, silver, copper and bronze objects. Applied plastic ornament in the shapes of monsters, sphinxes, mermaids and so on, and internal divisions in vessels, are evidence of the declining value of pottery and the general feeling that it must be made to imitate metal.

Cipriano Piccolpasso wrote a three-volume treatise around 1556–57 in which he describes in detail the techniques used by the majolica potters. Shapes, colours, glaze recipes, and decoration are all detailed and the books give a fascinating account of contemporary workshop practice.

Venice and Ravenna in the north were subject to intensive influence from Byzantium, as were Sicily, Apulia and Calabria in the south. It was here that the lead-glazing tradition was continued and developed, and around A.D. 1300, in imitation of and in competition to the white opaque glaze being used in other parts of Italy, white slip was used to give a white ground. The design was

Sgraffito Wares

Plate, majolica, showing the potter's wheel. From Arte Del Vasaro, The Three Books of the Potter's Art. *Cipriano Piccolpasso. 1524–79.* Victoria and Albert Museum.

159

Dish, earthenware. Sgraffito decoration of two youths in a garden scratched through white slip showing dark red clay body with touches of colouring oxides on transparent glaze. Bolognia. 1480–1500. Diameter 14 inches. Wallace Collection.

A History of Pottery

scratched through this to reveal the dark body underneath and subsequently glazed in a clear lead glaze. Some fine plates with modelled border patterns of leaves were made. Later green and brown colouring oxides were painted on to the glaze but these ran on the lead glaze and the rich mottled effect produced was quite unlike majolica. The designs, too, were different, being related to Gothic influences rather than Renaissance ones. The work reached its height in the sixteenth century when complicated shapes with modelled ornament were made.

Netherlands

NETHERLAND, FRENCH AND GERMAN MAJOLICA

The earliest majolica made in the Netherlands was at Antwerp when production started at the beginning of the sixteenth century in a pottery established by a friend of Piccolpasso from Castel Durante in Italy. Majolica was painted in the Italian style of decoration. The industry centred itself almost exclusively at Delft near Rotterdam in the second quarter of the seventeenth century and the ware became known as Delft. The founding in 1609 of the Dutch East India Company resulted in large amounts of blue and white Chinese porcelain being imported into Europe and this was imitated by the Delft potters. It is significant that the Guild of St Luke admitted potters to its ranks for their skill at painting and decorating rather than potting.

Two-handled vase, majolica decoration. Delft, Holland. The early Delft wares showed strong Italian influence. Early sixteenth century. London Museum.

160

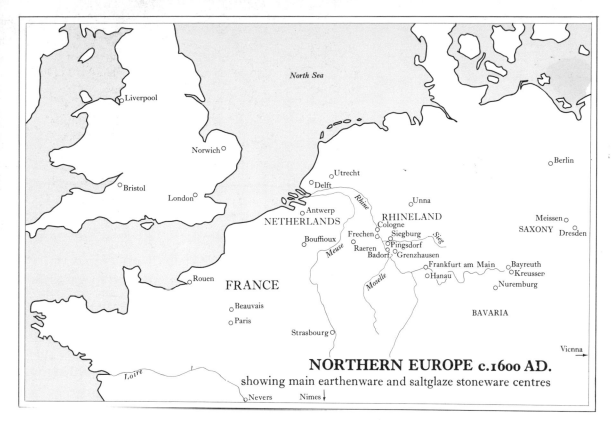

Map: NORTHERN EUROPE c.1600 AD.
showing main earthenware and saltglaze stoneware centres

Around the middle of the seventeenth century the pottery industry in Delft expanded rapidly, due to two events. One was the fall of the Ming dynasty in China which disrupted trade and so caused a drastic fall in the number of Chinese pots arriving in Europe, and the second reason was the availability of suitable pottery premises due to the lapse in the brewing industry in Holland. The Dutch potters used finely prepared clays and Chinese designs painted in blue. They also used a transparent lead glaze over the decoration, known to the Dutch as "kwaart", which gave the pots an even gloss, and the colours greater depth; this resulted in wares almost identical in appearance to the blue and white wares of China. Later, decoration was influenced by the work of contemporary oil painters. European landscapes, portraits and figure subjects were interpreted by the Delft potters. In the eighteenth century green, red and yellow were added to the earlier palette of blue and purple. Polychrome wares, imitating the

Six-sided dish, majòlica. Dutch, Delft. Painted and gilded design imitated that of the Japanese Arita wares in both form and style. Early eighteenth century. Diameter 13½ inches. British Museum.

161

enamelled porcelain wares made during the reign of K'ang Hsi (A.D. 1662–1772) in China and the rival Arita Japanese porcelain, known in Europe as Imari ware, were also produced.

France Though records exist that show the Duc de Berry took Valencian potters from Spain to central France around 1332 to produce tin-glazed earthenware, little is known of the wares they made there. There is evidence, too, that muslim potters fled from Catholic Spain to southern France where they made tin-glazed wares. Some of the earliest French majolica, known to the French as faience, was decorated with geometric painted designs in copper green and manganese purple and is similar in style to early Italian wares. Regular production, however, seems to have started in the sixteenth century and again the work produced shows a strong Italian influence. Immigrant Italian potters settled and worked at Nîmes in Provence and at Rouen near the west coast, and made pots which in their shape, decoration and general style are almost identical to contemporary Italian wares. At both centres the wares showed the influence of the work of the Royal gold- and silver-smiths. Large, decorative dishes, surrounded by ornate borders, and vases of elaborate forms were made.

At Nevers in central France, an industry was established towards the end of the sixteenth century and developed a naturalistic style of decoration in which birds and sprays of flowers were painted in blue and white on a white or a pale yellow

Europe

ground. Painted designs on imported Chinese blue and white porcelain wares were also imitated.

Towards the end of the seventeenth century the expanded industry at Rouen flourished and developed a unique, decorative style known as "style rayonnant". It was based on the work of ornamental engravers and the designs were painted mainly in blue on a white ground. Drapery, foliage and other Renaissance motifs were incorporated into the designs which were painted on finely moulded shapes closely imitating the work of the silversmiths.

During the eighteenth century the industry again expanded and the Italian influence was largely superseded by the imported Chinese porcelains and the Dutch Delft wares. Ruinous French wars resulted in edicts, in 1689 and 1709, which said all gold and silver vessels should be melted down, and the French faience industry was accordingly stimulated by the demand for replacement wares. At Rouen the "style rayonnant" was enriched by the use of further colours such as red and yellow, and the range of vessels extended to include many more accessories for the table such as fashionable ice-pails, dredgers for powdered sugar, boxes for precious spices and stuffs, salt cellars and basins.

The middle of the century saw the adaptation of the rococo style of decoration which reflected the influence of contemporary painters such as Watteau and Boucher. Garlands of naturalistically painted flowers and shells framed finely drawn pictures with amorous or pastoral subjects.

At Strasbourg, near the German border, technical changes were introduced in the second half of the century. Hitherto, colours had been painted directly on to the raw tin-glaze in the process sometimes known as in-glaze decoration. The new technique, copied from the porcelain factories, was that of using enamels in which the specially prepared coloured enamel glazes were painted on to the fired glaze and fixed by a third low-temperature firing. The main advantage of enamels was the wide range of bright colours which could be obtained.

Porcelain painters from Germany brought with them the necessary knowledge and skill and adapted the style of naturalistically painted flowers and finely modelled figures which had been used on porcelain to that of majolica. Tureens modelled in the shape of vegetables or animals – a popular shape was a boar's head – were also made for sideboards or banqueting tables.

Germany In Germany some of the earliest majolica pottery was made at Nuremberg in the sixteenth century, though majolica tiles, often for stoves, had been made much earlier. Dishes and drug jars were produced and, in their designs and shape, showed a strong Italian influence. The majolica industry at Kreussen, however, while imitating Italian designs, often made shapes similar to those of the local stoneware industry.

164

Europe

Two important German factories were established in the second half of the seventeenth century, the first of which was in 1661 by Dutch religious refugees at Hanan. At first the style was predominantly that of the Dutch Delft wares made in the Chinese style, but gradually European designs were developed. In these, patterns of scattered flowers interspersed with small exotic birds and groups of dots were painted on typical jugs which had tall, narrow necks and handles in the form of "twisted rope". By the 1750s designs were painted with the traditional in-glaze majolica decoration and also enamel over-glaze.

The second major factory was established, in 1666, by a French potter at Frankfurt-am-Main. Here German majolica flourished into a rich, highly decorative and ornamental ware which contrasted favourably with the more mundane products of nearby Hanan. Decoration, usually painted in blue, was covered in the clear glaze known as "kwaart" to give added depth and shine. Plates and dishes with smooth, ribbed or nine-lobed rims, vases, jugs and basins were made. Typical Frankfurt designs were of strong Chinese influence and showed, for example, a scene in which Chinamen were set in a stylized landscape with rocks, shrubs, birds, butterflies and insects. Naturalistic designs, more European in character, such as were made at Hanan, were also painted.

Majolica factories continued to be established in Germany in increasing numbers during the early

165

Jug with short tubular spout, wheel made. Traces of red painted decoration. This ware was imported into England where it was copied by the English potters. Eighth or ninth century. Excavated Burstow Castle, Sussex. Height 7 inches. Hastings Museum.

eighteenth century. Changes in drinking habits resulted in the widespread manufacture of tea, coffee and chocolate services and this, combined with the discovery of porcelain by Bottger in 1709 and its subsequent commercial production, affected the design and decoration of majolica in general. For example, the fine naturalistic painting known as "German flowers" first employed on Meissen porcelain was adapted to the use of the tin-glaze potter at Strasbourg in France, where the style of decoration became known as "Strasbourg flowers". This in turn affected the German products. Influence, too, was felt from the Du Paquier porcelain factory at Vienna which existed at that time.

Majolica factories throughout Europe adapted themselves to and even expanded under the changed conditions of eighteenth-century Europe. Their products existed by the side of fine porcelain wares which fulfilled the need that existed for luxurious goods while majolica provided a cheaper but acceptable alternative. It was, however, the large-scale introduction into Europe of English cream-coloured wares with their high quality and fantastically low prices which finally brought about the collapse of the industry throughout Europe around 1800.

GERMAN STONEWARES AND SALTGLAZE

Early Period
(c A.D. 400–1000) Following the disappearance of most of the technology introduced by the Romans in Germany

166

Europe

around the fifth century, coarse pottery, some of it reflecting Roman forms, continued to be made for domestic use. No new technical developments appeared until the ninth century when improved firing methods enabled higher temperatures to be reached. A productive industry developed in the Rhine valley around the seventh century A.D. when pots for domestic use, elaborated with simple painted decoration in red clay, were made. Forms were simple and sometimes incised decoration was included. Pots made in the Rhine Valley at Pingsdorf and Badorf were imported into England around the tenth century. Higher firing temperatures and more carefully prepared clay resulted in a harder and more vitrified body which in time became known as stoneware or "steinzeug".

The development of high-fired ware for the first time in the West was the culmination of a long pottery tradition in the Rhine Valley. It was made possible by the availability of good sandy plastic clay able to withstand high temperatures and a plentiful supply of wood and, later, good-quality coal; the Rhine made it possible for the wares to be transported easily. Stoneware is characterized by a hard, dense, impervious body which emits a clear ringing sound when struck. In some ways stoneware is similar to porcelain in that both are vitrified and non-porous, but stoneware is not usually white or translucent. Glazes capable of being fired to a high temperature were unknown to the early German stoneware potters and rela-

Thrown and wheel-turned pot, frilled foot, hard buff clay. Decoration painted in red vitrified slip. Pingsdorf Kilns, near Cologne. Ninth century. London Museum.

Early High-Fired Wares
(c A.D. 1000–1200)

167

tively unimportant as stoneware is impervious to liquids. This no doubt encouraged the use of salt-glazing when it was discovered. Early stoneware forms changed from being squat to ones which were more slender and Gothic in character. Jugs, cooking pots and cooking utensils seem to have been most common. Washes of a more fusible red clay were used both as decoration and to improve the surface texture of the pot by making it more smooth.

Saltglazing Technique Saltglazing was developed around the late fourteenth or early fifteenth century and is Germany's most important contribution to European pottery. The clay which lay in vast quantities in easily accessible beds in the Rhineland was found to react well with common salt thrown into the kiln towards the culmination of the firing. At a high temperature (1200°C) salt (sodium chloride) volatilizes into sodium and chlorine and the sodium combines with the surface of the clay to produce a chemically simple but extremely tough and resistant glaze. Occasionally the glaze so formed was smooth and brown, at other times it had a surface like orange peel and sometimes it was mottled brown and cream. Its colour and texture depended to a large extent on the clay body on to which it went, different sorts of clay slips giving different colours, but the glaze coating was always thin. Salt for the process was imported up the Rhine or came from the salt-mines of Unna in Westphalia.

Apart from the availability of raw materials two

168

Europe

other factors influenced the development of the industry. The first was the metal-working industry which was well established in Germany by the thirteenth century. This stimulated potters to copy the metal forms as well as the fine engraved designs. Saltglazing, because the glaze is formed from vapour, is very thin and tends not to obscure fine detail but to heighten and pick it out. The fine contemporary designs used on precious-metal-work were used with equal success on the salt-glazed pottery. At Raeren, the centre where brown-ware was made, a glaze almost identical to bronze was developed and, though its resemblance to metal may have been fortuitous, the popularity of the ware was possibly due to this resemblance.

The second factor which stimulated the industry was the increased consumption of ales and wines throughout Europe. Around A.D. 1500 a coarse, malt liquor drink was greatly improved by the addition of a new ingredient, hops; the result was a widespread increase in the drinking of ale. Inns and taverns became popular and the new saltglaze pottery drinking vessels were in great demand. England, too, enjoyed this new drink and a large trade was established to provide her with the necessary drinking vessels. Wine, too, was exported throughout Europe, including England, in stoneware wine bottles. The demand for drinking vessels of all sorts, especially the "canette", a pint pot, and the tall tapering

Tall drinking mug or "canette". Saltglaze ware with coat of arms in relief. Raeren, dated 1622. Wallace Collection.

169

"schnelle", encouraged the production of saltglaze stoneware which was preferred to earthenware or metal tankards.

Saltglaze wares fall into four groups, each group having a main manufacturing centre and each having its distinct characteristics. Raeren, in the Low Countries, was the main centre for the production of brown-ware. Here the art of saltglazing was fully developed and the rich, bronze-like colour was very popular. Ware was specially made for, and exported to, France, Sweden, Norway, Spain, Poland, Hungary, Denmark and England and it was often decorated with royal coats-of-arms. The best pots were made in the second half of the sixteenth century.

The vessels most commonly made were the pint drinking mug or "canette". Round-bellied mugs of fine clay with little or no decoration other than a band of pattern in relief round the neck were produced with a rich, brown glaze. Large jugs, turned on the wheel to remove throwing marks and perfect the profile, were made in three separate pieces — neck, body and foot — and joined together before the clay had fully dried out. Other popular forms were the three-handled Kaiser jugs, nearly a foot high, pilgrim flasks for holding spring water, pocket flagons in the shape of prayer books, puzzle jugs and jugs in the shape of cannons.

Friezes of relief decoration were popular motifs and these depicted classical scenes, often copied

Saltglaze Brown-Ware

Brown saltglaze jug. Raeren. Wheel made and turned with an applied moulded decorative frieze showing peasants dancing, after the style of Hans Sebald Behan. 1590. Height about 12 inches. Victoria and Albert Museum.

170

Europe

from engravings specially produced by German masters, religious scenes and scenes recording social events such as parties or festivities.

The so-called Bellarmines, full, round-bodied jugs with narrow necks, often with a large capacity, were decorated with a grotesque bearded face modelled on the neck and were perhaps the most famous of the brown-wares: they were so called after Cardinal Bellarmine, a medieval priest who forbade drinking, though the grotesque face had been a popular decorative motif long before Cardinal Bellarmine made his pronouncement.

Pots made in Cologne were similar to those produced at Raeren in that they were made from similar brown clay with a brown saltglaze, though the decorative subjects were different. Some white-ware was also produced in Cologne. Decoration tended to imitate precious stones in metal settings, and the influence of the Italian Renaissance can be seen in busts set under arcades. Texts, such as "Drink and eat, do not forget God", in Gothic script were often combined with classical acanthus leaves and medallions. Early in the sixteenth century potters were banished from the city of Cologne because the poisonous chlorine fumes emitted by the kilns during the salting process were thought to be excessive, and the potters moved to the nearby city of Frechen. Here, good, plastic clay and a welcoming city saw the growth of an industry which by 1650 was to rival that at Raeren. Decoration was characterized by applied

Saltglaze wine jar or bellarmine, supposedly showing the face of Cardinal Bellarmine on the neck. Coat of arms in relief. The mottled glaze effect is the result of the salt thrown into the kiln. Raeren (?). Height 7 inches. Excavated in Westminster. Ministry of Works.

171

Saltglaze White-Ware
(*c* A.D. 1550–1800)

White saltglaze jug. Siegburg, Germany. Found in the City of London. Throwing rings, the splayed foot and the tall elegant shape are typical of the early white wares of this area. Fifteenth century. Height 10 inches. Victoria and Albert Museum.

scrolls of foliage, leaves and rosettes stamped symmetrically over the full-bodied pots. Medals and acanthus leaves continued to be popular motifs. Siegburg, on the River Sieg, was the centre at which white-ware was developed around A.D. 1550. Accounts involving potters are first found in 1427, which would indicate a well-established industry. Guilds protected both the potters and the industry, and long family traditions over hundreds of years are recorded.

Early ware, produced in this area before about A.D. 1400, was hard and vitrified and made from brown or dark grey clay. Later, jugs, thrown on the wheel and left with finger mouldings at the base, often known as pie-crust decoration, and embellished with simple applied rosettes and grotesque faces, were made. Around A.D. 1400 clay was more carefully prepared and moulds of wood or metal were used to make relief decoration, known as sprigs, which were applied to the pot. Tall red jugs, "Roit Kroichen", with clay rings in the handles, were also made until the production of white-ware became most popular and the production of red jugs ceased at Siegburg.

Around the middle of the sixteenth century the finest white-ware was developed. The white body used for the pots did not react too well with the salt, and the glaze was thinner and less shiny than that on the earlier brown-wares. The forms included tall, slender, tapering drinking mugs and ewers, with long spouts imitating metal forms, for

172

White saltglaze tankard. Sieg-burg, Germany. The applied moulded relief design represents Philip II of Spain and Henri II of France with their coats of arms. About 1550. Height about 7 inches. Victoria and Albert Museum.

Europe

dispensing the best wine, puzzle jugs, large candlesticks and baluster jugs. Fine detailed relief decoration included religious subjects such as the Garden of Eden, Temptation, Annunciation, Last Supper and Flagellation; in contrast anti-Catholic scenes showing clergy and monks in scenes of wild debauchery, mythological scenes and heraldic devices were also popular.

Larger or more complicated pots were made in moulds, but pots thrown on the wheel were often left with the throwing marks, giving them a pleasant and lively appearance. Tall thrown jugs were graceful and elegant.

In the district known as "Kannenbäckerland", or "Country of Pot Makers", Grenzhausen was the centre to which many potters fled from the ravage of the Thirty Years War (A.D. 1618–48). Thus, in the early seventeenth century, a long established but undistinguished pottery industry here was suddenly given life and vitality. Saltglaze ware made in this area had, until then, been brown, white or cream, depending on the body used, but the new Grenzhausen potters introduced the use of cobalt-blue and manganese-purple backgrounds. A prosperous industry developed which was to flourish for some 200 years. Saltglazing does not favour the development of bright colours and the ultramarine, navy blue and aubergine purple combined with the grey background to give a startling if sombre effect. The pots were made out of light, bluish-grey clay and were

173

Saltglaze stoneware jug made in grey clay. The regular moulded and stamped design shows scenes from the Parable of the Prodigal Son and are picked out in manganese purple and cobalt blue. A metal lid has been fitted. German. Grenzhausen. 1618. Height 13½ inches. V. and A.

Coloured Ware

Saltglaze tankard with enamel decoration
shows the Emperor of Germany and the
Electors. Kreussen, Germany. 1696.
Height 7 inches. V and A.

A History of Pottery

decorated with bold, relatively unskilled designs
of notches, plain circles and rosettes, depending
for their effect on the added colour. The ware
proved very popular throughout Germany and
other parts of Europe. The drinker, it seems, no
longer wanted amusement from the friezes of
relief decoration, or instruction from the texts,
but colour. Dishes, plates, tableware, figures and,
later, modelled objects such as inkstands were
produced.

Kreussen, in Bavarian, was the centre of the fourth
and most costly saltglaze style. Majolica wares
from Italy had been coming into Germany for
some time and the use of colour by the Kreussen
potters may have been influenced by such ware.
The long-established glass-painting industry in
Kreussen had developed opaque low-temperature
lead glazes, known as enamels, which were
adapted for use on pottery by the Kreussen
potters. These were fixed on to the pots in a
second, low-temperature firing. The style started
around 1620 and lasted some 130 years. Pots
were made out of grey clay and saltglazed
Shapes were kept fairly simple and the two most
popular ones were the shallow and broad canette
or drinking mug and the plain oviform jug. The
bright coloured enamels were painted on to the
plain, pale grey background and, when the designs
were carefully controlled, gave a pleasant effect.
Glass-painters were often employed to decorate
the pots, and simple bands of figures, such as

Enamel Ware

Saltglaze jug with mould decoration
painted in black and white enamels.
Freiberg, Saxony, Germany. Height 8
inches. c 1650. V and A.

174

Europe

"The Planets", were very successful. In later work the whole body was covered with enamel decoration and the effect became crude and overbearing.

A fine, if simpler, style similar to Raeren was developed at Bouffioux. Large pieces such as barrels, Bellarmines, chemist's jars and boxes for holding medicines, pills and powders, as well as canisters, pocket flasks, cruets, inkstands and teapots, were made. Ornamentation was kept to a minimum and consisted of medallions and simple raised lines and popular grotesque masks, imitating those made at Frechen.

It was from Germany that John Dwight and the Elers brothers saw and probably learnt the art of stoneware which they brought to England in the second half of the seventeenth century. The technique had a profound effect on seventeenth- and eighteenth-century pottery in England, where German saltglaze wares were highly regarded. German saltglaze ware was, for example, presented to Elizabeth I. Great technical skill was required to achieve the clean, sharp relief decoration and careful kiln control to obtain a good glaze. Artists who worked out relief designs became well known and their designs can be recognized; such masters as Balden Mennicken, Jon Emens and Jan Baldems became well known. The finest saltglaze pots were often mounted on stands and the rim covered with finely engraved metal; in the case of jugs, ornate metal lids were also fitted.

Other Styles

175

GREAT BRITAIN
showing some of the pottery making centres

North Sea

Glasgow

Newcastle
Sunderland

Belfast

York

Irish Sea

Leeds

Dublin

Liverpool

Chesterfield

Trent

Lincoln

Tunstall
Longport
Burslem
Cobridge
Hanley
Bradwell Wood
Shelton
Fenton
Lane End
Lane Delph
Longton

Stoke on
Trent

Derby

Nottingham

Tickenhall

Stamford

Castor

Thetford

Grand Union Canal

Worcester

St. Neots

Ipswich

Colchester

St. Albans

Harlow

London

Thames

Cheam

Wrotham

Bristol

Glastonbury

Rye

Barnstaple
Fremington
Bideford

Old Sarum

NEW
FOREST

Chichester

Plymouth

St. Ives

Chapter 6

Great Britain until A.D. 1750

Beaker with incised cross-hatched and triangular design. Soft grey body. Aberdeenshire. c 2000–1500 B.C. Height 7 inches. Anthropological Museum, University of Aberdeen.

NEOLITHIC AND BRONZE AGE

It is probable that pottery was introduced into Britain around 2000 B.C., though recent excavations and improved carbon-dating methods indicate that it may have been earlier. Pots at that time were hand-built with distinctive rims; some had incised decoration. Vessels with a distinct shoulder developed soon afterwards which were to serve as models for later cinerary urns. Around the first part of the second millennium B.C., drinking vessels in the form of beakers were made, copied from wares brought by migrations of the so-called Beaker people who probably originated in southern Spain. Simple, incised chevron designs on the sides of the beakers helped to provide a better holding surface as well as being decorative, and some were inlaid with white clay or paint of some sort.

177

(a) *Pot, roughly built and fired. Lake Villages of Meare. Iron Age. Salisbury. Height 6 inches.* (b) *Pot from same area made after the introduction of slow wheel during the Iron Age. Incised curvilinear decoration. Form imitates that of iron. Height 3 inches.* Somerset County Museum, Taunton.

Coarse pottery barrel beaker, with roulette pattern. Evidence of turning on foot. St Albans pottery. c A.D. *200. Height 6 inches.* Ministry of Public Buildings and Works.

Cinerary urns with a prominent shoulder and sides tapering to a narrow base began to be made around 1500–1000 B.C. Larger urns were produced in the late Bronze Age.

Pottery, as a whole, became more sophisticated during the Iron Age (500 B.C.–A.D. 43). Invaders from Gaul brought knowledge of iron-working, and pottery was made thinner in imitation of the metal objects. A simple potter's wheel was introduced at this time, and forms generally became more symmetrical and developed an elegance and finish hitherto lacking.

ROMAN OCCUPATION

The Roman invasion and conquest of Britain in A.D. 43 brought a vastly superior technology, which included the more careful preparation of clay, a more sophisticated potter's wheel and improved kiln design, and the Romans imposed this on the more primitive British. Roman red-gloss wares, made principally in Gaul, were imported into Britain in fairly large amounts. Recent excavations at Chichester indicate that wares imitating them were made there. Coarse unglazed pottery was made in fairly substantial quantities at a number of sites in Britain and, strange to say, each site produced pottery with its own characteristics.

Castor Ware One of the largest and most important sites for the production of coarse-ware was that at Castor in Northamptonshire: its development was due to

178

Great Britain until A.D. 1750

Castor-ware hunt cup with design of hare trailed on side. Roman pottery. Third century. Height $3\frac{1}{2}$ inches. Richborough Museum, Ministry of Public Buildings and Works.

the proximity of the London–York Ermine Street and the excellent plastic clays which were available. A whole range of wheel-thrown pots were made for domestic use out of the local clay which fired a pinkish-buff colour. Basins, jugs, mixing bowls and beakers were among the pots produced.

Slip was used to decorate these pots, especially the beakers. Scrolls and leaping animal designs were trailed in thick slip on to the pot, a process known as barbotine decoration. Designs were freely carried out and the results had a pleasant liveliness, though the decoration often resembled that produced by the silversmiths. The decorated pot was dipped in dark brown or black pigment to colour the surface, though occasionally purple or red tones were achieved.

Potteries in the New Forest area produced two sorts of ware. One was a dark coloured, plain ware of distinctive form, often with impressed sides recalling the shape of leather bottles. The other group was decorated. Pattern was impressed in the form of rosettes, stars or crescents, or painted in slip in abstract designs built up exclusively of straight lines and circles.

New Forest Ware

DARK AGES

The withdrawal of the Roman legions saw the lapse of most Roman technology, and Saxon pottery forms reflect those made before A.D. 43. Cinerary urns, with high shoulders and decorated

179

with incised designs, applied clay and impressed patterns, seem to represent the highest achievement.

Major technical advances, however, were made around the seventh and eighth centuries. Trade with the Continent increased and in due course the fast wheel was brought to England as well as galena glaze. In the Low Countries and the Rhineland the use of both the fast wheel and lead glaze had been either maintained from their introduction by the Romans or reintroduced from the Byzantine Empire. It is significant that the east coast of England, particularly near the Wash, was quick to import and use the technological improvements, leaving the remainder of the country to continue with hand-building production methods and either open firing or very simple kiln arrangements.

Saxo-Norman Wares
(c A.D. 700–1066)

Three distinct wares have been found in the so-called Saxo-Norman type of pottery. The first, St Neots ware, was soft, grey, soapy to touch and had substantial amounts of powdered shell mixed with the body. It was bright red, purple, brown or dark purple in colour, which suggests it was open fired. Deep bowls, shallow dishes, cooking pots, six to eight inches high, and jugs with rouletted decoration were made.

Secondly, Ipswich ware, made as early as the eighth century, was the forerunner of Thetford ware, made from the tenth to the twelfth century. It was the first ware to show marked European

180

influence. The body was hard, sandy and grey, and the forms reflect closely those produced in the Rhineland. Cooking pots, bowls, storage vessels, decorated with applied and impressed bands of clay, and spouted pitchers were made. No glaze was used.

The last and most interesting type is Stamford ware, first found at Stamford on the borders of Northamptonshire and Lincolnshire and made from the local estuarine clay. This ware was both finer and whiter than the other two wares. However, what makes it so exceptional is that parts of the cream-coloured pots were glazed a pale, transparent yellow colour and this was perhaps the first glazed pottery to be made in England. The glaze was made by dusting lead in the form of galena, which is a natural sulphide of lead, on to the shoulders of the damp pot. Glazed bowls and spouted pitchers were made here as well as unglazed cooking pots. The spouted pitcher, by far the most common form, usually had three strap handles, a tubular spout and a rounded base trimmed with a knife round the edge. Stamford ware was widely distributed and was sold throughout the east Midlands.

MEDIEVAL POTTERY (A.D. 1066–1600)

The Norman conquest of A.D. 1066 is usually considered to mark the beginning of the medieval period in Britain. To some extent pottery reflected

181

Left: *Fine grey bowl with spout at rim. Thetford ware. Height 4 inches. British Museum. Below, top:* *Pottery ewer with convex base, tubular spout and small handles. Yellow, lead glaze. A rare example of the first group of English glazed wares, copied from imported ware from the Rhineland. Height 7½ inches. East Anglia, tenth or eleventh century. British Museum. Bottom:* *Pottery ewer with three handles and short spout. Thetford ware. Ninth century. Height 13 inches. M.P.B.W.*

Castrel from site of Saxon town. Thetford, Norfolk. Clearly wheel made with great skill. Early eleventh century. Height about 9 inches. Ministry of Public Buildings and Works.

Jug, excavated at Pevensy Castle, used for mulling wine and linked with the red wine trade with Bordeaux. Norman. Neck restored. c A.D. 1100. *Height about 11 inches.* Hastings Museum.

the architectural activity of the period, becoming bigger and technically better. Pottery was never highly regarded in Britain by the wealthier classes until the eighteenth century, when fine, white, industrially produced pottery, imitating the fineness of Chinese porcelain, was made. In medieval Britain the poorer people tended to eat off wood and drink from horn or leather containers, leaving pewter, silver and gold utensils for the use of the rich.

English medieval pottery is artistically of great interest and historically is the forerunner of the later Staffordshire wares. Jugs and pitchers form the majority of this medieval ware and are distinguished by a rare dignity and strength of form. The introduction of the fast wheel, improved kilns and the use of lead glaze formed the basis of its production.

These jugs were made at various sites, many as yet unidentified, and fired in comparatively simple kilns to a temperature of around 1000°C, having been previously dusted with dry powdered galena. The clay body varied in colour from red to buff, depending on the local clay source, and usually had ground shell or sand added to improve its throwing qualities. The fast wheel was used for the manufacture of these pots, which are remarkable for their lightness and thinness. A common feature of the earlier jugs is the convex or sagging base. This is thought to have been a continuation of the tradition of rounded bases which would sit firmly

182

Tall pitcher of the baluster type with splashed green glaze. Late thirteenth century. Height about 12 inches. London Museum.

Great Britain until A.D. 1750

on uneven earth floors or, more probably, in the embers of a fire. The introduction of wooden tables and flat surfaces necessitated the thumbing of the bottom edge of the pot and this is often found on many of the later jugs. Occasionally, small tripod feet were added.

The finest jugs were made during the thirteenth century in forms which were tall and slender and preceded the development of smaller, more squat ones in the fourteenth and fifteenth centuries. Handles generally were sturdy and well placed both aesthetically and functionally. They were always firmly joined on to the pot and occasionally were splayed out to form a pattern. Both round and flat, strap-like handles were made. Decoration was simple but effective, with the forms of the jugs remaining dominant and uncluttered. On some jugs coloured slips were trailed or painted on to the pots, sometimes combined with applied strips and pads of clay. At Cheam and Rye simple designs were painted in slip of a contrasting colour. On most pots the yellow-brown glaze, occasionally tinted green with copper, was the chief decoration.

Other pots made at this time included cooking and storing vessels, pipkins, saucepans and flat frying pans. Flasks and pilgrim bottles in many sizes and forms, some flattened, have been found at Old Sarum, Wiltshire, and were probably made locally. Aquamaniles or water holders with short spouts, some in the form of animals, were produced to

Pitcher with applied pattern of green lattice and red pellets with large red rosettes. Yellow glaze. Fourteenth century. Height about 14 inches. London Museum.

183

Pitcher, simple modelled face as neck similar to imported German jugs. Glossy dark green glaze. Fifteenth century. Height about 12 inches. London Museum.

Tudor Pottery
(c A.D. 1500–1600)

Tiles

Cistercian Ware

hold water for washing hands during or after meals. By Tudor times the range of vessels had widened to include cisterns, stove tiles and candle brackets.

Finely moulded relief decorations of Tudor roses and shields-of-arms imitated the decorative technique of imported German saltglaze ware. Jug forms became much more squat and were glazed in a rich moss or speckled green cucumber glaze: both form and colour of the pots imitated contemporary metal flagons, which were very popular.

The production of medieval tiles should also be mentioned, though, strictly speaking, outside the range of this book. These were usually made in red clay with a design impressed into the soft clay which was subsequently filled with clay of a contrasting colour, usually buff or white. Simple heraldic motifs, shields-of-arms, stylized flowers and animals were common designs. The tiles were often used for the floors of cathedrals and abbeys. An early example from Halesowen Abbey is dated 1290. Examples still in their original position can be seen in the chapter houses of York Minster and Westminster Abbey. Production, at various sites, lasted until the end of the seventeenth century.

The so-called Cistercian ware, found on or near the sites of Benedictine monasteries, may have been made by the monks. Production seems to have been reduced by the dissolution of the monasteries in 1540, and finally ceased in the

184

Left: *Red earthenware tiles with contrasting inlaid designs in white clay of heraldic animals. Mainly used on the floors in churches. Keynsham Abbey, Somerset, England. Thirteenth century.* Victoria and Albert Museum. Right: *Jug with decoration painted in white slip, Rye, Sussex.* c A.D. *1300. Height 8 inches.* Hastings Museum.

seventeenth century. The ware is hard, indicating a fairly high firing temperature, and characterized by a dark red body, glazed inside and out with a dark brown glaze stained with manganese. Occasionally, trailed white slip and applied pads of white clay were used for decoration. Drinking cups with several handles were made and preceded the much more common tyg. To a large extent this tradition of hard-fired, slip-decorated earthenware was continued from around the beginning of the seventeenth century until about 1700 at Tickenhall in Derbyshire.

Two-handled tyg with glossy brown glaze. Cistercian ware. Early sixteenth century. Height 5 inches. Hastings Museum.

ENGLISH EARTHENWARE (c A.D. 1600–1750)

Earthenware, fired only once and glazed with powdered galena dusted on to the leather-hard pots, continued to form the basis of much of the pottery made in England until the late eighteenth century. Its method of production was, with one or two exceptions, relatively unaffected by either the techniques introduced from the Continent of tin-glazed earthenware in the sixteenth century or of saltglazed stoneware in the seventeenth century. However, the impulse towards refinement in the eighteenth century and the production of white saltglaze ware and cream-coloured ware eventually brought about a reduction in the amount of this type of earthenware made until its production virtually ceased at the end of the nineteenth century.

185

Watering jug, yellow lead glaze. Probably fifteenth century. Height 11½ inches. Hastings Museum.

A History of Pottery

Lead-glazed earthenware was essentially produced for local markets, and the use of local materials and the development of local traditions resulted in a variety of decorative methods on a wide range of pots. Much of the earthenware had a peasant charm which derived from the simple practical forms and the fresh vigorous slip decoration carried out in the different but limited range of clays. English lead-glazed earthenware forms, artistically, one of the great achievements of English folk art.

Staffordshire Slipware

Staffordshire was the largest and most important centre where slip-decorated earthenware was made. Excellent local clays and wood for firing the kilns probably accounted for the establishment of potteries in the area in the first place. The earliest known examples of Staffordshire slipware date back to the first half of the seventeenth century, though the production of lead-glazed earthenware generally seems to have been well established here before then, with a market beyond that locally available. Staffordshire butter pots, for example, were well known throughout the Midlands. Wares for farm and household use were the main products made out of red clay and glazed with the lead galena glaze.

Slipwares are so called because they are decorated with liquid clays of different colours in the form of slips either poured or trailed on to the pots. Though the technique was highly developed in Staffordshire it was used in other areas as well.

Pottery money box with pale yellow lead glaze. Excavated in Abingdon. Seventeenth century. Ministry of Public Buildings and Works.

186

Staffordshire slipwares reached their peak around the end of the seventeenth century and the ware falls into three groups: flatware, such as plates and dishes; hollow ware, comprising drinking vessels, jugs, lidded pots; and miscellaneous ware, such as candlesticks, cradles, money boxes and chimney ornaments.

It is the flatware, comprising dishes and shallow bowls some twelve to twenty-two inches across, wheel thrown and turned and decorated with such vigour and robustness, that are the finest and best known pieces. The large dishes, usually made for special occasions such as weddings or christenings, reached the peak of their achievement in the work of the Staffordshire Toft family, and much so-called Toft ware was made by other potters imitating them, so great was their fame.

Toft Wares

Reddish buff clay was used for the body of the dishes and covered with a layer of white or cream slip which formed the background for the trailing of red, dark brown and tan slips. Designs were outlined and filled in with a wide variety of patterns. Human figures were drawn with little or no regard for anatomical detail and, like those painted on the tin-glazed blue-dash-chargers, had the naïve quality associated with talented but untrained artists. As such, the dishes have unique charm. Favourite subjects included royal scenes, such as King Charles II hiding in the oak, as well as portraits of popular figures and cavaliers. Coats-of-arms, mermaids, Adam and Eve, and the

Slipware dish by Thomas Toft. Trellis work border of black and tan slip on white ground. Clear lead glaze. c 1675. Stoke-on-Trent Museum and Art Gallery.

187

Slipware dish with design of owl, six little owls and another bird. c 1715. Stoke-on-Trent Museum and Art Gallery.

Jug with design carved through layer of white slip, clear lead glaze. "Drawn by me Thomas Amman, made by me Edward Reed." North Devon. 1741. Height 13½ inches. Stoke-on-Trent Museum and Art Gallery.

Other Centres making Earthenware

Pelican in her Piety, symbolizing the eucharistic sacrifice of Christ's death on the cross, were also popular. Designs were beautifully balanced within a rich trellis border pattern. Ralph and Thomas Toft often incorporated their name into the border as part of the pattern.

One development in the eighteenth century made by Samuel Malkin was the use of moulds with patterns incised into the surface. Clay was pressed over the mould and the pattern was left in slight relief. The pattern was subsequently decorated with slips of different colours, and quite complicated designs could be repeated easily.

Other imitators of the Toft style of decoration included Ralph Simpson, Richard Meir, Robert Shaw and Ralph Turner.

Many local pottery centres existed throughout the country in the seventeenth and eighteenth centuries. All made lead-glazed earthenware, but each developed its own styles, as well as methods of decoration, related to local needs. None of the centres achieved the mastery of the Staffordshire potters in slipware decoration, though some centres used similar slip techniques. There were various other methods of decoration. White clay was often applied in relief and slips were occasionally coloured dark brown or black. The use of green slip or glaze was not widespread until the late eighteenth and nineteenth centuries.

Potteries at Barnstaple, Bideford and Fremington in Devon used the highly plastic local red clay.

188

Large harvest jugs were made, some of which were dipped in white slip and designs scratched through to show the red body, using the sgraffito technique. Decoration included coats-of-arms, lions and unicorns, ships in full sail, mariners' compasses and floral designs.

Wrotham ware, which was made as early as the beginning of the sixteenth century in Kent, continued to be made until the end of the eighteenth. It reflected the influence of imported German stoneware in both form and decoration, and sprig-moulded decoration, usually made in white clay, was applied to the red pots. Fleurs de lis, roses, crosses, stars and masks were common motifs, as well as bucolic inscriptions. The forms produced included tygs, posset-pots, two-handled mugs and candlesticks. Handles, made by weaving different coloured clays together, were a distinctive feature of Wrotham ware.

Printer's type was used for decorative purposes on late eighteenth-century Sussex pottery. The type was pressed into the soft clay and the impression inlaid with clay of a different colour.

At Harlow in Essex the so-called Metroplitan slipwares were made from around 1630 for the London market. The decoration tended to be more sober and to reflect the political opinions of London, especially in the occasional use of pious inscriptions such as "Be not hy minded but fear God 1638".

Left: Cup with trailed slipware pattern and inscription. Clear lead glaze. 1696. Stoke-on-Trent Museum and Art Gallery.

Above: Puzzle jug in red clay with trailed slip and modelled decoration. To empty the contents the spout has to be sucked. Wrotham, Kent. 1669. B.M.
Below: Slipware tyg with decoration of white clay applied and stamped. Style shows influence of contemporary imported German saltglaze wares. Wrotham, Kent. 1653. Stoke-on-Trent Museum and Art Gallery.

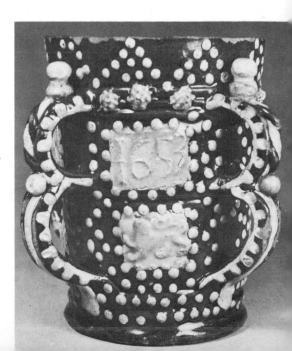

189

Left: *Drinking mug or canette. Metropolitan slipware with design trailed in white on red body. Clear glaze. About 1650. Height 8 inches.* London Museum. Right: *Small alba-rello-shaped drug jar of the kind made by Jasper Andries, an early majo-lica potter, in London. End of sixteenth cent-ury. Height 2½ inches.* Hastings Museum.

Early Tin-Glazed Earthenware

WHITE TIN-GLAZED EARTHENWARE

The sixteenth-century increase in European trade saw the importation into England of two major continental wares and the subsequent use of similar manufacturing techniques in England; one was saltglazed stoneware from Germany which is dealt with later, and the other was European tin-glazed earthenware. White tin-glazed earthenware was imported via the Low Countries where it was made by Flemish potters. The industry was later centred in Holland at Delft and the white tin-glazed pottery was often known in England as Delft ware. In France, tin-glazed ware was known as faience after the Italian city of Faenza which was one of the principal centres of manufacture in Italy.

White tin-glazed earthenware was first recorded as having been made in England by the Dutchman Jacob Janson, in London, around 1571, though it is not known whether or not he was responsible for introducing the technique into the country. Dishes, drug jars, vases and jugs were made and decorated with stylized floral and bird designs very similar to contemporary continental designs.

Widespread production did not begin in England until the early seventeenth century when potteries were established at London, in Southwark and Aldgate, and later in Lambeth, and at Liverpool and Bristol. It is significant that all were ports and so particularly subject to foreign influ-

190

Bristol majolica plate painted in blue, green, yellow and brown with the cypher of Queen Anne, a crown, a rose and a thistle. Diameter 8¾ inches. c 1706. British Museum.

ence. Clay, from Norfolk and Suffolk, was excellent for the production of this ware and, as well as supplying the English centres, it was exported to Holland during the seventeenth century for the use of the Delft potters. Cornish tin-mines were the source of tin for both England and Holland.

The greatest attraction of tin-glazed earthenware was its white surface, which was easy to obtain, smooth and pleasant to handle and provided an excellent surface for painted decoration. It also resembled Chinese porcelain, which was beginning to reach England in considerable quantities and was greatly admired.

Unfortunately, tin-glazed ware chipped easily, revealing the red porous body; only a limited number of forms were made, of which the commonest were flat dishes or chargers because they presented a suitable surface for painted decoration. Many of the dishes were decorated with blue strokes round the rim and were known as blue-dash-chargers. Blue, green, yellow and brown were the chief colours used in the decoration. Early designs copied those of Renaissance Italy, but an English style developed, characterized by bold, freely drawn designs often possessing a naïve simplicity. Portraits of kings and queens and personalities, which were almost caricatures, decorated the dishes; other subjects were biblical, especially Adam and Eve, and formal floral designs of tulips and carnations.

New drinking habits arose during Common-

191

A small bottle for holding decanted wine, in the shape of contemporary imported German saltglaze pots. The device, painted in blue, carries the initials E.C. 1640. Height about 8 inches. British Museum.

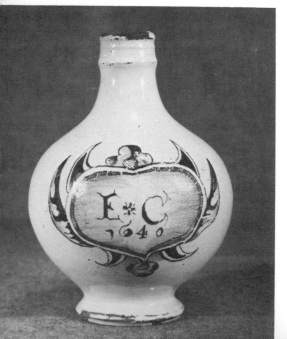

wealth times in the mid-seventeenth century, and tea, coffee and chocolate were often preferred to alcoholic drinks. Cups or mugs were made to hold the non-alcoholic drinks, and the production of the full, round-bodied wine bottles with narrow necks, imitating the form of contemporary German stoneware bottles, which had hitherto been very popular, ceased.

Continuing the oriental tradition, a wide range of vessels for the use of apothecaries was made which included spouted pots for syrups and oils, globular drug jars, cylindrical and squat jars for powders, pills, ointments and confections, and pill slabs. Decoration often included the name of the contents as well as floral designs. Barbers' bowls were another popular form; they were often decorated with scissors, combs and other tools of their trade, painted in blue on the white glaze.

Towards the end of the seventeenth century, the palette used by the tin-glaze decorator was becoming brighter and had been extended to include red; shapes became more diverse, some being modelled and moulded after the work of the French potter Bernard Palissy (c 1510–90), who supplied rustic pottery to the King and Queen Mother of France. His work included pots and dishes modelled with snakes, fish, shells, coloured with lifelike colours. Constant contact between Dutch and English potters brought other foreign influences into Britain, though the English potters never attained the sophistication of the Dutch

192

work which, in some cases, managed to imitate Chinese porcelain almost exactly. The naïve combination in England of Chinese and English design motifs has a unique charm. One design, for example, had English soldiers set in an English landscape with a band of Chinese mythological heads as a border.

Towards the end of the eighteenth century the colours developed a softer look and took on a pleasant watercolour quality. Forms had been extended to include rectangular flower-holders, pen-and-ink stands, puzzle jugs and the full tea drinking equipment of cups and saucers, sugar bowls, milk jugs, teapots and tea caddies. The introduction and success of industrially made cream coloured ware in 1765 by Josiah Wedgwood brought about the decline of tin-glazed ware until its production virtually ceased around 1800.

STONEWARE AND SALTGLAZE WARE

The early production in England of stoneware and saltglaze stoneware is slightly confused as potters often made both types. Stoneware is made by firing pottery to a temperature above that of 1200°C when the clay vitrifies and becomes non-porous. Saltglaze stoneware (usually known as saltglaze ware) is fired to a similar temperature but is glazed by introducing common salt into the kiln at maximum temperature. The technique of firing pottery to a high temperature was introduced

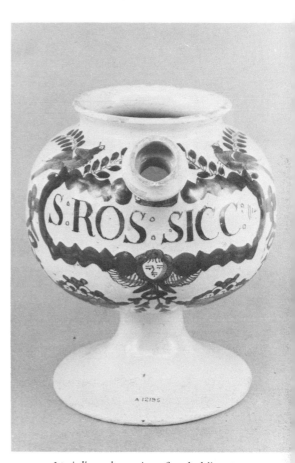

Majolica drug jar for holding liquid medicine and carrying its Latin name. Containers for use in the apothecaries were made by the majolica potters and so continued the tradition started in the Middle East by the Islamic potters. Mid-seventeenth century. Height about 8 inches. London Museum.

193

into England from the Continent, and two types of ware were made. One type, based on ware which came originally from China and known as dry red stoneware, was not glazed but was made from carefully prepared red-firing clay. The other was saltglaze ware from Germany. While giving the pottery a glassy surface, saltglaze also limited the colours to cream and brown as no colouring oxides were then used.

Saltglaze ware had reached England in large quantities from the Rhineland as early as the fifteenth century and by the sixteenth century many pieces were being manufactured in Germany specially for the English market, some having English coats-of-arms and the like as relief decoration. The finest of these pieces were highly prized and often beautifully mounted with silver. The large quantities of Rhenish imported saltglazed bottles and drinking mugs were curtailed in 1671 when war broke out between England and Holland. This encouraged the efforts of potters in England to make saltglaze ware for themselves.

The second major stoneware influence came from China. The activities of the Dutch East India Company in that country had resulted in large quantities of Yi-hsing ware being imported into Europe during the seventeenth century. Yi-hsing ware was hard, unglazed, dry red stoneware made mainly in the form of teapots, and in England and the Continent encouraged the popularity of tea. Many experiments were carried out both in

194

Great Britain until A.D. 1750

Holland and in Germany to discover how the ware was made, and the successful results were brought to England.

A patent is recorded in England as early as 1636 for the manufacture of stoneware, though little is known about its subsequent production. John Dwight (1637–1703), a university graduate and man of letters, took out a patent in 1671 for the manufacture of stoneware in London, though his real interest lay in the search for the secret of porcelain manufacture. Employing immigrant potters from the Continent he worked at a pottery at Fulham, London, where he made saltglaze mugs and bottles following the German style. Unlike the softer tin-glazed ware, stoneware could be made thinly without loss of strength, though the high temperature required in its manufacture precluded the use of lead glaze and colours painted in the tin-glazed earthenware style. Following the German example, Dwight decorated the pots with relief decoration known as sprigs made in metal moulds. The fine detailed modelling on the sprigs of such things as busts, animals and foliage was picked out and heightened by the saltglaze. Dwight continued his search for the production of white porcelain and, attempting to produce a white body, he mixed calcined flint with his clay which enabled him to produce a hard white stoneware. Unfortunately, his ignorance of china stone, an essential ingredient of porcelain, prevented the discovery of true porcelain.

John Dwight

Saltglaze mug with moulded relief decoration with hare hunting scene and inscription
On Banstead downs
A hare wee found
Which lead us all
A smoking round
Top half has iron pigment. Fulham. Dated 1721. Height 4 inches. Hasting Museum.

195

A History of Pottery

Elers Brothers

Tankard, thrown and turned, dry red stoneware. Applied moulded decoration of prunus spray. c 1610. British Museum.

Staffordshire Saltglaze Wares

Dwight was not alone in manufacturing stoneware in England. John Philip and David Elers, brothers of high Saxon-Dutch descent, and originally silversmiths, are said to have studied the art of saltglazing at Cologne and, following the crowning of William of Orange, came to England and worked in Dwight's pottery in Fulham, London. In the 1690s they moved to a remote part of England, Bradwell Wood near Newcastle-under-Lyme in Staffordshire, and produced, by methods they tried to keep secret, unglazed red stoneware in the Chinese style. Their processes of careful clay preparation and the use of relief decoration made in sprig moulds were soon discovered by the local potters, who used the technique themselves. Elers ware is characterized by fairly simple clean forms, based on the Chinese Yi-hsing wares. Small teapots, coffee pots and jugs made from finely prepared red clay were first thrown on the wheel and were then turned on the wheel or lathe while leather hard to give them a smooth, sharp contour. Some were left plain and on others sprigs of relief decoration, often with Chinese motifs, were subsequently added. Plum blossom was the most usual motif.

The discovery that calcined flint, when added to a clay body, could enable it to withstand higher temperatures still, as well as whiten the body, has been attributed to various potters, and it is possible it may have been made by more than one.

196

The production of fine white porcelain continued to challenge the pottery industry and the high-temperature white-clay body was widely adapted by the potters as an alternative to porcelain. Following the success of the Elers brothers at achieving high temperatures and their possible introduction into Staffordshire of the saltglazing technique, a good white domestic saltglaze ware was widely produced in Staffordshire by about 1720. It is said that when salt was being thrown in the kilns the whole area was covered in a thick grey fog, indicating the widespread prevalence of the technique. At its best, Staffordshire white saltglazed stoneware rivalled porcelain in its thinness, delicacy and refinement of decoration.

The so-called scratched blue saltglaze ware was developed around 1720. Designs were scratched into the surface of the white clay before it dried and the scratches filled with cobalt-blue stain. The limited blue and white palette and the unsophisticated designs prevented the fairly crude decorative technique from looking harsh or gaudy and the finely thrown and turned pots were, in many cases, further enhanced.

Brown saltglaze ware was manufactured in the Midlands at three main centres: Nottingham, Chesterfield and Derby. Loving cups, mugs, puzzle jugs and jugs in the form of bears with removable heads, which were used as cups, were made. The suitable Midland clays and the master-

Other Centres making Saltglaze Wares

Above: *Saltglaze teapot decorated with a portrait of Frederick the Great of Prussia in enamels. The shape of the spout and handle imitates wood and was popular with many potters. 1757. Height 5 inches. Hastings Museum.*

197

ing of the technique gave the saltglaze wares produced here a rich smooth brown lustrous quality, and decoration, instead of being in relief, consisted of scrolls, foliage and flowers scratched into the soft clay.

Unfortunately, the hard, slightly rough surface of saltglaze abraded silver cutlery and production of most saltglaze wares stopped towards the end of the eighteenth century in the face of the growing popularity of cream-coloured ware made by the larger pottery industries which developed in Staffordshire. The production of the more decorative saltglaze ware continued throughout the nineteenth century and culminated in the saltglaze ware made by the Martin brothers from 1877 to 1914.

Chapter 7

Great Britain
c A.D. 1750–1900

S ocial and economic conditions began to change
rapidly in the middle of the eighteenth century.
Population was expanding and industrial changes
were imminent. The wares which had been made
in small potteries for local needs were not suited
to mass-production methods. Tin-glazed ware
chipped easily, saltglaze ware wore away silver
cutlery while country earthenware was not accepted by the well-to-do, who preferred the imported Chinese porcelains.

CREAM-COLOURED WARE AND THE INDUSTRIALIZA-
TION OF POTTERY IN STAFFORDSHIRE

As we have seen in chapter six many small
potteries were firmly established by A.D. 1700 in
north Staffordshire. The subsequent development
here of the industrializing of the pottery industry
is marked in the eighteenth century by three

199

stages. The first was brought about by the Elers brothers making fine red stoneware, and the second stage was the addition of calcined flint to the body enabling the production of a near-white saltglaze. Stage three was the production of cream-coloured earthenware with a nearly colourless glaze and its manufacture on an industrial scale by Josiah Wedgwood in 1765. Cream wares, as they are often known, eventually replaced tin-glazed earthenware throughout Europe and caused the production of country earthenware to be greatly reduced.

Until the second half of the eighteenth century the Staffordshire potters tended to work in small family units employing about eight people. Overcrowding and soot and smoke pollution resulted in the working conditions in the area becoming worse as the industry grew bigger. Clay was dug as near the pottery as possible and clay pits often grew to a dangerous size. Usually the home and workshop were one and the same building. Roads were little more than tracks and during wet weather degenerated into quagmires. It was not until serious attempts were made in the eighteenth century by the industry to form itself into larger units that conditions in the area began to be organized and improved. Most of the ideas for these changes came from Josiah Wedgwood.

Many of the technical developments which were introduced in the eighteenth century have

Great Britain c 1750–1900

become identified with individual potters, mainly through the writings of Simeon Shaw in the early nineteenth century. Though it is convenient to use much of his information, developments cannot all be so clearly classified.

In 1710 the Elers brothers left Staffordshire and John Astbury (1686–1743), who is said to have worked for the Elers brothers and learned many of their manufacturing secrets, established his own pottery. Much of Astbury's work resembles that made by the Elers brothers in thinness and in the use of applied and stamped relief decoration. However, Astbury made earthenware and the reliefs are commonly made out of white pipe-clay with the vessels finished in a lead glaze with a yellowish tone. The clay used to make the pottery varied in colour from red to buff and appeared much darker under the transparent glaze. The stamped reliefs, often crudely done, had motifs of harps, stags, birds, lions and shields-of-arms.

In 1725 Astbury, with his son Thomas, established a pottery at Shelton where they are credited with having used white Devonshire clay to make lighter-coloured bodies. They are also said to have introduced the use of calcined and ground flint as an ingredient of the body, which gave an even lighter-coloured body. Early pieces made from this body could be the earliest cream ware made, though the glaze was still tinged brown or yellow. One of a large family of Cobridge potters, Ralph

Astbury

Ralph Daniel

201

A History of Pottery

Daniel is said to have brought the method of making plaster of Paris moulds, for casting pottery forms, to Staffordshire around 1740. Hollow wares were cast by pouring liquid clay slip into plaster of Paris moulds previously made from a "block" or model. Aaron Wood (1715–72), who was the most famous "block" cutter, worked for several potters, and was responsible for many contemporary designs.

One of the foremost potters of his day, Thomas Whieldon started his pottery at Fenton Low in 1740. He incorporated the technical developments made, primarily by Astbury, into his work and extended them. He is known chiefly for the production of "agate" and "tortoise-shell" wares. Agate ware was made by combining clay of different colours with the result that the finished pot had a marbled look which resembled agate stone. Tortoise-shell ware was made by dusting colouring oxides on to the glaze. At first only manganese, which gave brown, was used, but the method was soon extended to the use of other colouring oxides, which were dusted on to the body and were absorbed more or less irregularly into the thick soft glaze. Green, yellow, dark brown, purple and grey were employed in this way.

Saltglaze wares were another of Whieldon's products, including the so-called "scratched-blue" ware.

Further technical improvements and refinements were made during 1754–59 when Josiah

Thomas Whieldon (1719–95)

Wedgwood was Whieldon's partner. A green glaze was perfected and used over teapots and other vessels in natural forms, known as "pineapple" and "cauliflower" wares. Fine workmanship and richness of colour prevented these wares from appearing crude; they possessed a freer, less restrained quality which is absent from much of Wedgwood's later work.

A potter in Tunstall, Enoch Booth, is credited with having introduced into Staffordshire, around 1750, the practice of biscuit firing earthenware. This made the ware easier to handle as it was stronger, and gave it a suitable surface to absorb the glaze of lead and flint which was now mixed in liquid form. The practice of biscuit-firing had been used long before by the potters who made tin-glazed majolica wares.

Enoch Booth

In 1753 the Battersea enamel factory started using transfer-printing, which is thought to have been invented by John Brooks (*c* 1720–60). These transfers enabled detailed designs to be mass-produced for the first time. Colour was applied to a glued paper and transferred to the raw glaze. Messrs Sadler and Green further developed the process in Liverpool where many pots were taken from Staffordshire to be decorated.

Transfer-Printing

It was mainly due to the endeavour and skill of Josiah Wedgwood that the universal acceptance of the English cream-coloured earthenwares came about. Wedgwood had an extraordinary gift for organization and this, combined with a high

Josiah Wedgwood (1730–95)

A History of Pottery

standard of technical excellence, resulted in the industrialization of the pottery industry – the first major step of the industrial revolution.

The thirteenth child of the potter Thomas Wedgwood, Josiah became an apprentice potter at the age of fourteen to his brother Thomas. In 1754 Wedgwood joined Thomas Whieldon of Fenton and in 1759 opened his own factory at Burslem, making pottery of all the contemporary Staffordshire types. Wedgwood incorporated all the eighteenth-century technical improvements in his work and continued to develop the successful production of cream wares. In 1764 he secured the patronage of Queen Charlotte and renamed his ware Queen's ware. In 1769 he opened a brand new factory at Etruria where he further developed his cream wares by adding china stone and china clay to the body he was using to give a whitish-blue, more resonant body which could be made even more thinly without loss of strength. This pearl ware, as it was called, rivalled porcelain in its delicacy and colour.

Strong simple shapes formed the basis of Wedgwood's cream ware and, though the work of the silversmith was often emulated in the decoration, the clay was used in a straightforward and successful way. Decoration was limited to simple feather-edged mouldings and beading and some pierced designs, but little or no painting. Only later did Wedgwood apply transfer and enamelled designs to his wares.

Cream ware, Staffordshire. Teapot and stand with pierced decoration. At their best, cream-coloured wares were refined and elegant. Late eighteenth century. Victoria and Albert Museum.

204

Contemporary excavations at this time at Pompeii and Herculaneum held the public interest and encouraged Wedgwood to develop his neo-classical taste. He made dry, unglazed pots which in surface quality and colour imitated stones such as jasper, basalt and onyx; these were decorated with fine translucent applied reliefs with classical motifs such as draped figures and garlands of flowers.

Leeds was the main centre for the production of cream ware outside Staffordshire. Some of the ware had heart and diamond shaped pierced decoration and small moulded flowers often decorated the junction of handle and pot. Handles were often made of woven strands of clay. The clear glaze used by the Leeds potters tended to run pale green in the angles and crevices. Much of the work is, however, very similar to that of Staffordshire. Liverpool and, later, Bristol were also sites where cream ware was made at this time.

The result of all this activity and the developments in the production of cream ware was that during the eighteenth century the pottery industry changed from a pattern of small, locally based potteries, often producing rich folk art, to a major industry mass-producing large quantities of pots for home and export markets. In north Staffordshire the potteries had spread from the original five towns of Burslem, Stoke, Hanley, Tunstall and Longton to include Longport, Fenton,

Leeds and Other Cream Ware Centres

Teapot, cream-coloured ware, with double reeded handle, moulded flowers and floral knob on lid. Enamel floral design. Leeds. c 1775. Height 5 inches. Hastings Museum.

205

General view of the International Exhibition, London, 1862, showing one of stands displaying pottery and porcelain. Victoria and Albert Museum.

Porcelain

Bottger, fine red stoneware jug with moulded face design on neck and at base of handle. This ware was thought at the time to have been porcelain. c 1708–10. Height 5 inches. Hastings Museum.

Cobridge, Shelton, Lane Delph and Lane End. In 1774 the completion of the Grand Union Canal ensured easy access for the transport of raw materials and products and encouraged the growth of the industry. The success of the industry was such that in France in 1788 imported Queen's ware was cheaper than French pottery.

The discovery of the manufacture of porcelain in Europe in the eighteenth century had an effect on the design and production of contemporary earthenware. In 1709 Bottger in Germany discovered the secret of Chinese or hard-paste porcelain and on the basis of this discovery the Meissen factory was established. In other countries the so-called soft-paste porcelain, made by adding a glassy frit to the clay, was invented. This led to production difficulties owing to the ware losing its shape in the firing. However, the advantage was that a thin, translucent body resembling true porcelain was obtained at earthenware temperatures. The first soft-paste porcelain factory using a frit of this kind in England, was founded at Chelsea in 1745 by Nicholas Sprimont. The three English factories which did succeed in making hard-paste porcelain were Plymouth, Bristol and New Hall, Staffordshire, though none produced porcelain of great technical sophistication or design.

The invention of bone china, a form of porcelain, was peculiar to England and is attributed to the first Josiah Spode around 1800. This discovery

206

overcame most of the earlier difficulties of loss of shape, since bone ash is not in itself a glass but reacts with the other ingredients of clay, flint and feldspar to produce a translucent body.

A porcelain factory was founded at Worcester in 1751 and established an impressive tradition of finely made and decorated wares. Porcelain never appealed to the English in the way that the less romantic and more robust earthenware had done, no doubt due in some part to the success and cheapness of the cream wares made by Wedgwood and his followers.

THE NINETEENTH CENTURY

Many social and economic changes were reflected in the production and design of pottery during the nineteenth century. Mass-production techniques were brought to a high degree of refinement and locally made wares lost their popularity. Soft-paste porcelain was widely produced and the manufacturers of cream wares sought to imitate its fineness and colour. In Britain the expansion of towns, the increase in population and the huge overseas markets encouraged the growth of a pottery industry which was to lead the world both in the quality and quantity of its products. One technical improvement quickly followed another. There was little the pottery industry could not do and all too often ingenuity seems to have been used to produce

207

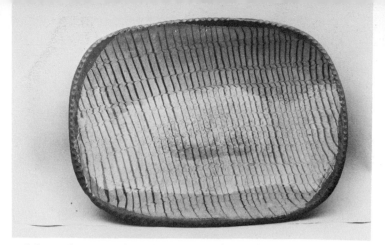

Vegetable dish with slip-trailed traditional decoration and decorated edge. Sussex pottery. Nineteenth century. Length 12 inches. Hastings Museum.

Flagon, red clay, with impressed and inlaid design, commemorating a wedding, 1819. Sussex pottery. Height 12 inches. Hastings Museum.

Country Potteries

odd and complex forms rather than those which were good and simple. Apart from the sumptuous and expensive porcelains made by such firms as Derby and Worcester, less expensive pots of a more individual kind were produced by a few smaller factories such as Rockingham. Stone china or ironstone-ware, made by mixing china clay, china stone, flint and bone ash, was introduced by Masons around 1800. It was a utility ware which was both hard-wearing and cheap to produce.

The pottery used by the mass of the population was made by the large industrial firms centred in Stoke-on-Trent and is outside the scope of this book, reflecting, as it does, the successful application of machines rather than the more human qualities of pots made in small workshops.

Country earthenware potteries continued throughout much of the nineteenth century to make a wide range of pots, usually on the potter's wheel, for local markets and Llewellyn Jewitt's *Ceramic Art of Great Britain* of 1877 lists numerous small potteries, many of which lasted for only a short time. Main products seem to have been pitchers, mugs, bottles, bowls, vinegar kegs and settling pans with simple but strong forms, well suited to their use. Candlesticks and tans or carpet bowls were also in common production. The local styles which had developed during the eighteenth century were often maintained during the nineteenth century. For example, many Kentish potteries, some using the dark red firing wealden clays, con-

208

tinued the slipware tradition started in the seventeenth century. In Sussex, Burgess Hill was noted for its agate ware which included goblets, posset pots and basins. At Rye and Brede, large full-bodied jars and pipkins were decorated with impressed patterns, sprigs of leaves and printer's type. Fuddling cups with intertwined handles, and basins and salt pots with incised decoration, were made near Ilminster in Somerset. From Devon came pilchard pots, harvest jugs, ovens and lamb feeders, while spice chests, money boxes, puzzle jugs and cradles were made in Yorkshire.

Saltglaze wares continued to be produced by many small potteries in the London area, notably at Mortlake, Lambeth and Vauxhall. Outside London, production centred on Nottingham, Bristol, Waverley Pottery, Portobello, Glasgow, and at Crich, Chesterfield and Denby in Derbyshire.

Cottage earthenware, cheaply produced in small factories, reflected the popular taste of the time. The enlarged populations of the towns seem, in some way, to have encouraged a taste for novelty, and mocha and lustre wares were made as a result of this interest. Wedgwood had first used lustre on a large scale around 1780, though its use only became widespread during the first part of the nineteenth century. When applied thickly, the lustre took on the appearance of metal and was used on forms copied exactly from silver, though this technique lost favour when electroplating

Mocha and Lustre Wares and Other Novelty Wares

Butter churn. Local potteries continued throughout most of the nineteenth century to supply local needs, in particular those of the farmer. Sussex pottery. Height 18 inches. Hastings Museum.

Above: *Coloured saltglaze Doulton ware humorous "Votes for Women" inkwell. Late nineteenth century. Height 5½ inches. Doulton Museum, London. Right: Jug with copper lustre and transfer printed scenes of Mariners' Arms and Sailor's Farewell. Such decoration was common and popular on Sunderland pottery. c 1810. Height 7 inches. Hastings Museum. Below: Saltglaze jug with moulded design of vine leaves, masks and scrolls. Impressed W. Ridgway. Hanley. Height 6 inches. Hastings Museum.*

was discovered. When used thinly, lustre took on an iridescent quality with bluish, reddish, purple or mother-of-pearl reflections. Its use was often combined with other techniques, notably those of transfer-printing and "resist" which left parts of the pot without lustre. Verses and quotations were common forms of decoration and were usually applied to jugs and plates. Swansea, Leeds, Newcastle and Sunderland were principal centres of manufacture. The printed designs, apart from their decorative quality, also have a documentary interest, reflecting contemporary events, celebrities, pious expressions and licentious verses.

Mocha ware was so called because of the dendritic patterns resembling ornamental quartz called mocha stone. By careful preparation of the slips, patterns of trees, feathers and moss which seemed to have a natural quality could be obtained. Backgrounds of brown, cream, orange and green were usually decorated with brown or black designs. Ale mugs, chamber pots, jugs, pitchers and shrimp and nut measures were the forms most usually decorated.

Another novelty ware was the ornately moulded jugs usually made of an unglazed white-clay body, though occasionally terracotta was used. The tradition was started by Josiah Wedgwood towards the end of the eighteenth century but emulated by many other firms. An advertisement of 1855 shows a wide variety of these jugs with titles such as Stag, Apostles, Oak, Grape Gatherer and Babes in the

Earthenware mugs in white clay with a ground of chestnut-brown slip with black Mocha decoration under a transparent glaze. The moss-like pattern is achieved by carefully balanced chemical effect of pigment on wet slip. c 1810. Height of tallest mug 4½ inches. City Museums, Stoke-on-Trent.

Wood; each jug was modelled in the appropriate Gothic, rococo or Renaissance style and the jug and modelling were cast as one.

Transfer-printing, especially of the very English blue and white willow pattern, was also a novelty feature. Transfers were mainly of pictorial subjects and pots were made especially to show this decoration to its best advantage. Local or exotic scenes with Chinese details, a rural cottage with crows and rustic figures, intricate baroque borders, and Gothic designs were all used at different times.

Parian porcelain, made by mixing feldspar and china clay, was first used for figures and later for hollow wares, notably at the Belleek factory in Ireland where it was covered with a white iridescent glaze. It was a low-temperature type of porcelain and the various pots were made extremely thin in quite complex shapes. W. H. Goss, in Stoke-on-Trent, using a similar body, made what was known as Heraldic China chiefly, it seems, for seaside souvenirs. The demand for these no doubt came about through the increasing popularity of holidays and day trips to the seaside advertised by the railways.

Ironstone china plate, M. Mason. Blue transfer decoration in the "willow pattern" style. c 1825. Diameter 9 inches. Victoria and Albert Museum.

Majolica, the term which had been used to describe the technique of painting coloured oxides on a white opaque tin-glaze, was now used to describe pots decorated with coloured glazes painted on to moulded forms with raised decoration. Minton's factory introduced the new technique around 1850 using designs based on vege-

211

table and floral forms. Green glazed plates with moulded leaf designs are another example of this so-called majolica.

In the Great Exhibition of 1851 much of the work on show was typical of contemporary design, especially with regard to pottery. While the objects displayed at the Exhibition served to show new and magnificent technical developments in the production of pottery, the standard of design generally could not have been lower. French Sèvres porcelain was imitated slavishly by the large English factories; the work seemed to have lost any sense of the capabilities and limitations of clay, whilst the reproduction, though technically excellent, seemed mechanical and lifeless. Vessels, badly designed, were overloaded with decoration. In 1857 the South Kensington Museum was established with the aims of showing the "application of fine art to objects of utility" and "the improvement of public taste in design". As a result the Museum tended to display forms which were fashionable rather than those which were well designed.

Two major influences distinguished the second half of the century from the first in the field of pottery design: one was the ideas and teaching of William Morris and the other was the establishment of the first pottery studio by the Martin brothers in London.

Arts and Crafts Movement
William Morris William Morris (1834–96), friend and colleague of Burne-Jones and D. G. Rossetti, and follower of

212

Photograph of three of the Martin brothers working in their studio at Southall. A wide variety of their work can be seen, including the "owl pots" and "face pots". Late nineteenth century. Victoria and Albert Museum.

John Ruskin, was one of the first advocates of the Pre-Raphaelite school of painting in the 1850s. He lectured and wrote extensively to spread his ideas which, as far as the making of pottery was concerned, echoed ideas that had been started in France. The effects of his teaching were far-reaching and no doubt were instrumental in encouraging many of the experiments made by individuals such as William de Morgan or by pottery firms such as Doultons.

Morris was a socialist whose ideas on reforms were inspired by the dislike of ugliness and the soul-destroying effects of industrialization. He thought art, ideally, should be made by the people, for the people, for the enjoyment of both the maker and user. He was one of the founders of the Morris, Marshall and Faulkner Company in 1861, a group of men working in painting, furniture and metals whose products proved so popular that a factory with larger premises was opened at Merton Abbey, Surrey, in 1881.

Martin Brothers

The Martin brothers were the first group of potters to start an entirely new method of working. Hitherto, all potteries had been either of the country or the industrial type; the Martin pottery, however, constituted the first break with this system in England, although each of the four brothers specialized in a particular aspect of production rather than carrying out all the processes involved in the making of a pot. Robert Wallace Martin (1843–1923) was the eldest of the brothers, and

213

Vase with incised decoration, saltglaze. Mottled blue with white dragon outlined in black. Martin brothers. Dated 1909. Height 16½ inches. Ernest Marsh Collection, Kingston-upon-Thames.

organized the studio. He trained first as a sculptor and later worked as a modeller at Doulton's factory in Lambeth. In 1864 he attended the Royal Academy Schools, and the terracotta sculpture he made was subsequently fired at Doulton's saltglaze factory. He gained production experience from a pottery in Devon and afterwards, around 1871, in Staffordshire. Later, he decorated pots which were fired at Dwight's old Fulham pottery. In 1873 he set up a decorating studio in Fulham; on the strength of its success he opened a fully equipped studio at Southall, Middlesex, in 1877.

The pots were saltglazed in subdued colours. Painted oxides were used to give dark blue, purplish-brown and dark brown. Decorative vases and jugs were made with relief, incised or painted decoration.

The pottery at Southall continued production for some forty years and the products can be roughly divided into three chronological periods. Angular shapes, with decoration carved in deep relief together with incised patterns, marked the first period which lasted until the early eighties. In the middle period the pots were more carefully thought out and the colours and decoration were very subdued. Cobalt-blue colour painted on a grey stoneware body as well as a rich, deep brown glaze were popular. Shapes became simpler and more rounded. Incised patterns were used sparingly and Renaissance designs of formally arranged foliage also appeared. In the last period,

Great Britain c 1750–1900

Earthenware dish painted in underglaze and rich red lustre with design of deer and tree. William de Morgan. Victoria and Albert Museum.

Plate with red lustre and majolica decoration on a white ground. William de Morgan. The swirling background derived from foliage and the mythical monster are typical decorative themes of de Morgan pottery. Diameter about 15 inches. Leighton House, London. By Courtesy of the Royal Borough of Kensington and Chelsea.

from around 1895 until 1914, attempts were made to integrate form and decoration. A wider range of colours and textured surfaces derived from plant forms and fish, were used with considerable success.

Face jugs and pots in animal form made throughout the forty years are a particular feature of the Martin products. The grotesque, fantastic, almost medievally styled animals seem to conjure up the ideas of a mysterious underworld. The heads of these owl-like creatures were removable from their bodies. Face jugs, in much the same spirit, had the modelled features leering out of the side of the jugs. Of the four brothers, Charles died in 1910, Walter in 1912 and Edwin, the youngest, in 1914, after whose death Robert closed down the workshop.

William de Morgan (1839–1917), a follower of the Pre-Raphaelite school and a friend of Burne-Jones and Rossetti, established his own pottery studio in 1872. His main interest was in decoration rather than form and in particular in the lustre colours on the Hispano-Moresque pots and the bright Persian underglaze colours. He decorated many tiles with complex designs of animals, strange beasts and ornate swirling foliage. Flat dishes also appealed to him for the opportunity they offered for decorative treatment.

His so-called Persian colours had a vivid yet harmonious quality, especially the blues, greens and turquoises which were painted on to a white

William de Morgan

215

slip under a clear glaze. Pots of oriental form were decorated with ships, foliage, animals and other motifs. De Morgan organized his workshop carefully, employing skilled craftsmen to carry out his instructions and to paint his ornate designs. His importance in the world of pottery lies in his studies of the use of lustre colours and underglaze colours and their use on decorative tiles and vases.

Minton In 1872–3 the large pottery firm of Minton established their Art Pottery Studio in Kensington Gore with a curious kiln designed, so it was claimed, to consume its own smoke. Pots made in Staffordshire were brought to London to be decorated. The decorators could make full use, it was announced, of both the local horticultural gardens and the South Kensington Museum. This was one of several experiments which tried to relate the industrial production of pottery with the work of the artist.

Doulton of Lambeth Doulton had established a pottery in 1815 at Lambeth, producing brown saltglaze ware. During the 1820s and 1830s the factory produced flasks with ornate decoration, but their rough finish eventually caused them to lose favour. The factory, however, continued to produce utilitarian wares such as oven pots, water filters, ginger-beer bottles and drain pipes. Under the management of Doulton's son, Henry Doulton, the factory was brought into close contact with the Lambeth School of Art. The then headmaster and Henry Doulton worked out a scheme whereby students from the

Top: *Biscuit barrel and lidded pot with incised decoration by Hannah Barlow, 1895.* Doulton Museum, London. Bottom: *Saltglaze Doulton stoneware Vase decorated with birds, by Florence E. Barlow, 1883.*

Great Britain *c* 1750–1900

school could use the facilities of the factory to produce art pottery. The results of the liaison were displayed in 1871 and 1872 in exhibitions in South Kensington. The pots were greatly admired and Professor Archer of Edinburgh, writing about the exhibition in the *Art Journal*, a contemporary magazine which reviewed the arts, said that no tricks were played with the clay by trying to make it do more than it was capable of doing well.

Following the success of these exhibitions the Lambeth factory employed decorators to work on forms specially made in the factory which were fired in large saltglaze kilns. Hannah B. Barlow is especially noted for her incised animal designs; her brother Arthur and sister Florence also worked in the factory as decorators. Later, experiments in the factory were extended to include the making of faience, using it as a term to describe any earthenware with relief modelling decorated with coloured glazes.

Division of labour, however, continued to be practised in all aspects of the production of art pottery and the makers were quite separate from the decorators. No workshop had yet been set up in which one person carried out all the processes from start to finish or one in which form and decoration were related in any meaningful way. Meanwhile the Art and Craft movement gathered momentum in the later part of the Victorian period and many art potteries were started through-

Other Art Wares

217

Earthenware vase, designed by Christopher Dresser, William Ault, Swadlincote. 1892–6. A fine example of the art pottery of late Victorian times. Victoria and Albert Museum.

out Britain. The pottery established in 1879 at Linthorpe near Middlesbrough by Henry Tooth is typical. His so-called Peruvian pottery, based on pottery made in ancient Peru, was highly glazed and characterized by speckled, richly flowing colours. In 1889 he moved and established the Bretby Art Pottery at Woodville in Derbyshire, where umbrella stands, "jardinières", vases and hanging pots were made. Earthenware, made to resemble hammered copper, bronze and steel, as well as carved bamboo was also produced.

The London store, Libertys, in 1879 sold and popularized the Barum wares of Devon in which thrown shapes were decorated with sgraffito or painted slips. Aller Vale wares made at Newton Abbot from 1881 were heavily decorated on fashionable shapes. Students from the local art school carried out the decoration. In Somerset the Elton wares, dating from around 1882, followed many ideas of the Pre-Raphaelites. Asymmetrical relief patterns of flowers and foliage built up of coloured slips with sgraffito outline stood on a background of mottled shades of blue and green. From 1894 to 1906 the Della Robbia pottery at Liverpool produced white opaque glazed ware decorated with painted majolica

218

Great Britain *c* 1750–1900

decoration. Much of it was in the form of tiles for architectural use, though hollow wares with vivid green glazes on modelled shapes were also made. The art nouveau style first made its appearance around 1883. The ideas of William Morris and of the other Pre-Raphaelites encouraged, especially in France, an extravagant art style employing plant forms in an exotic linear manner. New ideas associated with, and developing out of, the renewed contact with Japanese art encouraged the new style. Trade had been re-established with Japan in 1859 and large quantities of Japanese artifacts were brought to Europe. In pottery, as in other fields, art nouveau was evidenced by a break away from imitation of the past. Shapes from nature were adapted into stylized decorative patterns and a new feeling for colour was developed which continued to influence designs in the manufacture of pottery in the twentieth century.

Earthenware pot, with foliage design built up of coloured slips, in style of Pre-Raphaelites. Elton wares, Somerset. c 1895. Victoria and Albert Museum.

The Art Nouveau Movement

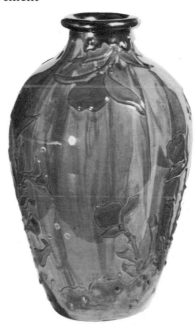

Two earthenware vases by Bernard Moore. The smooth shapes, echoing those of the later Chinese dynasties, have extremely rich red glazes which were only then being obtained for the first time in England. 1904. Victoria and Albert Museum.

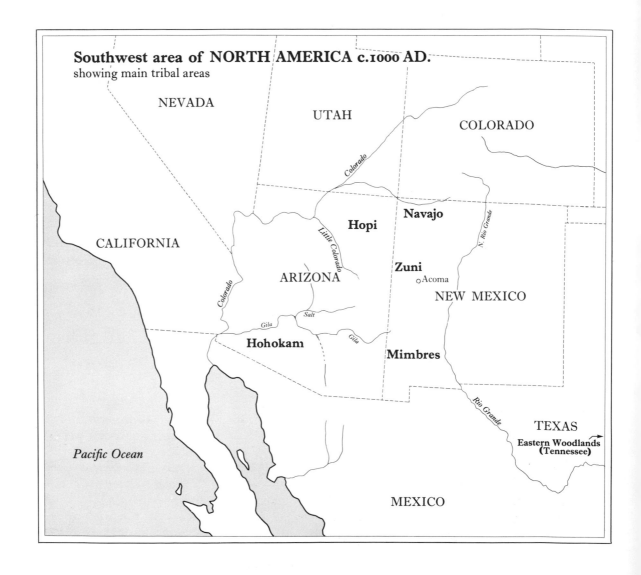

Southwest area of NORTH AMERICA c.1000 AD.
showing main tribal areas

NEVADA

UTAH

COLORADO

Colorado

CALIFORNIA

Hopi

Navajo

N. Rio Grande

Little Colorado

Zuni

○Acoma

ARIZONA

NEW MEXICO

Colorado

Salt

Gila

Gila

Hohokam

Mimbres

Rio Grande

TEXAS
**Eastern Woodlands
(Tennessee)**

Pacific Ocean

MEXICO

Chapter 8

The Americas

THE EARLY AMERICAS

Geographically, the areas in which the majority of pottery have been made in America are diverse and include hot, swampy lowlands, deserts, highlands and cultivated valleys. Early nomads, probably of Mongol descent, coming from the north of America, settled in the warmer areas of Central America, and it is here that most pottery was made. Early American pottery is unique in several ways. Separation from the remainder of the world for some thousands of years allowed a Neolithic-type society to develop without help or hindrance until visited and, in due course conquered, by invaders from Europe. The invaders found a fantastic and totally alien society, with artistic standards quite different from their own.

Metal-working was not developed in America until the ninth or tenth century A.D.; the wheel was either unknown or not developed, and mules and sleds were used for transport generally, while litters carried the rich or important. Basket-making developed very early, preceding pottery in many areas, and a similar technique to the coiling method of building baskets was used for making pots. Glaze was unknown except in rare cases and then it was used for decorative rather than functional purposes as, for example, on pottery made in the south-west of North America.

From out of this rather primitive background a distinctive pottery style, using only hand-building methods, emerged. The pots were decorated in a wide variety of ways using either incised or relief decoration or coloured slips. Kilns were primitive, but in some areas they were sufficiently developed to allow the atmosphere to be controlled, enabling the black colouring associated with reduced firing to be obtained. The pottery shapes themselves tended to be squat. Seed and maize, their basic food, had to be stored and many pots were made for this purpose. Cooking pots, which constitute the largest group of wares, show the characteristics of pots used by a primitive society living at ground level; for example, rounded bottoms, to sit in the fire or rest on soft surfaces, are common, as are bowls with tripod legs to stand on uneven floors. Faces modelled on pots point upwards so they can be clearly seen when the pots are sitting on the ground.

Basket-making undoubtedly played a large part in influencing pottery form. Three methods of building pottery – coiling, moulding and model-

Water bottle, orange ware with painted spiral design in dark pigment which was typical of the eastern woodlands area of the U.S.A. as a whole. Perry County, Tennessee. 10 inches high. Courtesy of Museum of the American Indian, Heye Foundation.

222

ling, used separately or in combination – allowed almost any shape to be made. This is in strong contrast to the use of the wheel which imposes a limit on the shape of the pot.

Decoration was rarely naturalistic, in that it did not attempt to reproduce natural forms such as animals or flowers as they exist in nature. Such motifs were interpreted stylistically and adapted to the medium of clay. In Mimbres ware, for example, insects were simplified and shown as patterns and designs. Scenes on Mayan pots were highly stylized while depicting the events accurately. Geometric designs were the most common motifs and occurred throughout most of the region. In some areas the patterns were clearly influenced by contemporary textile design, while in others they seem fairly basic geometric shapes used in satisfying divisions of space.

The custom of burying pots with the dead, practised by many tribes, has preserved much pottery, often in good condition. Most other evidence of the long-departed groups of people has been destroyed either by the sixteenth-century conquistadors or by the very nature of the material; for example, adobe, a mixture of mud and straw used for building houses, has not the permanence of stone.

The form and design of the pots made by individual groups of people closely reflect the contemporary way of life. In some groups, notably in the Mochica culture of Peru, the pots were painted

Bowl with design of insects painted in black pigment in white slip. A beautiful example of Mimbres ware, New Mexico, U.S.A. Diameter 9 inches. Peabody Museum, Harvard Uni-

223

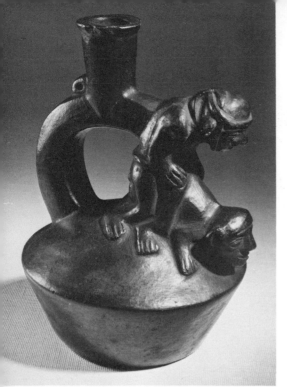

Stirrup vase, black reduced ware. Peru, Inca period. Height 7 inches. Anthropological Museum, University of Aberdeen.

with, or had modelled on to them, many aspects of contemporary life, from eating and hunting scenes to ones of love-making and punishment. The pottery of early America not only serves as a social record uniquely preserving in detail events otherwise unrecorded, but it is also an art form in its own right, reflecting the thoughtful and aesthetic success of communities following a unique stream of development. Three natural geographical divisions provide three convenient groups of American pottery.

SOUTH-WESTERN NORTH AMERICA

Pueblo Indians The south-west area of North America roughly covers the modern states of Arizona and New Mexico. Here Indians settled in villages or pueblos and were given the general name Pueblo Indians. Maize was the staple diet and pottery was one of the main art forms. Early pottery was coil-built and the outlines of the coils were often left on the outside, showing quite clearly the method of construction. Made from grey clay, the pots formed the basic cooking vessels and are known as corrugated wares. Later, coloured slips, mainly black and white, were used for simple geometric designs of rectangles, triangles, zig-zags, frets, spirals and chequers either hatched or painted.

Thin-walled bowls, cylindrical jars, ollas (jars with rounded sides and necks), handled pitchers,

224

ladles and mugs were all made out of carefully prepared pink or red clay. Although the local pottery techniques have undergone some changes, much of the traditional pottery made today employs methods similar to those used hundreds of years ago. Decoration has probably changed slightly and shapes have developed, but basically they are much the same. Each tribe had a distinctive style of decoration. Zuni pottery, for example, made in the upper Little Colorado, comes from an area occupied continuously by Indians. Zuni pottery had characteristic painted decoration which often covered the whole of the pot. Black and dark red paints were used on a pale grey background. Designs often showed deer enclosed in a structure which could be a house, near to a sunflower which is thought to be its food. On the deer, the internal organs of the throat, mouth and thorax were indicated. The base of the Zuni pots tended to be rounded, unlike the more pointed bases on the pots from Acoma, nearby.

Acoma pottery was decorated with a band of pattern covering the upper two-thirds of the pots. The design, often floral, was painted in black and yellowish-red. At Santo Domingo a white slip background was decorated with pure geometric and more openly spaced black designs. Hopi pottery, made in north-east Arizona, was decorated with black designs on a yellow slip.

In the Gila and Salt valleys in Arizona lived the Hohokam tribe who developed the use of the

Three bowls. Pueblo Indian Zuni. Designs painted in black and dark red on a grey white background. 10 inches high. British Museum.

Hohokam Indians

225

Two jugs from the Upper Gila area and Salt River Valley, Arizona, U.S.A. The sharp shoulder is often found in this ware. Height of tallest jug 5 inches. British Museum.

The so-called "duck" pot, probably for cooking. Pueblo Indians, New Mexico, U.S.A. British Museum.

Bowl with painted geometrical design. Tacoma, New Mexico, U.S.A. Height 3 inches. Hastings Museum.

paddle and anvil method of pot building. A sharp shoulder on the pot, formed by the junction of the rounded base with the straight walls, which probably developed out of the building method, is characteristic. In the Mimbres Valley in the south-west of New Mexico, Mimbres ware was made. Technical and cultural influences combined to produce one of the most beautiful and distinctive wares of America. Bowls are the chief form which have survived, probably because they were buried with the dead. Often they had a small hole knocked in the base, no doubt to render them useless to robbers, though there is a theory that certain tribes, believing that the inanimate as well as the animate possessed souls, deliberately broke burial objects in order to release their souls. The bowls, fairly simple in form, are notable for their painted decoration. Some had complex and beautifully executed geometric designs in black and white slip in which solid black and hatch work designs were combined and covered much of the surface. Other bowls had realistic though slightly stylized animal designs which are, perhaps, the most characteristic. These designs are not only beautifully drawn but spaced in such a way as to imply tension and a concern for the finer aspects of art. Frequently shown in opposite pairs, creatures such as insects were painted in black on a white background. The black was quite often replaced by dark brown. Production of the ware ceased around the fourteenth century.

226

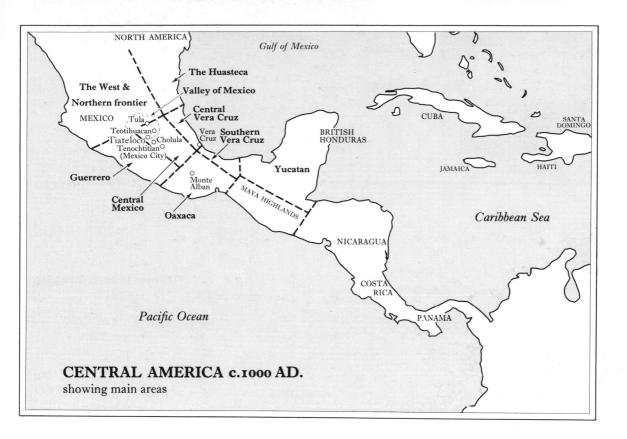

CENTRAL AMERICA c.1000 AD.
showing main areas

CENTRAL AMERICA

The development of the area which chiefly comprises modern Mexico can be broken down into three phases after the archaic period. The period from 1500 B.C. to A.D. 300 is known as the formative, A.D. 300–900 as the classic, and A.D. 900–1520 as the post-classic. Geographically, the area is large, with many local tribes and customs and it is only possible to mention the main centres. Though each group developed an individual style of decoration and customs, they all had a common background; this included hieroglyphic writing, bark-paper or deerskin books, maps and calendars, astronomy and a curious ball game, tlachtli, played with a rubber ball in a carefully prepared court.

During the classic period each city state existed peacefully. Independent cities were controlled by the priesthood and all the advantages of peace

Mexico

227

Three-legged bowl, probably for cooking. One broken leg shows clay rattle inside. Similar pots were common throughout much of the area of Central America. Costa Rica. Diameter 5 inches. Hastings Museum.

were enjoyed: trade flourished and pottery was widely sold. The end of the classic period is marked by the fall of Teotihuacan, the fantastic city in the Mexican highlands, and heralded a period of violence and aggression in which wars were waged to secure sacrificial victims and large-scale human sacrifice took place. Eventually the Aztecs gained a dominance they retained until overthrown by Cortez (A.D. 1519–21).

Mexican Formative Period
(c 1500 B.C.–A.D. 300)

During the formative period, most basic pottery shapes were common throughout the area. Bowls, neckless jars, long-necked bottles, spouted trays, bowls and jars with three tall feet and jars with stirrup spouts were all made. Hollow "mammiform" legs, in the shape of breasts, were often used on flat dishes.

Decorative techniques involved covering the pot in a fine slip of black, brown, red or white. This was often burnished by rubbing with a smooth pebble to produce a shine (sometimes called polishing). Some pots were left plain while others had simple geometric patterning. Incised designs were carried out, sometimes before the pot was fired, sometimes after: the latter gave a finer, drier line. "Negative" painting was a method of decoration in which the design was painted on to a pot with hot wax or another similar resist substance; the pot, subsequently dipped in a different coloured pigment, was left with the design in the colour of the body showing through. The wax burnt away in the firing.

228

Cylindrical tripod vase with hieroglyphic design incised through layer of dark slip. Similar technique to that of "fresco" decoration in which coloured slips were inlaid in the walls. Teotihuacan, Mexican highlands, classic period. Height about 6 inches. British Museum.

The classic period is marked by the growth of independent cities in which much time was spent in the study of astronomy and the service of numerous deities. Large temples and pyramids were built, and sculpture, pottery and painting were used for ritual purposes.

Teotihuacan, in the Mexican highlands, is a typical example of one of the cities. Here the pottery was technically accomplished if, in its early stages, dull and uninspired. Later, a polychrome style of decoration developed in which the "champlevé" technique was used. In this technique pots were covered in a dark brown or black slip which was scraped away to show the dark body which was sometimes painted in with cinnabar. A stucco technique was also used in which the surface of the pot, usually a cylinder with three feet, was covered with plaster; this was carved and the design filled with coloured clays. The result, fragile and impractical, seems to have been highly regarded, more for its technical virtuosity than for its artistic importance.

The Maya tribe, geographically situated in the Yucatan Peninsula, Guatemala and British Honduras, developed fairly independently in an area relatively secure from invasion. They showed little interest in military expansion until the postclassic period. Early work shows strong influence from Teotihuacan, but after about A.D. 600 a decorative effect, involving the use of coloured pigments of great brilliance, was developed by fir-

Mexican Classic Period
(A.D. 300–900)

The Maya

229

Twelve small pots joined in circle with modelling of gods or animals. Oaxaca, Monte Alban, Zapotec culture. Probably made during the classic period of the Mayas. British Museum.

ing the pots to a lower temperature. Durability was sacrificed for aesthetic beauty. Hieroglyphics and animals were used as decoration, but the most beautiful designs are the scenes of Mayan ceremonial life. Sacrificial cups in the shape of animals were also made.

Mayan Post-Classic Period (c A.D. 950–1325)

The Mayan post-classic period is reckoned from about A.D. 950. War was generally glorified during this time and an air of militarism prevailed which resulted in an expansion of the Mayan tribe. Tough, professional warriors, taking their names from such animals as the coyote, jaguar and eagle, led the tribe into Mexico. The main group, called Toltecs, meaning the artificers, established their capital, Tula, near Teotihuacan in Mexico and were led by King Topiltzin who claimed the title Quetzalcoatl, or Feathered Serpent, the hero of Mexican mythology.

The style of the decoration on their pots generally became more severe and abstract. While many local pottery styles continued, two styles predominated. The first, known as the Mazapan style, is characterized by a decoration of painted parallel wavy lines in red or white slip. Plates, jars, cylindrical vases, bowls and bi-conical cups were made in fine orange ware and had a hard, lustrous surface. The second main group, known as plumbate ware, so called because its black lustrous appearance was originally thought to come from lead, was in fact the result of careful kiln control. Forms were varied but all were black, hard and shiny.

230

In 1325 the Aztecs founded Tenochtitlan (Mexico City) and became the dominant ruling tribe. They founded a society based primarily on ecclesiastical rather than secular power, involving horrible rituals in which priests carried out mass human sacrifices; children, for example, were sacrificed to bring rain and the more they cried the more effective they were thought to be.

Pottery consisted of thinly made, well-fired, orange-coloured ware. Bi-conical and chalice-shaped cups were made for the old men to drink pulque, a potent alcoholic drink made from the fermented juice of maguery. Decoration, painted in black lines, was often geometric, though later it included birds, animals and floral patterns.

Mixteca polychrome pottery was one of the finest and most esteemed of the Aztec wares. It was made at Cholula and was decorated with several coloured slips. It is said that this was the only pottery King Montezuma would use. It was primarily a luxury ware using cream, yellow, red ochre, burnt sienna, grey and black colours. Human figures, religious and secular symbols, feathers and scrolls were some of the decorative devices and the designs had a full, busy quality. Much pottery was traded and the Spanish soldier, Bernard Diaz, reported seeing "every sort of pottery, made in a thousand forms from great water jars to little jugs" at the great market at Tiateloco, near Tenochtitlan.

Aztecs (A.D. 1325–1420)

Pedestal bowl with ornate incised and painted geometrical design in coloured slips. Cholula, Aztec period. British Museum.

231

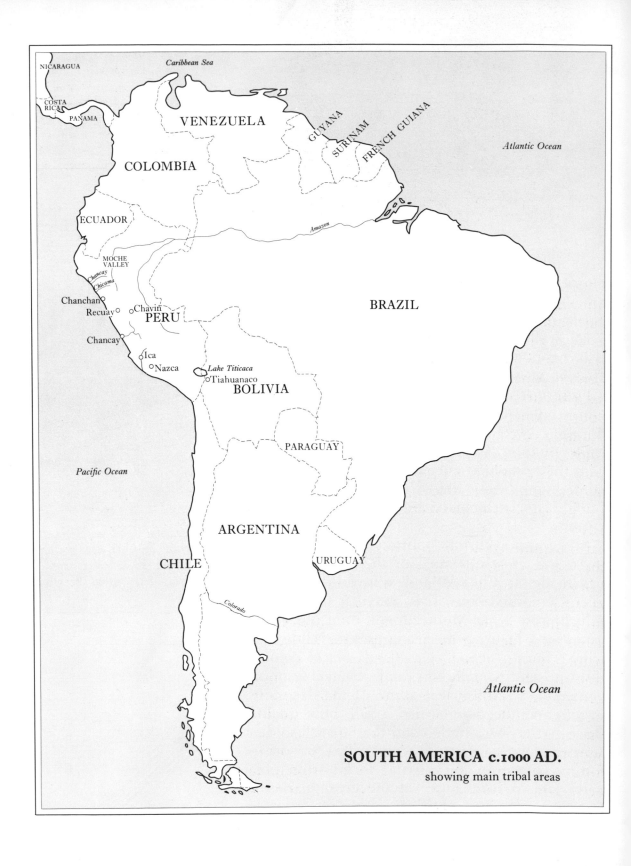

NICARAGUA

COSTA
RICA

PANAMA

Caribbean Sea

VENEZUELA

COLOMBIA

GUYANA

SURINAM

FRENCH GUIANA

Atlantic Ocean

ECUADOR

Amazon

MOCHE
VALLEY

Chancay

Chicama

Chanchan

BRAZIL

Recuay

Chavín

PERU

Chancay

Ica

Nazca

Lake Titicaca

Tiahuanaco

BOLIVIA

PARAGUAY

Pacific Ocean

ARGENTINA

CHILE

URUGUAY

Colorado

Atlantic Ocean

SOUTH AMERICA c.1000 AD.

showing main tribal areas

SOUTH AMERICA

The west coast and western mountains of South America, embracing Peru and Bolivia, known as the Andes, produced pottery which, though still made without the use of the wheel and lacking glaze, has a style different from that made in Central America. Little trading of goods seems to have occurred between the people of Central and South America, though raw materials were certainly exchanged. Because the land of the Andes is long north to south and narrow east to west it is possible to separate the north and south of the region on stylistic grounds.

In the north, the early or formative period from 1200 B.C. to about the birth of Christ saw the early beginnings of the Mochica culture centred in the north coastal valleys on the Chicama River. Chavin or Cuprisnique pottery, made around 800 B.C., was characterized by gourd-shaped pots in white or buff body sometimes decorated with a red inlay, topped by a stirrup handle. Resinous paint was often applied to the pottery to make it waterproof. "Negative" painting as well as incised decoration was used. The stirrup handle became a significant feature of later Mochica work made in this area and was so called because of its resemblance to a saddle stirrup, and provided both a comfortable carrying handle and an efficient drinking or pouring spout, as well as protecting the contents from dust and contamination.

Chavin or Cuprisnique Culture (*c* 1200 B.C.–A.D. 1)

233

Indian potter building coils on to moulded base. Mato Grosso region, Brazil, South America. Nineteenth century (?) British Museum. It can be assumed that pots have been made by this method for hundreds of years.

Mochica Culture (c A.D. 1–1200), Master Craftsman Period

The Mochica culture emerged around A.D. 1 and lasted until about A.D. 1200. The Mochica were master engineers and built complicated irrigation systems involving aqueducts. Adobe brick, rather than stone, was the chief building material and so no large masonry structures were built. Mochica pottery is well known through its careful preservation in tombs and has been closely studied for the light it sheds on contemporary life. Maize, potatoes, beans, peanuts, gourds, cotton, cocoa and fruit were the main agricultural crops and pots were often made in the shape of fruit of, for example, pineapple or squash. The pottery was distinctive and was made by different methods to those used in North or Central America. Moulds made out of fired clay were the chief method of production, though the pots often had additional modelling. Though technically excellent, the pots have a characteristic mechanical quality because of this. Designs, often taking on the appearance of human or animal figures, were carefully executed and well considered.

Mochica art had a strong stylistic tradition similar in many ways to that of the Egyptians. The human figure was conventionalized into three sections, each showing its broadest aspect. Legs were shown from the side, usually in a striding position suggesting movement. Bodies were shown frontally with shoulders square, while heads were depicted in profile, though the eye remained in full front view. Royal figures were

sometimes excepted in these rules, and this also applied to relief figures on pottery. Decoration on pots, as opposed to other forms of art, seems to have been allowed slightly more freedom of expression. Art, concerned with religious symbolism and secular ceremonial scenes of pageantry and warfare, contrasts strongly with animals and birds modelled on pots with refreshing directness which could only have come from close observation. No attempt was made to suggest perspective or volume in pottery decoration.

Modelled and painted scenes from daily life on the pottery provide superb documentary evidence of the contemporary life of this period. In warfare it seems the Mochica were vigorous and successful, using axes, clubs, spears, shields, helmets and drums. Architecture included religious and military structures, as well as simple thatched houses. Numerous gods are represented, indicating a polytheistic religion. The gods of maize and other agricultural products are shown and a feline deity is very much in evidence. Wind and percussion musical instruments made from clay, for religious and secular occasions, included the flute, trumpet, bugle and rattle. Though the roads were good, no wheeled vehicles seem to have been used. Instead, long trains of llamas were used, and the coastal islands had boats and rafts. Fish, a valuable source of food, were caught by a variety of methods—harpoons, hooks and nets supported by gourd floats. Dress, more elaborate and ornate for

Two vases from Peru, Chimu culture. British Museum. (a) *Vase with flaring spout, moulded in form of bi-valve shell. Black reduction-fired ware. Height 6½ inches.* (b) *Four small pots, stirrup handle with model of animal at base, burnished and reduction-fired ware. Height 7 inches.*

the men, especially the complex head-dresses, is shown in detail.

Portrait jars, enabling individuals to be recognized, had faces looking upward; while originally mould-made, the pots were embellished to show individual characteristics such as scars.

Whistling jars, in the form of birds, were common and were so built that when water poured from the spout it caused air to be sucked in through a whistle.

Chimu People
(c A.D. 1200–1450)

Following the gradual collapse of the Mochica culture after A.D. 1000 and the spread of influences from the south, a new state emerged around A.D. 1200 in the north with its capital at Chanchan. In many ways the Chimu, as the people are known, were successors to the Mochica, using moulds to produce forms similar to those made by the Mochica, but their pottery lacked the high quality of the Mochica work. The pots were mainly monochrome in grey, black or red, and many were burnished and reduction fired. The Mochica modelling tradition, reintroduced on Chimu pottery, perhaps by small independent tribes, lacked the spirit of the early work. Stirrup spouts and double whistling vases continued to be made.

Southern Area
Nazca Culture

In the south, the Nazca culture flourished at a time similar to that of the Mochica. Again, a lot is learnt about contemporary life from the pots, many of which have survived. Unlike the Mochica work, the Nazca pots rely for effect on their

236

Bowl with concave sides, hard, burnished orange or dull red with a pattern derived from woven textiles. Painted in black, white and red. This is characteristic pottery of the southern area of Peru. Inca period. Height 8 inches. British Museum.

decoration and the forms of the pots tend to be less interesting, having smooth contours which lack the strength of the Mochica forms.

The pottery may be described as colourful, as the slips were brightly coloured and wide ranging. Eight colours — black, red, white, yellow, green, brown, violet and cream — are known, though it was usual to use only five on any one pot. Designs were often outlined in black. Early designs were based on animals and fruit set on a plain red background. Gradually the themes were broadened to include religious and mythological subjects.

The Tiahuanaco culture, centred on or near lake Titicaca in Bolivia, was politically highly organized; evidence of huge gateways and walled cities has survived. The pottery is severe and lacks the warmth of other cultures. Tall, concave cylinders are typical pots of the city-building stage of this culture's development (A.D. 1000–1200).

In the Chancay Valley a distinctive if unambitious pottery style developed. Thin and porous jars were made in egg shapes with the bottom more rounded than the top. Humanoid features, often diminutive, were applied in relief and were often combined with black and white painted decoration.

The Imperialist period (A.D. 1450–1550) saw the rise to power of the Incas, who took and maintained control over the whole inhabited Andes region in South America. By building a network

Other Southern Cultures

Double spouted globular jar with polychrome painted design of heads. Nazca culture, southern Peru. Height 11 inches. British Museum.

The Incas
(c A.D. 1450–1550)

237

Vase with modelled features of corpulent man holding a cup. Red body, white slip, details painted in brown. Chancay, Peru. Height 14 inches. Anthropological Museum, University of Aberdeen.

A History of Pottery

of roads, conquered peoples were controlled, though they were not allowed to travel on them. Rigid bureaucratic control was exercised by the Incas, who seem to have had a genius for administration.

Technically, the Inca pottery was excellent. But though it was fine-walled, well made and strong looking, the forms and designs lacked the free and inventive qualities associated with the best pottery of South America. Nothing, it seemed, was left to chance; both forms and designs were carefully worked out and controlled. Shapes showed little change over a period of time and fall into three types: the aryballus or narrow-necked water jar, made in many sizes, the largest of which were carried on the back with a rope; plates with small, bird-head handles; jars and flat-based bowls, many for cooking purposes, with broad strap handles. Decoration, which was usually restricted to small areas, consisted of geometric shapes, carefully painted, and included bands, hatched diamonds, triangles, stylized plants and, rather incongruously, butterflies and bees.

The European conquest of America destroyed many of the ancient tribes and their cultures. Knowledge of these ancient societies has, in most cases, been the result of excavations and further work will no doubt increase this knowledge.

Two bowls with rounded bottoms and straight sides. Geometrical patterns painted in slip. Diaguite, northern Chile. Height 3 inches. British Museum.

238

UNITED STATES OF AMERICA A.D. 1500–1900.

Much of the early native American pottery ceased to be made after the Spanish conquest except in remote protected areas. The Pueblo Indians in the remote areas of southern North America, for example, continued to make their traditional shapes and designs until the late nineteenth century. During the sixteenth and seventeenth centuries European settlers arrived in large numbers on the east coast of North America and in Mexico tin-glazed earthenware was made which showed the strong influence of Hispano-Moresque in both shape and decoration. Gradually home producing industries were established, stimulated by the high cost of importing European goods which were too expensive for the majority of the population and by the needs of a growing society. Skills, too, were taken to America by trained workmen looking for better opportunities and a new life.

By 1614 building bricks were being made in Virginia and by the end of the seventeenth century many potteries were producing a variety of lead-glazed ware. Dutch settlers in New York were making tin-glazed earthenware which was reputed to be as skilled as that made by the Delft potters in Holland.

During the eighteenth century a pottery producing stoneware was established in New York at "Potters Hill" by an immigrant German, John Remmey, and remained productive until 1820.

239

A History of Pottery

Slip-decorated earthenwares made in Pennsylvania were decorated with bold designs trailed in white or red clay and covered with yellow lead glaze, and developed a unique style. The discovery of china clay in the Cherokee Indian territory led an immigrant potter from Bow, London, to produce soft-paste porcelain, but after two years the factory failed financially. American china clay, however, was imported into England during the eighteenth century until the large deposits in Cornwall, England, were discovered.

By 1800 a wide range of pottery was being produced in America, though the rich continued to favour imported wares from England and Holland. During the nineteenth century industrial wares continued to develop in scope and quality. All manner of pots were produced from "red and black glazed teapots and coffee pots" to lustre pitchers. True porcelain was made for the first time by William Ellis Tucker in 1825. By 1810 the range of cream wares made in Philadelphia was of equal quality to those made in Staffordshire. In Vermont the Bennington pottery, established by John and William Norton in 1793, eventually started producing decorative saltglaze wares and continued production until the twentieth century.

It was not until 1876 that the pottery industry responded to contemporary trends in more decorative wares from other parts of the world. The stimulus was an exhibition at Philadelphia in

The Americas

which were shown many different types of pottery from many countries. Miss M. Louise McLaughlin was so impressed by a group of novel faience pots from the Haviland potteries of Limoges shown at the exhibition that, with the help of twelve other women, she formed the "Pottery Club". This eventually became the world-famous Rookwood pottery at Philadelphia. As well as a range of cream-coloured wares with blue prints of fish and reptiles, the pottery produced a range of vases and ornaments, the forms of which showed a strong Japanese influence. The decoration, made by applying modelled flowers in asymmetrical designs on to grounds of coloured clay, was done originally by a Japanese, Mr Shirayamadani. Later, the influence of the Art Nouveau style was more evident in the form and decoration on the pots which were made. In 1889 and 1900 the pots were exhibited in Europe to international acclaim.

Other art potteries were started, some imitating traditional Indian pottery, in an attempt to create a uniquely American style. Among many other established potteries was one set up in Boston, Massachusetts, in 1897. The style of the pots was inspired by the work of the French potter August Delaherche and consisted of simple, hand-modelled, leaf-like shapes. These were integrated into the form of the vase and covered with a matt, usually green, glaze. Many potters who worked first at the Rookwood pottery moved to other potteries and so the influence of Rookwood spread.

Chapter 9

Modern Primitive Societies

Cooking pot, red clay, incised and roulette decoration. Morocco, North Africa. Modern. Height 8 inches.

In certain parts of the world, groups of primitive people have survived independently of other and more advanced civilizations. In many cases the civilizations are only slight developments of Neolithic models. Africa, Oceania, Melanesia and Indonesia are areas where such societies have continued until today. Many tribes have survived in areas heavily protected by natural barriers such as forests, mountains, deserts or seas. Their pottery, for the most part, reflects a social need which is either religious or functional, and is rarely made for its own sake. In many cases the hot climate and scarce water have resulted in an abundance and variety of vessels for water storage. In Nigeria, for example, pitchers, bowls, ewers, small flagons and large urns are all made. Generally these pots have rounded bases for resting on sandy floors or sitting in the embers of a fire.

242

Technically, the pottery is simply but skilfully made by hand-building methods. Local clay which, by experience, has proved suitable is ground and often mixed with sand, shell or grit to improve its working quality. Pots may be made by any one of a variety of hand-building methods brought to near perfection. The Eile tribe of East Africa, who were at one period slaves to the Arabs, learnt and retained from their former masters the use of a simple pivot wheel turned by hand, but this is a rare exception to the rule. Most tribes have either no knowledge of, or have not adapted, the wheel for the use of the potter. Women usually make and fire the pots.

In Nigeria, firings are usually one of three types: open bonfire, in which any number from one to a thousand pots can be fired; grate firing, in which a circular enclosure, eight feet in diameter with a wall four foot high and nine inches thick, is packed with pots and kindling wood and covered with dry grass; clamp method, which consists of a permanent structure of sun-baked mud built in the form of an elongated oven. In this last method pots and kindling wood are packed inside the oven and the heat is fairly evenly distributed throughout the kiln. None of these firing methods allows a glaze of any sort to be used and, in fact, the development or use of glaze is not associated with primitive societies. To give the pots a shine, vegetable resins prepared from such things as locust beans or tree bark are painted

(a) *Jug, rounded bottom, impressed textured surface, contrasting well with plain burnished neck. Nigeria. Height 9 inches. British Museum.* (b) *Round-bottom cooking pot. An almost ideal shape for cooking. Nigeria. Height 4 inches.* British Museum.

243

on to the pots, often while they are still hot from the firing. While the resins lack the permanence of true glaze and will not stand up to cooking use, they do add to the pots' decorative qualities as well as making them more waterproof.

The style of most primitive pottery is based on tradition. Over the years the pots that have proved to be most useful continue to be made. Most shapes are either copied from, or developments of, naturally occurring forms, such as gourds, though any primitive society will adapt new forms for their purposes. The tribes of northern Nigeria, for example, have incorporated into their pots the narrow necks from the pottery of the Islamic invaders from the north. Shapes tend, on the whole, to be rounded, full and regular.

It is in the decoration that local and even individual styles of pottery can be more clearly recognized. In West Africa each of some eighty tribes has its own style. Decoration is often limited to patterns that can be made in the clay, through incising, or applied clay patterns. Inlay work, made by filling incised patterns with clay of a contrasting colour, is made in, among other places, Ceylon.

The designs can have either religious, secular or abstract themes. Fingernails, corncobs, twisted vines, roulettes, shell fragments and hollow flower stems have been used to decorate pots by pressing them into the clay to give it a pattern. In the Sepik River area of north-west New Guinea, although

244

there are many local styles, the predominant motif is a highly stylized representation of the human face, carried out in a variety of ways. Decorated "appliqué" strips of clay are applied to the coarse red-brown pots in the New Hebrides in the form of geometric patterns.

Burnishing the clay by rubbing it before it is fired with a stone or small pebble smooths and polishes the surface and gives it a dull shine and strengthens the pot. It also helps to make the pots waterproof. The Hausa in Nigeria decorate many of their pots by this method.

Chapter 10

The Twentieth Century

BRITAIN

The twentieth century heralded a whole new era for the work of the potter. The large pottery industry centred in Stoke-on-Trent continued to adapt and improve its production methods and in terms of quality and price its wares were unrivalled throughout the world.

The only attempt before 1920, however, at a completely new approach in pottery design came from Roger Fry.

Roger Fry (1866–1934) started the Omega Workshop in Bloomsbury, London, in 1913, in association with Duncan Grant, Vanessa Bell and Wyndham Lewis. They made pottery which, seen today, seems to lack technical skill and craftsmanship but which is, from a design point of view, original and forward-looking. Clean white or rich blue glazes over simple shapes foretold the future of pottery design in an extraordinary way. But

Roger Fry (1866–1934)

Earthenware teapot and cup and saucer. Roger Fry. Omega Workshops, London. Though lacking in technical skill, the farsighted originality of the design can still be admired. c 1912. Victoria and Albert Museum.

England was not yet ready for that revolution and the work failed to attract much attention.

The First World War marked a turning point in the history of pottery. Many nineteenth-century country potteries, already severely diminished in strength and numbers by industrial competition, struggled on into the twentieth century but collapsed almost completely at that time. Lack of a market and men to run the potteries brought about a situation in which many traditional skills were in danger of being lost. Attempts by the art potteries to break away from functional wares and produce art pottery were, for the most part, brought to an end by the war. However, the climate of change brought about by such experiments eventually led to the establishing of the first studio pottery, under the leadership and influence of Bernard Leach – the first studio potter. Just as the East had influenced the development of pottery many times in the past, it again stimulated new interest in the West which was to have a far-reaching effect, especially in Britain and the U.S.A.

Bernard Leach (born in 1887) visited Japan after studying art in England. He returned in 1920 with the Japanese potter Shoji Hamada (born in 1892) and started a studio pottery at St Ives in Cornwall. Leach had studied pottery in Japan under the sixth Kenzan after a period of training at the Slade School of Art in London. In his pots he combined a great feeling and sympathy for the East with the

The First World War (1914–18)

Stoneware vase. Bernard Leach. Incised decoration under a transparent glaze gives this pot an extremely rich effect. St. Ives, Cornwall. 1951. Victoria and Albert Museum.

Bernard Leach

247

Stoneware casseroles. Leach pottery. Unglazed on the outside. For many years the Leach pottery has produced a range of consistently well designed functional pots. St Ives, Cornwall. Council of Industrial Design.

Stoneware lidded bowl. Bernard Leach. The iron oxide brushwork decoration has become lustrous in the reducing flame of the kiln. c 1930. Height about 2 inches. City Museums, Stoke-on-Trent.

Michael Cardew (b. 1901)

best qualities of traditional English slipware. Form, rather than decoration, became his principal concern and the pots he made were conceived from an aesthetic as well as a functional point of view. He carried out all the manufacturing processes himself, successfully combining the traditional work of the potter with that of an artist using clay as a means of expression. Much of his work shows a strong eastern influence, but he attempted to express this through understanding rather than emulation. At the St Ives pottery Leach organized the production of a well-designed and aesthetically pleasing, low-priced range of domestic stoneware made by a small team of potters of whom he was one. He also made individual pots with subtly incised, carved or slip decoration. His skill as an artist was especially evident in his control and use of brushwork.

Not only did Bernard Leach establish the first studio pottery in England but he took pupils who developed his ideas. Notable among these early pupils were Michael Cardew (born 1901), Katharine Pleydell-Bouverie (born 1895) and Norah Braden (born 1901). Since 1945 many foreign students have spread Leach's ideas internationally.

After working in the Leach pottery, Michael Cardew established his own pottery at Winchcombe in Gloucestershire in 1926. He sought out a retired traditional potter and revived the production of slipware. In 1936 he left the pottery in the hands of Raymond Finch, one of his students,

248

Right: *Vase and cover. Katharine Pleydell-Bouverie, Wiltshire. The sides have been carved and the ash glaze combines well with the simple but strong form. 1929–30. V. and A.* Left: *Stoneware pot and lid. Michael Cardew, Vume, Gold Coast. Iron oxide brushwork decoration has been used over a dark glaze to give spots of almost iridescent colour. 1948. V. and A.*

and after a visit to Africa he established in 1939 the Wenford Bridge Pottery in Cornwall. Further time spent teaching pottery and establishing a workshop in Nigeria formed the basis of his book *Pioneer Pottery* published in 1969, which covers in detail native Nigerian pottery and includes technical notes which are an invaluable guide for the studio potter.

Harry Davis, with his wife May, continued the tradition of making well-designed, functional ware started by Bernard Leach. In 1948 they started the Crowan Pottery in Cornwall where they combined enormous technical understanding with a sensitive feeling for form and produced a range of consistently well-designed and hard-wearing stoneware and porcelain until they left England in 1962 to start a pottery in new Zealand.

William Staite Murray (1881–1962) was an early champion of the studio potters, who worked to raise their status and promote them as artists rather than craftsmen. His ideas about studio pottery were different from those advocated by Leach. Originally trained as a painter and largely self-taught as a potter, Staite Murray's idea was that pots were works of art able to stand by works of the painter. To this end he successfully exhibited his own pots along with paintings in galleries which usually showed only paintings. His large, almost monumental high-shouldered vases with their swirling brushwork have strength of form but somehow fail to impress in the way Leach's work

Harry Davis (b. 1910)

Stoneware bread bin. Harry Davis, Crowan pottery, Cornwall. The design was painted on a light coloured glaze in hot wax and has subsequently resisted a second darker glaze with rich results. 1958. V. and A.

William Staite Murray (1881–1962)

249

does. Murray's greatest influence was as a professor of ceramics at the Royal College of Art where his ideas often made a lasting impression on many of his students.

The end of the Second World War in 1945 introduced, for the studio potter, a golden era. The work of Bernard Leach, the growth of his followers and his generosity in publishing *A Potter's Book* in 1940 making his working methods and ideas generally available, and the work of Staite Murray in promoting the value of studio pottery, encouraged individual potters to establish small studios, and art schools to start courses in studio pottery. The ideas of eastern philosophy continued to dominate much of the pottery design, but they were becoming less strong under such influences as Lucie Rie (born 1902), Scandinavian design, and the experimental use of clay by potters in the United States as a means of artistic expression.

Lucie Rie originally studied pottery at Vienna under Michael Powolny and came to England in 1939, establishing her studio in Paddington, London. Making oxidized stoneware and porcelain in an electric kiln she produces a range of simply designed domestic pottery as well as highly individual pots and bowls. Typically, her work is finely thrown and delicately balanced. Dry, gritty textured surfaces are combined with yellow or white glazes and decoration scratched on to matt dark brown pigment. Shape always seems to pre-

Stoneware vase. William Staite Murray. Iron oxide has been painted on to the glaze to give this rich metallic effect. c *1938.* Below: *Vase with incised foliage decoration through white slip. Charles Vyse, Chelsea.* Camberwell School of Art, opened 1898, became a centre where pottery was taught and many early potters studied and worked here, including Roger Fry, William Staite Murray and Charles Vyse who was particularly interested in producing Chinese glazes. *1930.* V. and A.

dominate and decoration, whether in the form of simple lines or bubbling textures, is always subservient to it.

Since the late fifties development of studio pottery has been along two lines. On one hand there is the production of well-designed useful pottery and on the other there are the experimenters trying to find out what else clay can be made to do.

Following the Leach tradition many potters have established workshops producing well-designed, hand-made domestic pottery at reasonable prices which does not celebrate handmadeness. Raymond Finch, at Winchcombe Pottery, Gloucestershire, and David Leach, at Lowerdown Pottery, Devon, are two potters in this tradition. The opening of the Craft Centre of Great Britain in 1948 and the Craftsmen Potters Association ten years later did much to bring the best pottery before the public. The fifties saw the beginning of a wider interest in pottery, following the work of T. S. Haile (1909–48) who had used slip decoration in a free and lively manner. William Newland, Margaret Hine, Nicholas Vergette and James Tower used traditional pottery materials to produce decorative bulls, birds and goats and pots which had a sculptural quality. While much of their work appears whimsical and amusing and, unlike the contemporary work made by Lucie Rie or Bernard Leach, lacks the classical quality of the best pottery, it does nevertheless mark a new dimension in studio pottery in England.

Recent Developments

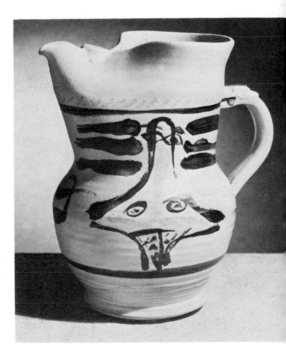

251

Stoneware pots. Hans Coper. Several firings and many different layers of dry white glaze are used to achieve the rich textured effect. Midland Group Gallery. Below: *Pinch rim bowl, raku. Walter Keeler. As well as making functional pots, Walter Keeler makes raku in which the unglazed black reduced body is contrasted with rich yellow or turquoise glazes. 1969.* Council of Industrial Design.

Stoneware double box. Tony Hepburn. White matt glaze with red enamel decoration. Such work owes a clear influence to the experiments of the West Coast potters, U.S.A. V. and A.

The sixties in Britain marked a time of expansion and experiment. Although the majority of potters continued to produce useful and often beautiful ware (Robin Welch, Richard Batterham, Gwyn Hanssen until 1963, Colin Pearson, Michael Casson, Geoffrey Whiting, Alan Caiger-Smith and the Boscean pottery are among these), a small number of experimenters arose more closely associated with the ideas of the United States of America (notably Hans Coper, Gillian Lowndes, Ian Auld, Dan Arbeid, Anthony Hepburn, Sheila Fournier and Walter Keeler). Perhaps the most successful of these is Hans Coper (born 1920), whose work is often linked with that of Lucie Rie, both having shared the same studio from 1947 to 1958 before he established his own. Coper's work, matt glazed and richly textured, explores a limited number of forms, each one building upon and illuminating that which has gone before. His work somehow manages to combine the best traditional craftsmanship with a rare degree of individual expression.

UNITED STATES OF AMERICA

Following the early success of the Rookwood pottery at making decorative wares, production continued in the twentieth century. The success of the Rookwood pottery encouraged the development of a number of large commercial art pot-

252

teries, notably those at Zanesville, Ohio, which made full use of the ideas of other art potteries.

During the twentieth century many studio potters followed the ideas of the Englishman, Bernard Leach, and established workshops producing repetition and functional wares. The pots generally showed a much stronger Japanese influence and the emphasis has been more on the individual rather than the repetition pot. Many students from America trained with Bernard Leach in England and took back his ideas to the States. Notable among these potters were Warren and Alex Mackenzie, who set up their pottery in Minneapolis in 1952. Other influences on pottery came from the Bauhaus in Germany, brought by, among others, Frans Wildenhain who worked in New York.

The most significant contribution of potters in the United States to international ceramics has undoubtedly been made since the Second World War. Without the strong influence of the ideas of William Morris many of the studio potters of the States have not felt the need to confine the use of clay to the production of a wide range of domestic wares, and have concentrated on its use as a means of artistic expression. Zen Buddhist ideas of asymmetry and spontaneity have also encouraged the breakaway from the major considerations of function and use. Such potters as Peter Voulkos, Paul Soldner, Jerry Rothman, Daniel Rhodes, Jun

Stoneware, coil-built pot. Ruth Duckworth. Until 1965 Ruth Duckworth worked in Kew, London, since when she has been working in Chicago, U.S.A. 1959. V. and A.

253

Porcelain teaset. Rosenthal, Germany. Designed by the founder of the Germany Bauhaus, Walter Gropius, in association with Louis A. McMillen. Principles of functionalism have been incorporated in the design, which is based on a convex bowl, inverted for the teapot. The knob in the lid is placed near the handle to allow it to be held in position while tea is poured. c 1968. Courtesy of Rosenthal.

Earthenware plate decorated with richly painted natural design. Theodore Deck, France. Like William de Morgan, Deck studied Isnik and Persian wares and attempted to reproduce the brilliance of their designs. 1860/ 1870. Victoria and Albert Museum.

Bauhaus

Kaneko and Michael Arutz have been some of the principal exponents.

More recently the West Coast, influenced by the ideas of pop art, seems to have become a centre for free, almost wild experiments aimed for the most part to shock rather than to please. Pots have combined almost every known ceramic decorative technique as well as the use of paint and acrylic pigment. It is as though for many American potters the exploration of clay were an end in its own right; the freedom and breadth with which the material is used have not yet compensated for its apparent lack of direction, though the experiments are having a wide influence on studio potters generally. It is too soon to say how this use of clay is going to affect the work of other potters, but the ideas of the experimental potters are powerful and the work produced, at its best, has a committed and serious quality.

GERMANY

After the First World War Walter Gropius (born 1883) established the Bauhaus in Germany. It was, primarily, a school of architecture but also embraced the design of furniture and all kinds of domestic utensils. In one sense the Bauhaus developed the idea of William Morris that machines should not emulate the work of the human hands: one of the aims of the Bauhaus was to find out what machines could do well. The result, sometimes

Stoneware bowl with decoration cut through a black slip to give a striking if sombre geometrical pattern. Émile Lenoble, France. c 1931. Victoria and Albert Museum.

Stoneware bowl with grey crackled glaze. Émile Decœur, France. Glaze effects, especially those of China, interested many French as well as English potters in the twentieth century. 1931. Victoria and Albert Museum.

called functionalism, swept away the old ideas of fussy ornament, and the designs, in comparison with what had gone before, look clean, naked and austere. So successful was the Bauhaus that today much design is based on the principles which the school established. The ideas of the Bauhaus, as far as ceramics was concerned, were expounded by several artists, notably Gerhard Mareks, Otto Lindig, Theodor Bogler and Marguerite Wildenhain. The attempt to link art and industry covered furniture and design generally. Many students throughout Europe came under the Bauhaus influence and potters were no exception. In Vienna, the teaching of Otto Wagner that an object which, from a practical point of view, was unsatisfactory could not be beautiful, encouraged the search for good as well as beautiful design.

FRANCE

France was perhaps the main centre of activity for nineteenth- and early twentieth-century art potters. Highly individual tin-glazed pottery had been made much earlier by Bernard Palissy (c 1510–90) and Charles Avisseau (1796–1861) of Tours emulated his work. Theodore Deck (1823–91), like de Morgan, studied Isnik and Persian pots and lustrewares and based his work on them. The late nineteenth century saw the development of interest in imported Japanese and Chinese pottery and the study of stoneware glazes, especi-

Flat stoneware vase and jug, wood-fired stoneware. Yves and Monique Moby, La Bourne, France. Two stoneware hand-built pots fired in wood kiln. Elizabeth Joulia. La Bourne, France. Meubles week-end, Paris. Below: Lidded porcelain box, fired in wood kiln. Gwyn Hanssen, Achere, France. In this box the soft mottled surface contrasts well with the smooth shiny inside glaze. 1970.

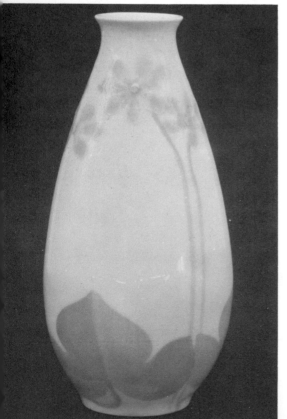

Porcelain vase, caladine flowers and foliage modelled in slight relief and painted in mauve and grey in the art nouveau style. Sweden, Rorstrand. Late nineteenth century. V. and A.

ally of the more spectacular sort, by such potters as Auguste Delaherche (1857–1940), Ernest Chaplet (1835–1909), Émile Lenoble (1875–1939) and Émile Decœur (1876–1953). Again, most of the pots which were made show a preoccupation with effects, whether achieved by moulded or added ornament or by carefully controlled glazes, rather than a unity of form and decoration.

More recently French studio potters have worked along two lines. One group was influenced by the work of painters who concentrated on decorating pots. Joan Miro was such a painter who worked with the Spanish potter Artigas. Following the successful work of Picasso at Vallauris who had used brightly coloured glazes on freely shaped pots and painted decoration on plates, many other earthenware potters continued to work in this area, centred mainly in Vallauris. The other major group works in La Bourne in central France, in an area with a 400-year tradition of wood-fired stoneware. The French studio potters have tried to develop a new style using the local clay and wood-firing kilns. Many of the pots have a richness of colour and texture on forms which, for the most part, have not yet broken away sufficiently from the traditional wares or from the more recent Japanese influence. Yves Mohy, Elisabeth Joulia and Gwyn Hanssen are three potters who have used the traditional methods in a creative way. Gwyn Hanssen, in particular, has

256

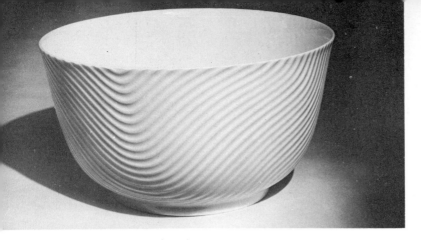

sought to combine richness and colour with quiet forms to give a peaceful style of great beauty.

NORTHERN EUROPE

Much of the pottery made in Europe has been influenced by the large porcelain factories established in the eighteenth century under royal patronage. Porcelain was highly valued and its manufacture was considered to be a mark of great prestige. In Germany the first porcelain factory at Meissen was established in 1709. The Rosenthal factory, established 1879, encouraged the consideration of the form of the pots rather than their decoration, though it was primarily a machine-made rather than a hand-made form. During the 1920s the functionalist ideas of design developed by the Bauhaus were applied to work made here.

Many students trained in the Rosenthal factories moved to other countries where they continued to work in similar ways. In northern Europe during the twentieth century the production of pottery in Finland, Sweden, Denmark and Norway has been done by a single large factory in each country. Production and design have been consistently good and the pots have reflected the best qualities of machine-made work. In Finland, the Arabia factory, one of the largest in Europe, established in 1874 has, since the last war, maintained a high standard of design based on plain, almost austere forms. The domestic range of pots has managed to combine the warmth of hand-

257

Group of stoneware pots by Raija Tuumi, Arabia, Finland. The technical resources of the Arabia factory are available to individual potters and the work is often in direct contrast to the factory products. Courtesy of the Finnish Embassy.

A History of Pottery

made ware with the best qualities of machine production. Recently, potters have been encouraged to develop their own ideas independently while working in the Arabia factory with full technical resources at their disposal. The work of the individual potters seems to be primarily concerned with decoration as a means of breaking away from the evenness of machine production and this is the best quality of the work.

The Rorstrand factory, originally founded in 1726 in Sweden, the Royal Copenhagen factory (1775) of Denmark and the Norwegian Porsgrunde factory have all played a major role in their own countries. Each has recently been concerned with encouraging the work of individual potters within their factories. This has led to the development of the so-called Northern School of pottery and the work is characterized by simple forms and rich decoration. Bright, rich glazes such as red and blue are often used on small areas set against dark textured unglazed surfaces on simple, often straight-sided forms. Designs, often of geometric shapes as well as stylized animals, are richly worked in relief decoration.

Recently, potters in Finland and Sweden have attempted to establish their own studios and break away altogether from the factories. It will be interesting to see how these experiments with clay develop in countries where good design is an accepted part of life and how the work of the potters will challenge that made in the factory.

258

Glossary

Alkaline glaze Contains soda or potash in some form and when small quantities of copper oxide are present gives a rich turquoise colour.

Amphora Pot form used in Mediterranean countries for holding liquids. Characterized by two handles linking the neck to the body of the pot.

Arabesque Ornamentation derived from a mixture of formal geometric and foliage patterns, characterized by flowing linear designs of leaves and scrolls.

Barbotine decoration Made by trailing thick slip on to the surface of a leather-hard pot.

Biscuit Pottery which has been fired once without a glaze in the biscuit-firing. It is usually porous and fairly soft.

Body General term for various clays from which pots are made.

Burnishing Sometimes known as polishing, made by rubbing the surface of unfired pots with a smooth surfaced tool such as a stone or a bone. The particles of clay, pressed flat and smooth, take on a dull gloss.

Carinate Pottery shape made by joining a rounded base and straight in-sloping walls.

China clay Pure white clay of theoretically correct composition. Essential for the production of fine porcelain.

China stone Form of feldspar used by the Chinese for the production of fine porcelain.

Clay Plastic malleable earth occurring over much of the earth's surface. It must be carefully prepared to remove foreign matter and be mixed evenly throughout.

Cobalt oxide	A metal oxide which gives blue over a wide temperature range. Imported from Persia into China where it was known as Mohammedan blue or Sumatran blue.
Colouring oxides	Various metal oxides when painted on or mixed into a glaze give different colours. Copper oxide gives green, manganese oxide gives brown or purple, iron oxide gives brown or green, cobalt oxide gives blue.
Combing	Incised parallel-line decoration made by a toothed tool such as a piece of comb.
Delft ware	English term used originally to describe tin-glazed earthenware made in Delft. Holland, and subsequently all tin-glazed ware made in England.
Earthenware	General term used for pottery fired to temperatures up to 1150° C. Characterized by glaze and body remaining as quite separate layers.
Enamels or **on-glaze decoration**	Glazes prepared in frit form to melt at low temperature which allows a wide range of colours. Painted on to a fired glaze and refired in a muffle kiln.
Faience (Egyptian faience)	An artificially made clay body made from an added fluxing agent, which was capable of being moulded into small objects or pots. The surface became glossy when fired and, if dusted with copper oxide, turquoise. A term also used by the French for tin-glazed earthenware.
Feldspar	Naturally occurring mineral consisting of alumina, silica and a flux of potassium or sodium. Melts at 1250°C to form a simple glaze.
Flux	Essential glaze ingredient which causes other ingredients to melt and fuse to form glaze. Different fluxes affect colouring oxides to give a wide range of colours.
Frit	Artificially produced glaze or body material made by heating two or more raw materials together until they melt to render them insoluble or non-poisonous. The mixture is shattered by being poured into cold water and subsequently ground to powder.

260

Glaze	A smooth waterproof glossy surface applied to pots, discovered in the Near East about 1500 B.C.
Green wares	General term for Chinese wares with green glazes, where the colour was obtained by small amounts of iron in the glaze. Often known as celadon wares.
Incised decoration	Pressed or cut into the surface of a pot or tile.
In-glaze painting or majolica painting	Technique of decorating pottery, brought to perfection by the Italians in the Middle Ages, in which colouring oxides are painted on to unfired opaque white tin-glaze.
Kilns	Sometimes known as the potter's oven, they are structures in which clay forms are fired until they become pottery. Developed originally in the Near East, they separate the fire from the chamber which holds the pots.
Kwaart	Technique used by the Delft potters to imitate Chinese blue and white porcelain in tin-glazed earthenware by using a clear transparent glaze over the white opaque glaze. This gave a greater gloss and depth to the colours.
Leather-hard	Half-way stage between wet and dry clay. Stiff enough to support its own weight but sufficiently pliable to bend slightly and be carved. The stage at which turning is carried out on unfinished pots.
Levigation	Process of preparing clay of fine particle size by reducing it to liquid and decanting finer particles which remain in suspension while heavier particles sink to bottom. Technique used by, among others, Greeks and Romans.
Liu-li	A glass frit probably of lead and sand, imported into China from the Near East in the Han Dynasty (206 B.C.–A.D. 220).
Lustre	A type of colouring decoration achieved by painting metallic pigment on to a fired glaze and refiring in a reducing atmosphere which gives an iridescent effect.

261

Majolica (maiolica)	General term for tin-glazed earthenware decorated with oxides painted on to the unfired glaze. Used specifically in the nineteenth century for moulded earthenware with relief pattern decorated with coloured glazes or majolica painting.
Monochrome pottery	Usually made in one colour or has decoration painted in a contrasting colour.
Muffle kiln	Protects pots from flames in a flame-burning kiln. Essential for production of enamels.
Natron	A mineral found in the Near East containing sodium oxide (Na_2O) which acts as a flux in a glaze or in faience.
Opacifier	A substance, usually a metal oxide such as tin oxide, which, when added to clear glazes, suspends itself and renders the glaze opaque and white.
Oxidizing atmosphere	Conditions inside a kiln when a clean bright flame burns with plenty of oxygen available. The resulting pots are often bright coral red and iron-glazes yellow or brown.
Paddle and anvil	Tools used for hand-built pottery. The anvil, often in the form of a stone, supported the pot wall inside while the paddle was beaten against the outside wall. Used in Indus Valley and America among other places.
Plastic	Clay which can be moulded without breaking is described as being plastic.
Polychrome pottery	Decoration painted in two or more colours usually with coloured slips or oxides.
Porcelain	High-temperature ware which is white and translucent. The body is made by mixing china clay, china stone and quartz together.
Potash	A form of potassium oxide (K_2O) found in wood-ash. Acts as a flux in glaze or in faience.
Quartz	A form of silica (SiO_2) such as sand, which when mixed with a suitable flux will form a glaze.
Raku	A method of firing pots quickly using an open body. Used extensively since the eighteenth century in Japan and more recently in Britain and the U.S.A.

262

Reducing atmosphere	Opposite to oxidizing atmosphere in a kiln. Oxygen content is kept to a minimum by burning damp fuel or closing air inlets. The resulting pots are often dark brown or black and iron-glazes green or blue.
Resist	Decoration where one area is painted in a substance such as wax which resists colouring pigment or glaze when applied to the pot and therefore fires a contrasting colour.
Rouletting	Two sorts of decoration. In antiquity made by allowing a tool to 'chatter' against the side of a leather-hard pot revolving on the wheel. Also used to describe the pattern made by a relief-decorated revolving wheel held against a turning pot.
Saltglaze	A thin glaze achieved by introducing salt (NaCl) into the kiln at high temperature. The chlorine as gas goes up the chimney and the sodium vapour forms a glaze on the surface of the pots.
Sgraffito	Decoration scratched through a layer of slip to show the body of contrasting colour.
Slip	Clay which has been softened down in water and put through a sieve to make it smooth. Usually has consistency of cream.
Soft-paste porcelain	A European imitation of Chinese porcelain made by mixing white clay with a frit or a flux such as bone ash or talc, which vitrifies at earthenware temperature to give a white translucent body.
Sprigging	Decorating technique in which relief-moulded decoration was applied to the leather-hard pot. Used extensively by Wedgwood in the production of his Jasper wares.
Stoneware	Pottery fired to a high temperature (up to 1350°C). Body is vitrified and glaze and body partially fused.
Throwing	Art of building up pots on the fast-spinning potter's wheel using centrifugal force.
Turning	Process of removing surplus clay from thrown pots by returning them, when leather-hard, to the potter's wheel and trimming with a metal tool.

263

Underglaze painting	A technique of painting colouring oxides on to unfired pottery which may or may not be subsequently glazed. The term is used occasionally to describe the technique of painting on to unfired glaze.
Viscous	A glaze which when melted remains stiff and does not run down the pot is so described.
Vitrified	Like glass, fused together.

Museums with Pottery Collections

Aberdeen University Anthropological Museum
Brighton Museum and Art Gallery
Bristol City Art Gallery
Cambridge Fitzwilliam Museum
Cambridge University Museum of Archaeology and Ethnology
Durham Gulbenkian Museum of Oriental Art and Archaeology
Glasgow Art Gallery and Museum
Hastings Public Museum and Art Gallery
London Bethnal Green Museum
        British Museum
        Guildhall Museum
        London Museum
        Martin-ware Pottery Collection, Public Library, Osterley Park Road, Southall, Middlesex
        Percival David Foundation of Chinese Art
        University College Department of Egyptology
        Victoria and Albert Museum and extensive Art Library
        Wallace Collection
Norwich Castle Museum
Nottingham City Museum and Art Gallery
Oxford Ashmoleam Museum of Art and Archaeology
        Pitt Rivers Museum
Salisbury and South Wiltshire Museum
Stoke-on-Trent City Museum and Art Gallery

Museums and Galleries in Great Britain and Ireland is a full detailed list of Museums, published annually by Index Publications.

264

Bibliography

GENERAL

CARDEW, M. *Pioneer Pottery*. London 1969. Longman

CHARLESTON, R. J. (Ed.). *World Ceramics*. London 1968. Paul Hamlyn

COOPER, E. *Handbook of Pottery*. London 1970. Longman

CUSHION, J. and HONEY, W. B. *Dictionary of European Ceramic Art*. London 1952. Faber and Faber

DODD, J. and ROGERS, A. *Exploring Pottery*. London 1967. Odhams

HAGGAR, R. *Pottery through the Ages*. London 1959. Methuen

HILLIER, B. *Pottery and Porcelain 1700–1914*. London 1968. Weidenfeld and Nicolson

HODGES, H. *Artifacts*. London 1964. John Baker
The Technology of the Ancient World. London 1970. Arthur Lane

HOLLAND, F. *Fifty Years a Potter*. London 1950. Pottery Quarterly

HONEY, W. B. *Art of the Potter*. London 1955. Faber and Faber

LEACH, B. *A Potter's Book*. London 1945. Faber and Faber

MITCHELL, L. *Ceramics – from Stone Age to Space Age*. New York 1963. McGraw-Hill

RIETH, A. *5000 Jahre Topferscheibe*. Konstanz 1960. Jan Thorbecke Verlag KG

ROSENTHAL, E. *Pottery and Ceramics*. London 1949. Penguin

Magazines

Archaeological journals such as:

The Antiquaries Journal, Society of Antiquaries, London (two editions a year)

Archaeological Journal, British Archaeological Association, London

Local Archaeological Societies, i.e. Surrey, Sussex, Durham

Transactions of the English Ceramic Society

The Art Journal (a magazine published during the nineteenth century 1849–1912)

Burlington Magazine

Ceramic Review (a review of the work of modern potters), 5 Belsize Lane, London NW3 5AD

The Connoisseur
Pottery Quarterly, Northfield Studio, Northfields, Tring, Herts
Studio Magazine
Oriental Art, 12 Ennerdale Road, Richmond, Surrey

PREHISTORY AND THE EARLIEST CIVILIZATIONS

ALDRED, C. *The Egyptians*. London 1961. Thames and Hudson
ALLCHIN, B. and R. *The Birth of Indian Civilization*. London 1968. Penguin
EYLES, D. *Pottery in the Ancient World*. London 1950. Doulton
POULIK, J. *Prehistoric Art*. London n.d. Spring Books
CHILDE, G. *What Happened in History*. London 1964. Penguin
HUTCHINSON, R. W. *Prehistoric Crete*. London 1962. Penguin
PORADA, E. *Ancient Iran*. London 1965. Methuen
SINGER, C., HOLMYARD, E. J. and HALL, A. R. (Eds.). *History of Technology*, Volumes I–III. London 1954, 1956, 1957. Oxford University Press/Clarendon Press

GREECE AND ROME

AMERICAN SCHOOL OF CLASSICAL STUDIES AT ATHENS. *Pots and Pans of Classical Athens*. Princeton, New Jersey 1958
BEAZLEY, SIR JOHN. *Attic Black Figure Vase Painters*. London 1956. Oxford University Press
  Attic Red Figure Vase Painters. London 1942. Oxford University Press
  Etruscan Vase Painting. London 1947. Oxford University Press
CHARLESTON, R. J. *Roman Pottery*. London 1955. Faber and Faber
COOK, R. M. *Greek Painted Pottery*. London 1960. Methuen
COUNCIL FOR BRITISH ARCHAEOLOGY RESEARCH REPORT NO. 6. *Romano-British Coarse Pottery*. London (n.d.)
LANE, A. *Greek Pottery*. London 1956. Faber and Faber
NOBLE, J. V. *The Techniques of Painted Attic Pottery*. London 1956. Faber and Faber
OSWALD, F. and DAVIES PRYCE, T. *Terra Sigillata*. London 1966. Gregg Press Ltd
STANFIELD, J. A. and SIMPSON, G. *Central Gaulish Potters*. London 1958. Oxford University Press

THE FAR EAST

BRANKSTON, A. D. *Early Ming Wares of Chingtechen*. London 1971.
Lund Humphries. First issued by Henry Vetch 1938

CHEWON, K. and GOMPERTZ, G. ST G. M. *Korean Arts*, Volume II.
Ceramics. London 1961. Korean Ministry of Public Information

FRANKS, SIR A. W. *Japanese Pottery*, 3rd edition. London 1912.
Victoria and Albert Museum Handbook

GARNER, SIR HARRY. *Oriental Blue and White*. London 1964. Faber
and Faber

GOMPERTZ, G. ST G. M. *Chinese Celadon Wares*. London 1958. Faber
and Faber

GRAY, B. *Early Chinese Pottery and Porcelain*. London 1953. Faber
and Faber

HETHERINGTON, A. C. *Early Ceramic Wares of China*. London 1922.
Ernest Benn

HOBSON, R. L. *The Art of the Chinese Potter*. London 1923. Ernest
Benn
*British Museum Handbook of Pottery and Porcelain of the Far
East*. London 1937. British Museum

HONEY, W. B. *Ceramic Art of China*. London 1945. Faber and
Faber

JENYNS, S. *Japanese Porcelain*. London 1965. Faber and Faber
Ming Pottery and Porcelain. London 1953. Faber and Faber

KORJAMA, FUJIO (Ed.). *Japanese Ceramics*. California 1961. Oakland
Art Museum

LAUFER, B. *Chinese Pottery of the Han Dynasty*. New York 1909.
American Museum of Natural History

MEDCALF, C. J. B. *Introduction to Chinese Pottery and Porcelain*. London 1955. Cresset Press

MILLER, R. A. *Japanese Ceramics*. Tokyo 1960. Toto Shuppan Co.
Ltd. Distributed by Charles E. Tuttle and Co., Rutland,
Vermont, and Tokyo, Japan

SANDERS, H. H. *The World of Japanese Ceramics*. Tokyo 1967.
Kodansha International Ltd

WU, G. D. *Prehistoric Pottery in China*. London 1938. Kegan Paul,
Trench Trubner and Co.

ISLAMIC POTTERY

BUTLER, A. J. *Islamic Pottery.* London 1926. Ernest Benn

HOBSON, R. L. *A Guide to the Islamic Pottery of the Near and Far East.* London 1932. British Museum

LANE, A. *Early Islamic Pottery.* London 1958. Faber and Faber
Later Islamic Pottery. London 1957. Faber and Faber

POPE, A. U. *An Introduction to Persian Art since the 7th Century* A.D. London 1930. Peter Davis

POPE, A. U. *Survey of Persian Art*, Volume II. London 1938. Oxford University Press

WALLIS, H. *Persian Ceramic Art* (two volumes). London 1891. Privately printed

EUROPEAN POTTERY

ARRIBAS, A. *The Iberians.* London 1968. Thames and Hudson

FORTNUM, C. D. E. *Maiolica.* Oxford 1896. Clarendon Press

FOTHINGHAM, A. W. *Lustreware of Spain.* New York 1951. Hispanic Society
Talavera Pottery. New York 1944. Hispanic Society

HONEY, W. B. *European Ceramic Art* (two volumes). London 1952. Faber and Faber

LIVERANI, G. *Five Centuries of Italian Majolica.* London 1960. McGraw-Hill

MORGAN, C. H. *The Byzantine Pottery (Corinth)* (American School of Classical Studies). Harvard 1942. Harvard University Press

PENKALA, M. *European Pottery.* London 1951. A. Zwemmer Ltd

PICCOLOPASSO. *The Three Books of the Potter's Art* (translated and edited by RACKHAM, B. and VAN DE PUTA). London 1934. Victoria and Albert Museum

RACKHAM, B. *Italian Majolica.* London 1952. Faber and Faber

RICE TALBOT, D. *Byzantine Glazed Pottery.* Oxford 1930. Clarendon Press

SAVORY, H. N. *Spain and Portugal.* London 1968. Thames and Hudson

SOLON, M. L. *Ancient Art Stoneware of the Low Countries and Germany.* London 1892. Privately printed
Italian Majolica. London 1907. Cassell and Co.

STEVENSON, R. B. K. *The Great Palace of the Byzantine Emperors.* Oxford 1947. Oxford University Press

TATLOCK, R. K. *Spanish Art*. London 1927. Burlington Magazine Monograph II

THEOPHILUS. *The Various Arts* (edited by DODWELL, C. R.). London 1961. Nelson

WALLIS, H. *The Byzantine Ceramic Art*. London 1907. Bernard Quaritch
Italian Ceramic Art. London 1897. Privately printed

AMERICA

BARBER, E. A. *Pottery and Porcelain of the USA* (3rd edition). New York 1909. G. P. Putnam
"Rise of the Pottery Industry in the USA", from *The Popular Science Monthly*, Vol. XI., No. 2, 1891, and No. 3, 1892

BUSHNELL, G. H. S. *Ancient Arts of the Americas*. London 1965. Thames and Hudson

BUSHNELL, G. H. S. and DIGBY, A. *Ancient American Pottery*. London 1955. Faber and Faber

COE, M. D. *The Maya*. London 1966. Thames and Hudson
Mexico. London 1965. Thames and Hudson

GODDARD, P. E. *Pottery of the South-western Indians*. New York 1928. American Museum of Natural History

HOYLE, R. L. *Peru*. London 1966. Thames and Hudson

LOTHROP, S. K. *Treasures of Ancient America*. London 1964. Skira

MASON, ALDEN J. *The Ancient Civilizations of Peru*. London 1964. Penguin

VAILLANT, G. C. *Artists and Craftsmen in Ancient Central America*. New York 1935. American Museum of Natural History
Aztecs of Mexico. London 1962. Penguin

WILEY, G. R. *An Introduction to American Archaeology*, Volume I. *North and Middle America*. New Jersey 1966. Prentice-Hall Inc.

ENGLISH POTTERY UNTIL 1800

CHURCH, A. H. *English Earthenware*. London 1911. Victoria and Albert Museum Handbook
Some Minor Arts. London 1894. Seeley and Co.

COOPER, R. G. *English Slipware Dishes*. London 1968. Tiranti

GARNER, F. H. *English Delftware*. London 1948. Faber and Faber

JEWITT, L. *Ceramic Art of Great Britain* (2nd edition 1883). London 1877. J. S. Virtue & Co.

KIDSON, J. R. and F. *Leeds Old Pottery* (first published 1892). London 1970. S.R. Publishers and *The Connoisseur*

RACKHAM, B. *Medieval English Pottery*. London 1947. Faber and Faber

RACKHAM, B. and READ, H. *English Pottery*. London 1924. Ernest Benn

TOWNER, D. C. *English Cream Coloured Earthenware*. London 1957. Faber and Faber

MODERN POTTERY 1800–1970

BEARD, G. *Modern Ceramics*. London 1969. Studio Vista

BEMROSE, G. *Nineteenth Century English Pottery and Porcelain*. London 1952. Faber and Faber

BIRKS, T. *Art of Modern Pottery*. London 1967. Country Life

CASSON, M. *Pottery in Britain Today*. London 1967. Tiranti

GAUNT, WILLIAM and CLAYTON-STAMM, M. D. F. *William De Morgan*. London 1971. Studio Vista

HETTEŠ and RADA. *Modern Ceramics*. London 1965. Spring Books

HUGHES, G. B. *Victorian Pottery and Porcelain*. London 1959. Country Life

KLEIN, A. *Moderne Deutsche Keramik*. Darmstadt 1956. Franz Schneekluth Verlag

NAYLOR, G. *The Arts and Crafts Movement*. London 1971. Studio Vista

ROSE, M. *Artist Potters in England*. London 1970. Faber and Faber

WAKEFIELD, H. *Victorian Pottery*. London 1962. Herbert Jenkins

WILDENHAIN, M. *Pottery Form and Expression*. New York 1962. Reinhold

Index

Index

Index